# OVER THE HILLS

BY

## PETER STEELE

OVER THE HILLS
Copyright © 2015 by Peter Steele
Image and cover copyright © Peter Steele
Cover design by Keara Hlewka
Digitization of cover image by Marten Berkman
Author photo by Cathie Archbould

Computer consultants: Ben Steele and Sasha Masson


ISBN: 978-0-9940614-0-9

peter.steele@northwestel.net

*For my grandsons Tim, Ben, Sasha and Felix*

*With thanks to the indomitable
Marcelle Dubé, who floated this book.*

*...over the hills and far away*
*she danced with Pigling Bland!*
Beatrix Potter, The Tale of Pigling Bland

# OVER THE HILLS

# ONE

**M**Y GRANDPARENTS SPENT most of their lives on foreign soil far from home—one grandfather was a businessman in India, the other a missionary in China. I recall their stern mien and the noisy way they lit their pipes. I remember less of my grandmothers because they died before I was ten years old, but they seemed to float in and out of the shadows of their Victorian husbands.

Visits to The Old Country—that is, England—involved, for Grandfather Walsh in Calcutta, a sedate month in the luxury of a P & O steamship (ticketed POSH—Port Out, Starboard Home—for a cabin on the shady side of the boat away from the unrelenting sun). For Grandfather Steele, home leave from China once every five years entailed a long, *clackety-clackety* ride on the Trans-Siberian Railway.

\* \* \*

I have a portrait of John Steele in black clerical gown with scarlet academic hood. A halo of wavy white hair, plentiful for a man in his ninetieth year, frames his angular face with its strong square chin. For twenty-three years he eked out a harsh life as a Presbyterian missionary in Swatow, a port of mainland China on the seacoast halfway between

Hong Kong and Shanghai. He waged his own private war against the opium poppy, and he suffered the Boxer uprising that caused outbursts of violent attacks on foreigners. Eventually, he was forced to return home because of failing eyesight due to undiagnosed glaucoma. Nearly blind in his later years, he would write his sermon notes, for the Presbyterian kirk at which he helped out, on pieces of cardboard, holding a pencil like a Chinese calligraphy brush.

I used to visit him at his semi-detached house in what is now the London suburb of Muswell Hill, where his strong presence seemed to deserve a larger and more dignified dwelling. The front parlour doubled as dining room and Grandfather's study. A roll-top desk stood in the lace-curtained window bay, and glass-fronted cabinets held books that reflected his scholarship. He spoke Chinese and Gaelic (both Irish and Scottish) fluently, and he could read parts of the bible in Hebrew. He had once been a lecturer at the London School of Oriental and African Studies, and he was awarded a Doctorate of Literature by Belfast University for his translation of the *I Li*, a classic of ancient Chinese manners and customs.

Grandfather smelled richly of tobacco, and sparks from his pipe had singed the front of his woolen waistcoat in a dozen places. His clerical collar was off-white and frayed around the chin, and its black bib had a coppery sheen of age. He would half-blindly finger the studs securing the leather arms of his special high back chair that stood beside the fire grate. Occasionally he loaded coals from a hod and stoked them into flame. Beside his chair stood a brass spittoon, half-filled with water, where nicotine-stained gobs of mucus floated.

Grandfather took his breakfast porridge the Scots way, sprinkling it with salt instead of sugar, and dipping a loaded spoon into a cup of milk. Then he slurped it back noisily, which vexed my father, who was fastidious about table manners.

Each day of my schoolboy visit, Grandfather would shuffle around the block of look-alike suburban brick houses with me, telling tales of China. I regret that I paid scant attention then to his maunderings instead of appreciating them as slices of history. He reminisced often about the time when he was a chaplain to a Black Watch regiment in the First World War and also translator for battalions of Chinese labourers. He gave me his rough, military-issue kilt that had a patch over a hole reportedly made by a bullet that had killed its former owner; the sporran, he told me somewhat fancifully, was picked up at the battlefield of Culloden. Later, when I was at university, I started climbing in his beloved Scottish Highlands, and he would sit me down and teach me to pronounce their Gaelic names correctly. However, he never mentioned his birthplace, Cork, in southern Ireland, because of his shame at Irish behaviour during The Troubles.

Being of stocky build, Grandfather was once a good footballer. When I saw him in Muswell Hill, he appeared frail; however, when preaching in the local kirk, he became a giant. His hooded eyelids drooped a little, but he spoke in a strong, clear voice with a slight Inverness accent—the purest tongue of the English language—acquired when he had once served a parish there.

Of his wife, my grandmother, I recall her regal poise. She wore a choker and necklace with a cut glass emerald at her throat, and a coiled bun fixed with long hairpins high on the back of her head. We "took" tea in the gloomy inner parlour, where half-drawn damask curtains and an aspidistra guarded French windows that led into a solarium. She would always produce scones larded with dripping from the Sunday roast, and thinly cut Marmite sandwiches.

* * *

By contrast, Grandfather Charles Walsh—Buppa, as my brother and I knew him—was a citizen of the Raj at the height of the British

Empire. He had made his fortune with a Calcutta jute company that employed legions of peasants from the Ganges-Brahmaputra basin of West Bengal. He played a good polo chukka at the Tollygunge Club, and was handy at tennis. In pre-monsoon early mornings, he used to exercise his string of ponies around the perimeter of Chowringhee, the huge park beside the Hooghly River. Photos show him in jodhpurs and a solar topi, with a syce—a stable-boy—running beside him, holding onto his stirrup. When summer temperatures soared in the city he migrated, along with the viceroy and most of the government of British India, to Simla, a hill station on the lower slopes of the Himalaya, where my mother was born. He was widowed when my grandmother died of typhoid fever, caught from cleaning her teeth with tap water on the Rajputana Express, heading for Bombay and the homeward-bound ship.

Grandfather retired to Dunsfold, a village in rural Surrey, and became the self-appointed squire. His neo-Georgian mansion, Burningfold Hall, seemed like a palace to me at age of six, with its billiard room, tennis court, and spacious grounds set about with monkey-puzzle trees and a stagnant lily pond, beside which lay a rotting rowboat. Doves cooed outside the window of the nursery—Nanny's domain—that overlooked stables from where arose a comfortable smell of horses. Brass-studded, green baize doors between the lobby and the servants' quarters swung with a soft *swish*. There my brother and I spent much of our time with Cook, who understood small boys as no one else did.

Grandfather's study lay behind heavy magenta curtains drawn over an alcove, where crossed mallets hung beside sepia-tinted photos of polo teams and memorabilia of bygone Indian days. Grandfather's photograph in the hall showed him seated on a hunter of seventeen hands, wearing Master of Foxhounds regalia—a scarlet "pink" coat, black top hat, and bunched white silk cravat fixed with a pearl-headed gold pin. He would summon my brother and me to his study on our Sunday visits from nearby Guildford, where we lived. On birthdays or special days, the summons was notable—for we knew we would receive our rupee. Waiting in the hall, we could hear lip-smacking noises as Grandfather puckered his cheeks while sucking on his pipe that he lit with many matches. Wafts of musty tobacco smoke drifted through the curtains. Once his pipe was alight, he would call us into his den, unlock a safe with ponderous ritual, and withdraw two shiny silver coins—one for each of us. We thanked him immoderately, always hoping for more than one rupee—but it never came.

Outside this sombre recess was the relative freedom of the garden where we balanced along the verandah wall and incurred the gardener's scolding by toppling into lavender bushes—that left a sweetness in the air—and trampling aubrietia beside his immaculate gravel paths.

Grandfather Walsh had a serene, somewhat bewildered face, crowned with a silvery tonsure. Dressed in white flannel trousers, white-chalked shoes with spats, and wearing a Panama hat, he sometimes walked me down to the revolving hut beside the grass tennis court, where the croquet set was kept among random deck chairs and tennis nets. We struck a few balls through hoops, but he soon became bored. Then he would drag himself up the path and usher me off to the nursery. It was as though he had left his life behind under an Indian sun and now had nowhere to go.

In their waning years, my grandfathers were dim reflections of their youthful vigour.

* * *

My father, Gerald Hector Steele, was born in China. Aged sixteen he was sent home by train to live with a guardian, a trusted friend of the family, for his education at Highgate School, from where he won a scholarship to University College Hospital. His career was studded with prizes, and he gained the stellar post of registrar to Sir Wilfred

Trotter, senior surgeon at UCH, and Surgeon to the King and the Royal Household. By age twenty-five, he had become a Fellow of the Royal College of Surgeons and Master of Surgery. He was appointed surgeon to the Royal Surrey County Hospital in Guildford in 1930, when he was still a penniless but eligible bachelor. He had round, tortoiseshell glasses, a boyish face, and curly black hair. He laughed readily when relaxed (which is how I like to remember him), but when serious, as photos during the war show, he furrowed his brow. His brilliant surgical career had engineered his entry into a much more affluent set. He met my mother, Sylvia Walsh, at a tennis party. Her shy smile and gentle face, framed with short, crimped hair, beguiled him, and they fell in love. She was quiet and timid because of her overbearing parents; her mother would often pry into her desk and read her private letters and diaries.

Gerald and Sylvia were duly married in 1931 at Dunsfold church, Gerald wearing a rented morning coat and top hat. He drove from Guildford in his Baby Austin coupé, together with his best man and colleague at UCH, South African Libero Fatti, whose family owned a huge spaghetti and grocery consortium in Johannesburg. Sylvia arrived in the Rolls Royce of her father, who hosted a posh reception in a marquee on the lawn of Burningfold Hall, to where he was then fully retired. A family photo album shows Sylvia going away wearing a cloche hat and waistless dress that were fashionable in the Swinging Thirties; Gerald leans casually against his car with one foot on the running board, hands thrust deep into the pockets of his baggy trousers with wide-bottomed turn-ups. On seaside holidays at Swanage, Gerald swims in a full-length, black bathing costume with shoulder straps, and he wears a suit when sculpting sandcastles with surgical precision, using a knife from a picnic hamper. His meticulous fortifications would nevertheless soon be demolished by the flooding tide. Sylvia has her crimped hair parted in the middle and laid flat against her ears, and she often wears a fur coat, brown stockings, and woolen ankle socks.

I was born in 1935, three years after my brother and four years before the outbreak of World War II. My brother and I were of the nannied class. Until I could walk, a uniformed nursemaid with puffed white sleeve cuffs and starched apron, pushed me in a boat-shaped, four-wheeler pram. Later, we went to other children's birthday parties dressed in double-breasted tweed overcoats with velveteen collars.

Our home was in Guildford, the county town of rural Surrey, then set apart from London by thirty miles of open farming country, now a suburban extension of London. The gold filigree town hall clock was cantilevered over the cobbled High Street. Nearby, on a mound overlooking the meandering River Wey, stood a ruined Norman castle keep on whose disintegrating walls we climbed. The Friday cattle market was held down by the Southern Railway station near the county cricket ground, where we could watch our heroes, the famous Bedser twins.

We lived on the outskirts of the city, beside Merrow Downs, a wilderness of sandy heath, wide-armed pine trees, and furze. There my brother and I flew kites and made secret houses in dense patches of bracken and bramble. Deep-cut lanes, with banks higher than a car and roofed by crinkly, ivy-clad oak trees, led towards Newlands Corner. This was *Winnie-the-Pooh* country, portrayed by Ernest Shepherd, to whose studio a mile away we used to bicycle. Shepherd wore a green visor cap and would point out the animals of his imagination on his drawing board. Our generation's fashion in double forenames was set by A. A. Milne's Christopher Robin, so we were christened John Michael and Peter Robert, shortened to our initials.

My father, an avid gardener, crammed our half-acre with herbaceous borders, copse, and lawns. A swing stood beside the vegetable patch that had been enlarged for the war effort. My brother and I learned to swim in a small canvas pool at the bottom of the garden. We built a den behind the privet bush around the rubbish heap and lay there on our backs, identifying real live Spitfires and Hurricanes engaged overhead in deadly dogfights with German Mesherschmits and Junkers. Periodically, one would spiral out of the sky and plunge earthward, trailing a slipstream of black smoke. It never occurred to us that a moment before it had held a living man. We were intrigued but did not register the tragedy of it.

Our back gate opened onto Merrow Downs, where an Italian prisoner-of-war camp had been built behind a barbed-wire fence. Once a week, a man wearing a brown jacket with a yellow circle painted on the back came to work in our garden.

After giving my brother and me a golf lesson, my father would take us for a ginger beer to the silent clubhouse, where the settees smelled of leather and tobacco and the *Illustrated London News* lay beside a billiard table. In rare snowy winters we tobogganed down the steep hill from the first tee, where a dog once chased my brother and nearly tore his ear off.

Our friend, William, lived nearby in a big house at One Tree Corner. There, a huge oak tree grew out of a brick plinth where we sat to wait for the bus. William and my brother spent many hours arranging toy soldiers in complicated battle formations; I was allowed to watch but was not invited to join in since I was so much younger. But I could wear a real soldier's cap that belonged to William's father, who was away in the army fighting Rommel in the North African desert. Among shoulder-high grass in a corner of William's large garden lay a defunct car in which we sat for hours, making engine noises and pretending we were a tank. All our games had strong overtones of war, which was, for our parents, uncomfortably close; but to us was merely exciting play.

On blackberry-picking outings on sunny days, my brother and I biked along narrow lanes to Newlands Corner, following the route of the Tillingbourne Valley bus—the *Tilley Anne*. Occasionally, for a few pence, we rode to its terminus, half our world away in the village of Wonersh, where we ate our sandwich lunches, and returned home in late afternoon.

Two sisters of our own age, daughters of friends of our parents, lived in downtown Guildford below the ruined castle in Quarry Street. Their house was perched on a steep hillside, where the garden stretched down to the banks of the River Wey. Their parents had built an air raid shelter in the basement and equipped it with bunk beds, blankets and a cooking stove. It became our favourite sleepover place, where we all crowded into the same bed and hid under the blankets and played rude games. The girls enticed my brother and me to the bottom of their garden, where, in turn, we dropped our pants and peed, agog with curiosity and mirth.

Our families rented punts for river outings. We took along a wicker picnic basket stocked with treats bought using precious wartime ration coupons. My father wore long white-flannel trousers. He paddled or punted upstream toward some locks that haunted me with visions of capsizing and being sucked through the lock gates by the current. Upstream, the ruins of St Catherine's Abbey stood on a high hill at a bend in the river where, in cold winters, flooded meadows made smooth ice for skating. There we found a gypsy's camp and stood around his fire, where a kettle hung from a green stick stuck in the ground.

Our privileged lives were firmly entrenched in the British middle class, yet my father was no snob and he allowed us to wander downtown in summer. One day, barefoot in Guildford High Street, we overheard an elderly lady remark haughtily to her companion, "…and those are Doctor Steele's boys." Our way home passed the Abbot's Hospital, Thorpe's second-hand bookshop, the Norman gateway of the Grammar School, and the Odeon Cinema.

When we went to the "flicks," my father would tell the ticket girl if he was on duty, so, should an urgent call come for him, a message would flash on the screen: "Dr. Steele wanted in the foyer." People would stare at the tall, gaunt figure extricating himself in the semi-darkness, and we felt very important. Pathé Pictorial News showed anti-Nazi propaganda clips from the war frontline accompanied by martial music and machine gun chatter. There was no doubt that there was a war going on.

As for thousands of other families, the war disrupted ours. Gerald was exempt from military service because Guildford hospital had to retain a skeleton staff to care for the many wounded expected from the evacuation of France and the ensuing European war. After Dunkirk, he worked ceaselessly and was rarely home until late, so we saw little of him. On dark winter evenings, my mother, my brother, and I would cook scrambled eggs on toast and eat them in front of a coal fire, having pulled the Chinese draught screens round our armchairs. This shared pleasure gave my mother some of the warmth she had lacked in her own childhood. However, she was often unwell and closeted in her bedroom.

My father was very strict about table manners—elbows off the table, eating peas off a fork, and taking soup off the side of the spoon. My brother and I giggled uncontrollably when the other was being scolded. Once, my father, exasperated by our incorrigibility, sent us down to the greenhouse to select our own bamboo cane for punishment. We sawed his carefully hoarded collection of bamboos into three-inch lengths, so he used the bristly side of a hairbrush instead. Corporal punishment for rambunctious boys by one of so gentle a nature seems strange; but in lighter moments, he used to horse around and wrestle—lambasting, we called it. Our mother took no part in disciplining us, and she was so shy and reclusive it was hard to get to know her.

My father operated at Mount Alvernia, a Roman Catholic nursing home at the top of a steep hill behind the cinema. Mother Francis, a beatific, roly-poly Franciscan nun with round glasses, founded the original

mother-house and nursing home in Guildford in 1935. She had the habit
of insinuating a forefinger under her double chin to ease the pressure of
her wimple. Her main assistants were serene Sister Margaret, tall and
stern Sister Leonard, jolly Sister Bernard, and tiny, hunch-backed Sister
Immaculata, who had a lilting Irish brogue. Twenty years later, by dint
of hard work, the order had more than thirty houses scattered across the
world.

My father was their first surgeon, who helped them to get started.
Being a Protestant—and moreover, a Presbyterian—never intruded in
their friendship, and Mother Francis loved my father for his loyalty.
Consequently, we boys could do no wrong. We ran free in the convent
gardens, played hide-and-seek behind the statues of St Francis and the
Virgin Mary, and raced in wheelchairs along the corridors, to the despair
of postulant nuns, with rolled sleeves on their knees scrubbing floors.

In the surgeons' changing room, beside the disinfectant-smelling
operating theatre, coffee and tea were served in china cups from silver-
plated pots. Gory pictures of operations, in a pamphlet advertising a
surgical instrument company, nurtured my fantasy of becoming a doctor. My father occasionally let me watch him operate, and I would stand
on a footstool looking over his shoulder. For my fifth birthday, the nuns
made me a suit of a green gown with a cap and mask. While an early
decision to become a doctor freed me from the anxiety of choosing a
career, later the high expectations of my father's admirers became a
millstone.

My father worked mainly at the Royal Surrey County Hospital,
where we had to behave more formally than at Mount Alvernia. Mr
Sheaf, the dour senior surgeon, disapproved of Gerald Steele's liberally
reared children. So, instead of being allowed into the operating theatre,
I helped the anaesthetist hold down struggling "tonsil" children, trying
to escape a mask sprayed with knockout, lavender-smelling fumes of

ethyl chloride. One Christmas the theatre sister, Miss Stanger, a large lady with a biting wit, allowed us to use our new football for a match in the operating suite hallway, where we knocked over and broke a stand-up telephone.

The hospital driveway led up a ramp to the front steps, where the medical staff parked their cars against the outer kerb. On our way home, my father often allowed me to start the car, a sleek Armstrong Siddeley with synchromesh gear transmission. One day I dashed ahead of him and turned on the ignition without first checking that the gearshift was in neutral. The car leaped forward towards the road that lay a dozen feet below. By good fortune, the transmission box caught on the kerb and the car hung in the air, its wheels spinning. That was the last time I was encouraged to start the car.

Once a week, my father operated at Farnham and Aldershot. I accompanied him, driving along the Hog's Back, where hundreds of vehicles and tanks were parked beside the road under camouflage, ready for the invasion of Europe. At my feet always lay a wooden, lead-lined box, containing radium seeds for treating throat cancer. Those were the days before the perils of radiation were fully understood.

We lived on the flight path to London of German planes, which would jettison their unspent bombs over Guildford on their return. Our home became so dangerous that our parents decided to send us to Canada. Bound by train to Liverpool docks, we were ready, packed with several brand-new Dinky Toy cars to play with on the sea passage. However, the ship that was to take us, the *City of Benares*, was torpedoed by a submarine in mid-Atlantic, with many casualties. And so, instead, we were sent to remote North Wales, well away from bombs. Despite occasional visits home during the war, long separation deprived us of getting close to our parents.

# TWO

IN 1940, AGED FIVE, I WAS ONE of several hundred evacuee children, who boarded trains from London bound for North Wales in order to avoid the bombs falling on southern England. My mother accompanied my brother and me, both with luggage labels hanging round our necks for identification in case we got lost. Our destination was Porthmadog, a small town on the Glaslyn Estuary at the crook of the long arm of the Lleyn Peninsula that points west towards Ireland. We lodged in a semi-detached boarding house, *Penrallt*, in the village of Borth-y-Gest, a couple of miles seaward from Porthmadog. My mother had to return south to our home in Guildford to look after my father; this was her contribution to the war effort. She left us in the guardian care of an elderly spinster, Miss Lyon Mackenzie, whom she had met by chance. Mother planned to visit us during several school holidays; however, when she did, she was then almost a stranger.

Miss Mackenzie was a tall, refined lady with a gentle Highland voice. Because of a heart condition due to rheumatic fever in childhood, she would stoop over her walking stick to catch breath halfway up the hill that led from the harbour, past the post office, to *Penrallt*. Although quite unused to handling young boys, she was patient with her boisterous wards. My day school was in a large house set in spacious wooded grounds a mile away on the road to Porthmadog. Walking there I would balance along the slate wall of a field where cows grazed.

"Why are they playing leap-frog?" I asked Miss Mackenzie on seeing them mounting each other. She became silently flummoxed and more breathless.

My brother, being three years older than me, was sent to a boarding school at nearby Penrhyndeudraeth. The village of Borth-y-Gest clung to the shore of an enclosed harbour where small boats sheltered from winds and rough seas that crashed on the outer rocks. At low tide the sea retreated to the harbour mouth, leaving anchored boats heeling over until they were refloated by the next flood tide. Miss Mackenzie forbade me to wade out in rubber Wellington boots searching for treasures because of the risk of being sucked into the squelchy mud and, we imagined, disappearing forever. So I went barefoot along the shore where I squeezed sand between my toes and trod on seaweed wrack that burst with a loud pop.

Schooners and brigantine sailing ships—Western Ocean Yachts as they were known locally—were built at Porthmadog around the turn of the century, and tiny Borth-y-Gest spawned many locally famous sea captains.

The narrow gauge railway carried roofing slates, quarried in the Ffestiniog mines on the slopes of Snowdon, to Porthmadog to be shipped around the world as far as Argentina, and even round Cape Horn to Chile. The ships returned with cargoes of wool, mutton, and beef, along with rock that created Ballast Island in the middle of Porthmadog Harbour.

One ship's crew, all teenagers, spent two months tacking into the teeth of the Roaring Forties, continually in view of Cape Horn, which they could not round. Eventually they turned to run with the wind, and made their first landfall in nine months in Australia. At Sydney the twenty-one-year-old skipper refused the crew shore leave for fear they would desert. As a result they mutinied.

The war seemed remote from this peaceful, secluded part of Wales until a shipload of Indian troops and transport mules arrived in Porthmadog. Many soldiers became sick from practicing mountain warfare training in wet and windy Welsh hills. Some died, lonely and far from home. One day when I was sitting on the harbour wall I met a turbaned Sikh, who offered me an egg saved from his sparse rations. He spoke little English but made a stilted attempt at conversation in order to be friendly. Some visiting Polish sailors gave to a friend and me several live rifle bullets as trophies that were promptly confiscated by the school headmistress.

During school holidays my brother joined me at Borth-y-Gest. We explored beaches, coves, and sand dunes, and scrambled over rocky headlands. We played hide-and-seek war games in tall bracken undergrowth, and built forts and secret houses in windswept dwarf oak trees. We were oblivious of the real thing happening half our world away in the skies over our Surrey home and on the beaches of England and France.

Despite my father's busy hospital duties, every week he wrote installments of a story about Max, a mouse, and Egbert, an elephant, which he illustrated with line drawings. Max and Egbert's adventures were our enduring fantasy, and a tenuous link with our mostly absentee parents.

After a year, I joined my brother at his boarding school, Deudraeth Castle, a baronial stone pile on the Penrhyndeudraeth peninsula a mile distant from the mock-Italian village of Portmeirion. At the outbreak of war, Ian Stuart—the eccentric, thirty-year-old headmaster—had evacuated the school from Frinton-on-Sea in Essex. On a whim he hired buses and trundled all the pupils and staff off to North Wales, where he rented the castle whose many rooms easily accommodated the school.

Life at Deudraeth Castle was quite informal compared with schools I would know later. Instead of a conventional uniform we wore grey shorts, corduroy bomber jackets, open-necked Aertex shirts, and sandals. We were free to roam the neighbouring woods where we built our scout camps.

One day a visitor arrived at the school while the headmaster, affectionately known as 'Mr Ian', was demonstrating a headstand in the front hall.

"Is this the Portmeirion Hotel?" asked the stranger.

"No, it's not," Mr Ian replied, still upside down. "It's Deudraeth Castle school, and I'm the headmaster."

After a boy wrote graffiti in chalk across the tennis court, Mr Ian summoned six suspects to his study. I was one of them by reason of my friendship with the leader.

"Would you do this sort of thing on the walls at home?" he asked.

"No, sir," we replied in unison, shaking our heads.

"Then don't do it here," he said, "Get a bucket of water and brushes and scrub it clean." We spent a couple of backbreaking hours reflecting on our misdeeds, but we bore Mr Ian no grudge as he was always fair. He had a singular understanding of small boys—at heart one himself—and we responded with love and loyalty.

Mr Ian held Latin classes in his bedroom, which occupied the octagonal tower of the castle. Wearing his dressing gown, he propped himself on pillows in a huge bed surrounded by a dozen small boys sitting cross-legged. While quizzing us over grammar he chain-smoked. If we knew the answer to a question, instead of holding up a hand to draw his attention, we flicked our fingers—index against opposed thumb and middle finger—that made a loud snapping noise. The loudest snapper was the winner. One hot summer's day our class was working through the *Shorter Latin Primer* (known as the Short Bread-eating Primer) when Mr Ian suddenly clapped his book shut and hurled it through the open window. Silence and tenterhooks followed.

"To the beach!" he yelled, "It's too nice for Latin today. You've got twenty minutes to be ready."

One ten-year-old boy, who owned a bugle, became homesick and ran away with one of the few girls in the school. They camped in a neighbouring farmer's field, less than a mile from the school. On return from his brief escapade, Mr Ian appointed him to blow *Reveille* each morning from the castle ramparts and at the close of our wide games. Proud of his assignment, the bugler settled down and never ran away again.

The slate slab floor of the castle's main hall made a smooth concourse for games of marbles. A craze swept the school and we repeatedly requested more marbles from home especially the prized blarneys with their central, coloured spiral. You rolled the marble underhand towards your opponent's marble, which became yours if hit. If you fell short, but within a forearm's length of your opponent, you could bomb him from eye height. A suit of mediaeval armour stood behind one of the doors in the hall, and marbles often rolled irretrievably under it. I was once sent out of class for bad behaviour and on hearing the approaching steps of the headmaster, climbed behind the armour to avoid detection.

"Good morning, Steele minor," he said, in passing, "Have you lost your marbles?"

We also played 'conkers' with shiny, mahogany-brown horse chestnuts. You bored a hole carefully with a penknife spike and threaded a string knotted at one end. You then dangled the conker at arm's length and an opponent swung at it. If he smashed your conker, his became a "one-er", if the smashed conker had already racked up several victories, that number was added to the winner's score and carried over to the next encounter. Someone discovered that conkers baked overnight in the kitchen oven became rock hard. They were then unbeatable, but this was considered foul play. Huddles of boys were scattered round the grounds and secreted in school corners, gambling at poker and *vingt-et-un* for high stakes with conkers and marbles. Soon Mr Ian decided it was bad for our morals and closed our clandestine casinos. Instead we turned to building balsa wood gliders of our own design, carved with razor blades and smoothed with sandpaper. We launched them from the castle tower and a good flight could reach a distant field beyond the tennis court.

The castle was designed as a hotel. Before the war, Clough Williams-Ellis built, in a natural vale looking across Tremadog Bay to Harlech Castle, a conglomeration of pastel-painted houses with ornamental follies, a barbican gatehouse, and campanile. A lighthouse and a concrete ship were set into a seaside wharf in front of the hotel. Clough, an ardent Welsh Nationalist, was a tall, gangly figure with a shock of curly, flaxen hair. He occasionally appeared at the school carrying a shepherd's crook and dressed in breeches and yellow stockings, with a cravat and yellow waistcoat. Before the war the village had become a fashionable Bohemian artists' colony. It was deserted during the war when only a caretaker remained to guard the empty buildings—a ghostly monument to its days of carefree splendour. Not a soul stirred where once writers, actors, and artists convened and sported. A mistress of the Prince of Wales once stayed there and kept regular contact with St James' Palace by a party-line telephone shared with the neighbours who could listen in.

The castle was set in spacious grounds, but had no level fields suitable for cricket and soccer. Instead we played "wide games" that ranged over the entire Portmeirion peninsula, a paradise of acres of open broom, gorse, and bracken heath, and neglected ornamental gardens. An overgrown arboretum, the Gwyllt, had cavernous tunnels burrowed through dense rhododendron, azalea, and bamboo plantations. Each boy became a battleship, a cruiser, a destroyer, or a submarine (valued with appropriate points), and two opposing sides tried to invade their enemy's naval base. Breaking a strand of wool tied round the arm of an opponent with lower points put him out of action. At game-over the bugler boy sounded *Retreat* from a gazebo on a hill overlooking the sea, where low tide left sand ripples stretching to the horizon. We then congregated in Portmeirion, a ghostly monument to days of carefree splendour for the rich.

To play cricket or football, according to the season, each week we took the Ffestiniog railway three miles across the causeway, from Minffordd station to Porthmadog. In an unfavourable wind an overpowering smell of blood wafted from the adjacent abattoir. This pleasant outing supposedly provided team discipline to offset the happy hooliganism of our wide games.

Each scout patrol and cub pack had its own camp among the thick oak and beech woods and scrub surrounding the school. We built huts from timber and any other material we could scavenge in the grounds. At weekends we were banished to our respective camps to cook and care for ourselves. We collected our allocation of vegetables and some flour from the school kitchen. Parcels of "tuck" sent from home, supplemented our rations with split lentils, porridge oats, and dried milk (farting powder). Over embers we baked "twists" of flour dough rolled on green sticks that tasted like warm concrete.

The school also enrolled a few girls. I became fond of one of them, the daughter of a renowned author who smoked dried Old Man's Beard—a lichen—in place of war-scarce cigarettes. He took us on a weekend outing way up in the hills to his stone farmhouse that had a secret hideaway behind a large, flaking oil painting. In a field in front of the school was a huge chestnut tree where together my paramour and I balanced along the low branch that recurved to form a natural bower. There, aged eight, I proposed marriage and was peremptorily rejected.

Each day after lunch we spent a "quiet hour" in the school common room, the main lounge of the former hotel. Dozens of small boys sat on tuck boxes (wooden trunks with metal-reinforced corners) knitting scarves for sailors with wool sent on request from a government office somewhere in the south of England. Knitting became furiously competitive, and, under the tuition of one of the teachers, we each tried to make the longest scarf. We imagined we were helping sailors win the war, bundled to the ears on corvette patrol in the gelid North Atlantic and wearing our mufflers that were often more than six feet long. I have never knitted since. Our tuck boxes, securely locked, held our private treasures, especially boiled sweets and chocolate sent from home. The matron, Mollie Keen, handed out our daily ration from jars labelled with our names, together with yellow calcium pills, which we pretended to swallow, then spat out into the toilet bowl.

The other teachers were strangely assorted and all excused from military service. Mr Sontag, an Austrian refugee, taught us carpentry and art, while his wife taught music. Fresh curlicued wood shavings lay on the floor of the carpentry shop, which smelled of the wood glue that bubbled in a cast-iron pot on a stove in one corner of the stables. There we boys built a flat-bottomed, double-ended, dory-style boat, named *Alouette*, which we launched from the quay at Portmeirion with great ceremony, all the school attending.

Mr Sontag lived on the opposite side of the peninsula in a low-roofed stone cottage that he had refurbished. Because there was no road nearby, the cottage was approached by a grassy track through woods, descending via a flight of steps cut into the bank. A slate-flagged terrace and retaining wall overlooked the sea that lapped the rocks below where Mr Sontag moored his home-built boat. A hundred yards to the right lay the Cob, the causeway where occasional steam trains of the Ffestiniog narrow gauge railway puffed towards Porthmadog. Mr Sontag, a meticulous craftsman, built all his own furniture. He fashioned seats from beer barrels that were cut at half their height; the remaining staves gave back support and were painted in Austrian style with exotic flowers.

Myopic Mr Hann, by reason of his rough guttural accent, we believed was a German spy. We imagined him signalling with his shaving mirror from the castle tower to enemy submarines waiting in the estuary.

Mr Crawshay Williams (also known as Cow-shit Long-legs), whose Adam's Apple oscillated during math class, lived in a local farmer's cottage. He was a minor philosopher and was writing a book, *The Methodology of Methodology,* inspired by Bertrand Russell. One day I met Mr Russell—a renowned pacifist, who spent the war in a nearby house on the Penrhyndeudraeth peninsula—striding over the gorse moor behind the school wearing a devilish black floppy hat and a tweed cape and bundled in a long scarf. We had no idea how famous the great man was.

Rarely my mother spent holidays with us in Wales; because of pressure of hospital work, my father came only once in the five years we were there. On the day of his visit my holiday job was to collect milk from Dai Jones's farm at nearby Penrhyndeudraeth, and to deliver it into churns stored in the dairy of the high-ceilinged, slate-floored kitchen. A cast-iron potato peeler was bolted to a scrubbed wooden table and, when cranked fast, it gathered momentum and whirred loudly. On hearing footsteps I tried to grab the gyrating handle near its axle, but caught my index finger in the gear and ripped off the nail. Unwilling to confess my crime, I wrapped my finger in a handkerchief, ran to collect the milk, and returned with a full churn. Meanwhile the pain and throbbing increased and blood seeped through the dressing. As I entered the hall I slammed the front door loudly and howled with pain pretending I had caught my finger in the door. The matron summoned my father, who took a cursory professional look and drove me to Porthmadog to see Dr Morris, the father of one of my school friends. He was so solicitous that I broke down and confessed. He removed the nail, the bed of which remains deformed, a reminder of exquisite pain and futile deception.

* * *

Newspapers were placed on a lectern in the school front hall for students to read. They told of the Blitz devastating London, of fathers called up into the armed forces to fight abroad and often not returning, and of wives trying to keep homes running in their absence with the added burden of ration books, air raid sirens, and the ubiquitous military. In tranquil north Wales it was difficult to relate to these daily horrors until the holiday in 1944 when we returned home.

On the day of my brother's and my departure, we assembled with other students bound for home in the front hall at 4:00 a.m. with small travelling bags and gas masks in cardboard boxes, awaiting taxis to take us to Penrhyndeudraeth station. The headlight beams approached along the school's avenue of chestnut trees shining like tigers' eyes. At the station, as the sun rose over Harlech Bay, the train puffed into view with sparks spewing from the funnel, and smoke rose over yellow gorse bushes beside the track. Beyond Barmouth the line swung inland, winding a devious course through mid-Wales before entering England. On the platform of Paddington Station, from where we had left four years before, I rushed to hug a stranger whom I mistook for my father. After a short holiday we were glad to return to North Wales. I don't recall missing our parents, because that was just how it was for all of us. We had strong friendships among the boys and a very happy atmosphere in the school.

Soon the newspapers were full of news of the D-day invasion of Normandy, and in geography class we charted the Allied armies edging slowly across France into Germany. Quite suddenly on 8 May 1945, three days after my tenth birthday, the war was over, and my brother and I returned south. Our blissful five years in North Wales was an evanescent dream.

# THREE

SOON AFTER MY BROTHER AND I returned home from North Wales, our parents decided we needed civilizing so they sent us to private schools—preparatory for me, public for him, both misnomers. This was because they were exclusive to high fee-payers, and preparatory only for the rigid social structure of Britain. It was like a prison sentence after the freedom and liberal teaching, or lack of it, that we had enjoyed for five years at Deudraeth Castle. I entered Aldro School (as weird to me as its bizarre name) in the village of Shackleford. This was once rural Surrey, a county of quaint pubs with cricket pitches on village greens, beech forests and broad furze heath, stockbrokers and upper-middle-class gentry. My brother's boarding school, Charterhouse, was only a few miles away near Godalming.

Aldro School was set in the spacious grounds of a Lutyens mansion, with lead-paned windows and assorted outhouses, stables, and vegetable gardens—reminders of its opulent days as a private house. In front of the main building from a stone-flagged terrace with a rose pergola and sundial, one looked over a sunken, walled ditch (known as a ha-ha fence) to the sports fields. Beyond was a small reed-fringed lake where we swam among weeds and watercress and squelched in gooey mud. The boathouse became a place of secret meetings where we boys bemoaned the school, the masters, and anyone who made us miserable. My uniform of white shirt and tie, grey shorts and pullover, long knee socks (usually around my ankles), school cap and blazer with the school crest felt like convict attire.

On Sundays we walked to church by way of a lane that led across fields through elm, oak, and beech woods towards Peperharow. Aldro School's headmaster, Frederick "Freddie" Hill, known to the boys by his initials—FEH—was a lay preacher. He fancied himself in the pulpit and indulged a passion for amateur dramatics by preaching in a black university gown and a shabby, silk-lined academic hood trimmed with rabbit fur. A diet of daily prayers and bible readings in the school chapel made for stodgy religion. Etched above the assembly room fireplace was the school motto, from a Kipling poem,—"If you can meet with Triumph and Disaster, and treat those two imposters just the same ... you'll be a Man, my son." It suggested the glory of Empire and a stiff upper lip, better to prepare us for greater trials ahead at our public schools, which were far from open to the public, being exclusively fee-paying.

The headmaster's wife—Octavia, alias Blanche—billowed like a galleon under full sail with her silvery bouffant hair, double chin, and vast bosom. She lived in the Private Wing, a cavernous room secluded from the noise in the Spartan corridors and classrooms behind a thick velvet curtain. After Sunday church Blanche dispensed our ration of sweets—tuck. Then she dispatched us on healthy walks in the school grounds that usually took the form of roaming round the lake telling each other smutty stories. In the evening we went to FEH's study where we sat cross-legged in the penumbra of his reading lamp listening agog to his theatrical rendering of stories like Dr Syn's baleful doings in the mists of the Romney Marsh.

In the corridors and classrooms our days were ordered by bells, and on the playing fields by whistles and the shouts of bossy older boys; one of their jobs was to tick off a record of the bowel movements of junior boys (inexplicably termed "going across"). The penalty for a first omission was a bowl of vegetable soup served by the housekeeper; for repeated failure, Matron dosed us with castor oil.

We ran everywhere because our life was thereby regimented. We ran to the hexagonal cider house in the orchard by the main gate for Latin with Alfie Tressler, who arrived every morning on his moped bicycle. We ran to the old village schoolroom down by the allotments for geography with debonair Peter Carpmel, who entertained us by changing the dressing of his amputation stump (the leg had been shot away in Corsica, something quite inexplicable to us boys). We ran to the stables for gym, and to the squash court for boxing with "Sarge" Lawrence, an ex-army physical training instructor, who did full forward aerial somersaults to impress us. I showed an early promise in boxing (I know not why) and in squash racquets.

I was always hungry because food was still rationed and continued to be scarce for several years after the war. We had kippers and porridge for breakfast, and heavy suet pudding called "boiled baby" or another sort with raisins called "spotted dick" for lunch. To supplement our lean diet we each had a small patch in the vegetable garden. There we grew lettuces and carrots from seeds out of glossy packages impaled for identification on bamboo sticks at the head of each row.

At Aldro I encountered a paedophile for the first time. Chain-smoking Mr Scott's fingers were nicotine-stained to the knuckles, his teeth were yellow-brown, and his clothes reeked of stale tobacco. Greasy, grey swept-back hair fell forward into his eyes, which were rheumy-red from cigarette smoke constantly curling up the side of his face. Scotty, as he was known, was habitually hunched, warming his

backside over the cast-iron radiator in the hall where we congre
round him between classes. We naively mistook pats on the head, or on
the bottom, for affection. Nonetheless he was popular among the boys
and none of us felt threatened by him.

A young matron known as Twinkletoes oversaw our baths making
sure we washed our faces and scrubbed behind our ears before washing
our nethers, which always had to be performed last. Even a face cloth
could not hide our nascent and unruly erections. During nature walks
Scotty gave garbled talks about birds and bees—our only sex instruc-
tion. But that was not then important to us, romping around like pre-
pubertal puppies oblivious of what awaited us at public school.

* * *

The weekly Sunday ritual of smart parents in smart cars arriving
after church to take boys away for the day was known as "going out."
One Sunday in May 1946 my father arrived in his beige-and-black
Armstrong Siddeley. He was alone, which was no surprise since my
mother usually stayed at home to prepare lunch. Driving along the
Hog's Back, my brother and I barely drew breath chattering on about
lessons flunked, goals missed, jokes played on some boys, fights with
others. Something felt awry as we coasted into our crescent driveway.
Our mother was normally at the front door to greet us; however, that
day the porch was empty.

"Where's Maw?" we asked together. (Our parents had adopted the
nicknames Maw and Paw from reading *Wee Macgregor*, the tale of a
Glaswegian boy brought up in the Gorbals.)

My father didn't reply immediately. His face was drawn and empty
of its usual sparkle as he led us into the living room where French windows opened onto the garden.

"Maw's died," he said. Then he hugged my brother and me close
to him and tears, huge tears, rolled from his eyes and dropped onto the

carpet. We were stunned into silence but were aware that some cataclysmic event was afoot even before its consequences overwhelmed us. When our sobbing abated, my father lifted a plain bronze box from the mantelshelf over the empty fireplace where I had so often stared at the flames in the grate during long, cosy evenings spent with my mother.

"Her ashes are in here," he said. "She was cremated yesterday." Then after long pause, "I think we should bury her in the garden."

I wondered why we had not been told nor invited to a funeral. Speechless, I never asked. He laid the casket on the sofa, knelt down, and drew my brother and me to either side of him. He said a prayer but I don't remember any of it. I just stared between my fingers at the box lying on a richly patterned red, magenta, and black Persian rug that was draped over the back of the couch. It seemed impossible that the box contained all that remained of my mother, who the week before had been her habitual timid self, but pretty, loving, and seemingly well.

"A dog barked in the road and woke me," said my father, who was a light sleeper. "I felt something was wrong. I put on my dressing gown and ran to Maw's bedroom. It was locked. I called and knocked on the door but there was no reply. So I went into the garden and climbed through her bedroom window. There was a note on the table beside her bed. Her pill bottle was empty."

Because she slept badly, my mother always kept a tray of medicine bottles beside her bed in a separate bedroom from my father at the opposite end of the house. He showed us the note, written in pencil, which read: "I'm sorry I've been such a drag on you all these years. Now you will be free again. Please forgive me, but I can't go on like this. I love you all very much. Sylvia."

I was bewildered that a mother, who said so often that she loved us, could do something so hurtful and shameful. Only later did I learn of the years of torment, anguish, and recurring depression that had brought her to this final, tragic act.

"Fetch a spade," my father said, guiding us into the garden. "We'll dig a hole over there under the maple tree I planted last year."

My brother and I collected the spade from the shed behind which we used to smoke cigarettes we had stolen from a silver box kept for guests. We walked in a daze down the lawn between herbaceous borders full of May colour to a coppice that my father was nurturing behind a beech hedge enclosing a small grove of trees. We took turns at digging a hole at the foot of the maple that he had chosen, cutting through some roots.

With his penknife my brother carved "Maw" into the bark of the tree. We placed the casket deep in the ground. Then my father read some verses from the Wisdom of Solomon. " . . . But the souls of the righteous are in the hand of God and there shall no torment touch them. In the sight of the unwise they seem to die . . . but they are in peace . . . and in the time of their visitation they shall shine, and run to and fro like sparks among the stubble."

I imagined a charred field with sparks flitting here and there like fireflies. One of those sparks was the soul of my mother. That image gave me profound solace.

We walked slowly back up to the house and my father told us about some of the events of the past sad week.

"There was a post-mortem examination," he said. "The pathologist said that some marks on her skin could have been caused by an injection. At the inquest the coroner reproached me for not reporting her previous attempts. He kept asking me about marks on her arms."

The insinuation that my father might have caused them himself upset him greatly, since every detail was reported in the local newspaper, the *Surrey Advertiser*. Eventually the coroner announced a formal verdict of "Suicide while the balance of mind was disturbed."

Sometime later my father's sister, Janet, spoke to him. "You must be terribly alone. I'm surprised you don't seem more shaken by Sylvia's death."

"Don't forget she's tried it before," he replied. "Thank God this time I didn't have to decide whether or not to revive her."

We boys were quite unaware of my mother's repeated bouts of melancholy that accounted for her sad demeanour. On each of her previous attempts my father had revived her with the help of the nuns of Mount Alvernia.

These events fell on us like blows on a floored boxer who stands up and is knocked down again and again. I went back to school drained, but school went on as normal. I sobbed at night under the bedclothes and often woke up with nightmares. No one mentioned my mother, neither my friends nor any of the teachers. I presumed that this incident—my mother's death—was best swept under the carpet. Crying was unmanly for boys, and grief unheard of. As for sympathetic counsel, there was none.

For several months after my mother's death, my father lost his normal zest and became quite withdrawn. I wrote a note to remind myself to bring back to school from home a "photo of Paw smiling." However, in none of the photo albums could I find one. His usually kind, handsome face, always hinting a smile even when serious, was stern and haunted with sadness.

One day during the holidays I returned home unexpectedly early through the lower garden gate from the direction of Merrow Downs. My father was on the garden swing seat with his arm around his lady house surgeon. Joan Leitch was a pretty redhead with a North Country lilt, young and vivacious and nearer to my age than his. She appeared more and more frequently at our home and I believed they were in love. I liked her and was excited by the thought that they might get married. It never occurred to me then that an affair between them might have been the cause of my mother's recent desperation.

My father still seemed worried over the coroner's report and how the bad publicity would affect his surgical practice. I overheard many long and acrimonious telephone conversations with my mother's brother about Grandfather Walsh's will. Their disputes seemed to be over my mother's share of the estate, who should get the Rolls Royce, who the pearl necklace. Generally things at home returned to normal, though my toys remained untouched in the playroom, which I could not bear to enter as it was adjacent to my mother's bedroom. I avoided the corner of the garden where we buried her ashes, and kept to the path opposite when walking towards the back gate.

* * *

My brother and I returned to our schools and outwardly life seemed to return to normal, although underneath it was clouded in sadness and bewilderment. One Sunday in November 1946, like any other Sunday, my father drove over from Guildford to take us home for a day out. First he collected my brother from Charterhouse and then came to Aldro for me. He seemed strangely preoccupied and spent much of the day sitting in a chair beside the empty fireplace, writing in his small, fine hand. As the dread hour approached for leaving the peace of home and returning to the zoo of small boys that was school, I became more apprehensive than usual. He dropped me off at Aldro with a parting hug, and then took my brother on to Charterhouse.

The following day during mid-morning break I was kicking a ball around the soccer field with a dozen other boys. A senior older boy approached me.

"FEH wants to talk to you, Steele," he said offhandedly. "He's up by the barn."

Any headmasterly summons was ominous, but a quick inventory of any possible recent sins produced nothing particularly heinous. I hurried along the crazy paving leading to the barn where we changed clothes before games. The headmaster stood where hundreds of schoolboy feet had worn the grass to mud by cutting across the corner. He stared at his shoes and avoided looking me in the eye. He continued his habit of biting the cuticle of a misshapen nail of his right forefinger, which he always did when nervous.

"Something has happened to your father, Steele." A long silence followed; then he said, "Come over to the house."

I didn't ask what had happened. I just imagined some sort of accident. I followed him through the school's double front doors into the hall, and past the heavy magenta curtain into the Private Wing. Blanche, in the gallery above the hall, came scurrying down the stairs and pushed aside the curtain. She clutched me to her vast bosom, into which I sank, almost suffocating.

"You poor boy," she said. "He was such a good man."

*Was* sounded sinister. She led me to a seat by the fire.

"We'll have to wait to hear from the police to be sure what happened."

Mention of the police was bad news, but I still didn't comprehend what she was getting at. I hoped it was just a car accident, and I guessed that my father was probably in hospital. I sat alone in the Private Wing for a couple of hours, oblivious of whispered comings and goings. It was a beautiful sunny day and the other boys were noisily playing games on the field outside the window. Late in the afternoon Blanche came in with a cup of tea on a tray—a dire sign indeed.

"Your father has died," she said. She gave no explanation. Then, as if there was no more to say, "You'd better go to your classroom and do your prep."

Dazed and numb, I returned to the cacophony on the other side of the velvet curtain. Sitting at my desk I stared vacantly through a pool of tears at the hinged lid of the desk, where generations of bored small boys had etched their names and scoured channels with their pencils between ridges in the wood grain. Tears, I knew, were for sissys. However, I cried gallons during the next weeks, either alone behind the boathouse, or under the bedclothes after lights-out.

I kept thinking, "Now I'm an orphan." The word was vaguely reminiscent of *Oliver Twist*, and conjured images of workhouses that compounded my bewilderment. Being an orphan had no real meaning. To my embarrassment several relatives—Grandfather John Steele and various aunts—visited the school outside the regular times for going out, which caused inquisitive gossip among my fellows. I was aware of my family's love and concern, but they seemed entirely absorbed with discussions over what should be done with my brother and me. He was at nearby Charterhouse during this time and I saw little of him. Certainly we never talked about our parents then, or even subsequently. No one talked to us about our parents; everyone skirted around them for fear of upsetting us. Grief was unmentionable and more comfortably left that way.

Some days later the headmaster told me that my father, too, had killed himself. I was utterly floored by this news, but I had no one with whom I could talk about it. Many years later I learned the circumstances from Dr Heward Bell, his best friend and a physician with whom he had worked closely. Together they virtually ran the wartime medicine of Guildford.

According to Dr Bell, the Friday before that Black Sunday my father met him in the hospital.

"I'd like to talk to you about an urgent personal matter," my father said.

"I'm rather busy at this moment," Dr Bell replied. "How about tea on Sunday? Come at 4:00 p.m. after you've dropped the boys back at school."

On returning to Guildford my father drove straight to Mount Alvernia nursing home where he asked for Mother Francis, the Mother Superior.

"Reverend Mother's away," said the nun who met him in the entrance hall. She noted that that he "looked like a ghost."

When my father did not arrive punctually for tea as arranged, Dr Bell became alarmed and phoned our home. On getting no reply he felt something was amiss, so he collected a friend and drove straight to our home, Stoney Cross. The garage was shut tight so they forced the door. The Armstrong Siddeley's engine was running and my father was slumped over the wheel, still holding a pencil in one hand. In the other was a piece of paper on which he had scribbled a few words that tailed off and became illegible.

My father was cremated somewhere nearby—Woking Cemetery is my guess—attended by his father and his sister Janet. My brother and I were not invited to the funeral. Presumably this was to spare us grief, but grief ungrieved may never go away. I don't know what happened to his ashes, nor if there is a memorial plaque in some gloomy Surrey cemetery. The tree in the garden at Stoney Cross under which we buried my mother's ashes has disappeared and with it my brother's penknife inscription.

* * *

Much of my teenage years passed in a haze of trying to come to terms with sadness that supplanted any happy memories of my parents. None of my friends or relatives talked to me of them, and the subject was always taboo between my brother and myself. I let down my guard just once and poured out the whole story to a friend while we walked round the school lake. It felt like opening a floodgate. But I soon clammed up, mortified with guilt at my confession to my friend, who did not know how to react. I never told my secret again, even to my closest friends.

One sunny day on a nature walk with Mr Scott, our class, full of high jinks, rested under a tree. I cannot remember how the subject arose, but one boy asked Scotty, "What's suicide, sir?"

"It's when a person kills himself," he replied.

"Why do they do that, sir?"

"I don't know, but it's a crime."

"What does that mean, sir? You can't punish them when they're dead." Giggles all round.

"Perhaps," he said. "But it used to be that people who committed suicide were buried at a crossroads with a stake through their heart."

This insensitive remark haunted me for years. Scotty must have known about my parents and it was strange that he could have been so insensitive.

Subsequently Scotty gave me a tartan tie for my birthday and asked me to visit him during the holidays at his cottage in Sussex. Fortunately I ignored the invitation because shortly thereafter he was gaoled for molesting a village boy less lucky than myself.

Because my father had not written a proper will, Lloyds Bank Executor and Trustee Department became our guardian and dispenser of his estate. At the start of every holidays my brother and I had to visit the manager, Mr Strange, to account for ourselves during the past school term. His bald pate shone and he twitched his nose while peering at me through thick tortoiseshell glasses. These interviews were so distasteful that I sat in front of him kicking my feet against the panels of his desk.

"Stop that, boy," he said testily when I gave another kick. After a suitable silence I lobbed a bombshell into his lap.

"A friend has asked me to stay with his family next holidays," I said. "They have a farm in Kenya."

"Oh, that would cost too much," Mr Strange replied, as custodian of our inheritance. "We've got to be careful with your money."

"But I may never get the chance again," I said.

"I won't allow it, boy," he replied. "That's final."

Various relatives discussed between themselves the future of my brother and me, and without consulting us Mr Strange alone decided who should be our guardian. I had become fond of Joan Leitch and would have liked her, but Mr Strange considered her unsuitable since she was a single lady doctor with a profession to follow. Grandfather had remarried and we were all devoted to his wife, but Mr Strange decided that Grandfather and Dorothy were too old to manage a couple of rambunctious teenagers. Aunt Janet Lack, my father's younger sister, wanted to have us but she was not thought affluent enough for the standards of Lloyds Bank.

So we ended up, reluctantly on both sides, as wards of my mother's brother, Arthur Walsh. He and his wife Joan had just returned from India; they now lived outside Godalming in a house surrounded by acres of garden woodland. No one had reckoned how much the intrusion into this paradise by two bewildered teenage orphans would disrupt the ordered lives of my uncle and aunt, who had two young children of their own.

# FOUR

UNCLE ARTHUR AND AUNT JOAN WALSH had recently retired from the jute business and returned from India where they had lived mostly in Calcutta. There they had servants, polo, and a busy social schedule. On sweltering afternoons they cocooned themselves from the slums that lay just outside the walls of the Tollygunge Club where turbaned bearers, on order, brought tiffin and sundowner chota pegs of whisky and soda, and uniformed ayahs kept children well out of earshot. In Grandfather Walsh's jute exporting business, workdays were short. Tennis and polo followed the noon siesta, and bridge filled evenings at the Gymkhana Club. When the pre-monsoon heat and humidity began to rise in the plains, the entire Government of India, and many civilian followers decamped to Simla. The women and children of the Raj followed shortly thereafter to various other Himalayan hill stations like Darjeeling, Mussoorie, and Nainital.

This enchanted life ill prepared the Walshes for a return to post-war Britain, with ration books, demob suits, and a new socialism that threatened to impoverish the independently wealthy. They lived in a large house, Munstead Grange, on the outskirts of Godalming in a dozen acres of manicured garden surrounded by woodland of oak, chestnut, and beech. A driveway flanked by rhododendrons led to a red brick house, typical of many luxurious Surrey dwellings designed in the thirties by Edward Lutyens. A red-tiled roof with ornate brick chimneys surmounted lead-paned windows that peered out over lawns and herbaceous borders to a laburnum pergola, the tennis court with its gazebo, and a high yew hedge surrounding the swimming pool.

A silver salver lay on the table in the front hall to receive visiting cards. Also it held the keys to my uncle's Rolls Royce. Kashmir carpets brought back from India were scattered on polished hardwood floors. In the sitting room were chintz-covered sofas and deep armchairs. Bookshelves flanking the fireplace held volumes on India, mainly concerned with horses and shedding the blood of India's prolific wildlife. Silver-embossed frames of family photos graced the baby grand piano, and on various delicate coffee tables stood carved ivory elephants. Sandalwood cigarette boxes gave off a whiff of exotic faraway places.

A married couple—cook and butler—occupied the servants' quarters, and a full-time gardener lived in a tithe cottage nearby. Nanny took care of the young children upstairs in the nursery from where they emerged around four o'clock—afternoon teatime—to pass an hour or so with their parents.

During the holidays my rapscallion brother and I stayed (rather than lived) in the guest bedroom of this immaculate household. Our belt buckles chipped the walnut footboards of the beds over which we flung our dirty clothes; we sorted our postage stamp collections on a glass-topped vanity table that cracked by us leaning on it; our shoes rucked the Persian carpet. By day our schoolboy treasures had to be tidied away into huge wardrobes; during term-time they were packed in cardboard boxes and stored in the attic in case the guest room was needed. It was never a homely pad and we felt ill at ease there.

My uncle bought a nearby farm and hired a bailiff to run it. He drove there daily in his Land Rover and walked around the farm looking as if he was working, dressed in traditional farmers' garb of a flat cloth cap, plus fours, and Wellington boots. He and my aunt tried to be kind to us, but they clearly rued the day they took on such unruly wards. In a corner of the spacious grounds Uncle Arthur had erected an old army hut for us to hang out in. However, lack of heating and a cold concrete floor rendered it suitable only for storing bicycles, sports gear, and assorted junk. The cost of the hut was added to the bill for our keep submitted monthly to Lloyds Bank Executor & Trustee Department. Our once-effusive gratitude shortly rang hollow.

* * *

My brother and I found temporary respite from unrelenting warfare between ourselves by building a tree house high in a huge chestnut tree that stood against the estate fence. We built it of wood, collected from a nearby coppice, that we nailed together. To reach the upper branches above the bare trunk, my brother, who was far more adventurous than me, tied a rope round a brick, hurled it over a horizontal branch twenty feet above the ground, and then climbed the rope. Meanwhile I made a ladder by tying clove hitches of stout hemp onto ash rungs that I cut from a clearing over the fence where a friendly forester was thinning a plantation. We hung the ladder from the stump of a sawn-off branch, so our feet swung away as we pulled ourselves up into the fork of the tree like Jack tar sailors aloft. Later we learned the trick of positioning the ladder against the trunk to stop it swaying.

We built the frame of the house with stakes nailed into the tree. For walls we tacked parallel slats of ash, leaving spaces for window lights. Being purists, we used no planks, boards, or corrugated iron. As chippie's mate, I cut and trimmed saplings on the ground and tied them in bundles, which my brother hauled up on a rope.

We worked hard throughout the summer and by autumn the house was complete with trapdoor and three seats built against the diverging branches of the tree. Even when the labour that bonded us was over, our tree house remained the one place where we did not squabble and were at peace. We sat up there in late autumn and picked ripe chestnuts from our parlour window; when the leaves fell we could hear rain drumming on the tar paper roof, and watch it dripping off the wide eaves. We invited my uncle to visit the house; he was scared of the rope ladder and just put his head through the trapdoor and retreated, shaking so hard that the rungs rattled and we had to guide him down foot by foot. But his visit reassured him why we were so quiet and well-behaved when secreted away in this corner of the grounds. I was now twelve years old and had moved to Charterhouse from Aldro, so I was quite used to being bossed about by older boys. My brother was unusually solicitous when I arrived at the school as I had left all my friends behind at Aldro.

During the summer holidays we were occasionally shipped off to Somerset to stay with our mother's elderly great-aunt Lil Hawkins, at Cowslip Green, Wrington. Her house looked over a ha-ha ditch, across fields where cows grazed, to the distant Mendip Hills. Aunt Lil spoiled us with teas of home-baked scones spread thickly with honey and fresh clotted cream known as "thunder and lightning." With gnarled arthritic hands, she delicately painted flowers on plain china cups and saucers to raise money for the local Women's Institute.

Uncle Fred watched us with benign indifference as we raced our bikes round the house on carefully raked and manicured paths. We circled the vegetable garden and the raspberry cages and swooped down past the cedar of Lebanon, skidding round the back yard beside the empty stables and potting sheds. A sharp corner at the end of the house brought us, in a shower of gravel, to the finishing line on the front lawn. We then tried to rake out the worst of our skid marks before the gardener complained. Our racecourses were increasingly complex as we became more competitive and our dirt-riding skills improved. Bike racing kept us happy for days on end and brought other children to play. I fell deliciously, unrequitedly, in love with a surgeon's daughter from a large house up on the hill. Nevertheless, I could beat her on my bike.

My relationship with my Munstead uncle and aunt cooled, froze, and finally came to an inevitable end after they sent me to an eminent London psychiatrist for a sex talk they evidently felt unable to give themselves. A bizarre chain of events came about thus.

At Nannie's behest, my young cousin rested on her bed for an hour every day after lunch. With nothing better to do, one day I innocently lay down beside her to read a story aloud. On leaving, I passed her clothes cupboard and, stopping at one, casually remarked, "That's a very pretty dress." Nanny must have overheard this.

I thought nothing of the incident until a few weeks later when I was summoned to my housemaster's study.

"Your uncle and aunt think you need a talk about life," said Freddie Ives. "We've arranged an appointment for you to see a doctor in London."

Telling my school friends caused hilarity and endless speculation on the need for such an elaborate introduction to sex.

"Lucky old Steele," they exclaimed, "the tosser gets a day off school and a trip to London for a sex talk. You can't beat that."

So on the appointed day I took the Southern Railway train to London. A brass plate beside the door of 118 Harley Street read "Dr H Yellowlees FRCP." A receptionist showed me into a waiting room where copies of *Country Life* and the *Tatler* covered the table. Dr Yellowlees was short and broad and built like a rugby footballer. He wore a black morning coat and pinstriped trousers, a starched white collar, and plain grey tie. He would become famous a few years later as the prosecution's chief psychiatric witness in the trial of Dr Bodkin Adams, accused of murdering elderly patients, who coincidentally left him large legacies, with drug overdoses.

"You play chess, don't you?" he asked in a distant but reasonably friendly voice as he set up a board on his consulting room desk. We played for about half an hour; that struck me as an expensive preface to a sex talk. Being quite expert for my age, I nearly beat him. This got us off to a bad start as he was evidently a poor loser.

Out of the blue he shot a question at me. "Do you have feelings towards your cousin? Do you often go into her room and look at her clothes?" Then the bombshell dropped. "Have you ever touched your cousin?"

In a flash the whole meaning of the visit became clear. I was flabbergasted at being suspected of evil intentions, perhaps even of dirty deeds.

"Was this what I came to London for?" I asked.

"Your uncle and aunt were worried about you," he blustered. "They think you shouldn't be showing such interest in your cousin. But they didn't feel comfortable discussing this with you themselves."

"That's ridiculous," I said, with anger boiling up inside. "I've been brought here falsely. That's a cheat. I'm leaving."

I astonished myself at my boldness in confronting this eminent man, having been educated to call my elders "sir," never to question their judgment, and to do what I was told. I stormed out of his consulting room and walked down Harley Street to Baker Street station, scuffing my heels on the pavement and kicking lampposts to vent my anger and frustration. This betrayal cooled to ice my relationship with my guardians and led to a tacit agreement that Munstead Grange was not the right place for me to spend the rest of my adolescence. I was now sixteen years old and went to live in Barnet, Hertfordshire, with my father's sister, Janet. My brother joined the Rifle Brigade for his National Service and our paths diverged, never truly to join again for any length of time.

\* \* \*

During all this turbulence I had one constant and faithful friend, Willie Scott. I first met him at Aldro School, but we continued to see each other in the holidays once our ways parted for different public schools—he for Eton, me for Charterhouse. Willie was an only child of wealthy parents who lived in a modest bungalow set deep in Surrey woods near the village of Shere. Mr Scott was the engineer, his wife the business brain of a small, highly successful machine tooling company in Clapham, South London.

Willie was hugely fat because each day he drank upwards of twenty bottles of Coca Cola, and was nicknamed Hippo by his unkind schoolfellows. His passions were model railways and fast cars. During school classes he bent his capable brain to designing endless new railway track layouts. His model railway was housed in a shed built in the woods close to his home, and dedicated only for his trains. The operator stood in the centre of an open square made of four tables, controlling a vast network of model trains with buttons and switches. Such a set, with every kind of engine, carriages, rolling stock, along with stations and lead figures to make up the panorama, outshone anything one could see in the model department of Hamley's toyshop in Regent Street, London. For hours we shunted and raced trains round Willie's elaborately designed tracks. Then when he became bored we dismantled the whole set, changed the layout, and rebuilt stations. It took several days to complete the new plan. When trains lost our fancy we built labyrinthine marble runs in his sandpit that passed through delicately carved tunnels and over bridges. Into the sand castle we inserted fireworks bought at a local toyshop. When the whim for marbles passed we would ignite the fuses and blow the whole structure to smithereens with whoops of destructive joy.

In his garage Mr Scott always kept a racing sports car. He regularly changed them for each new model that came on the market—Jaguar XK120, Aston Martin DB4, Ferrari—all appeared in the Scott stables. To avoid being ostentatious he never brought it to school, but he would often drive us at speed round the narrow Surrey lanes. Long before he was eligible for a licence, Willie had his own electric car, Bucephalus, which he drove round the perimeter of a neighbouring farmer's field. The car was a shell comprising only the front seats and a flat deck at the back. Its openness, and the narrow tracks overhung with branches that we followed, gave an illusion of tremendous speed at its maximum thirty miles per hour. After charging overnight, its batteries were good for a couple of hours of hard driving.

When Willie and I had exhausted the novelty of Bucephalus, we took to going out at night in one of his father's sports cars. We sped round the narrow, deserted, deeply cut lanes, headlights aglare, unlicenced, and thoughtless of other traffic. We would occasionally swop places and he would let me drive. The ultimate excitement was when we chased each other through the lanes in separate cars. One night on the way back from Birmingham, their chauffeur /handyman allowed me to drive a newly acquired Sunbeam Talbot coupé. Approaching a bridge too fast on a wet road, I missed the corner and rolled the car just before hitting a telegraph pole. No one was hurt but, sobered by this terrifying experience, I abandoned illicit driving. Mr Scott was amazingly phlegmatic and understanding over this episode.

The Scotts kept a suite at the Grosvenor Hotel for when they would spend evenings in London. Room service summoned a waiter with dinner on a trolley and champagne in a silver cooling bucket. Going to the theatre with them I felt very grand. I also accompanied them on holiday to Switzerland where on my first attempt at skiing I broke my ankle. That was set badly and remained deformed, causing me to limp slightly.

After Willie's father died of a stroke, his mother continued to run the firm and welcomed me during the holidays long after Willie and I had gone off to our respective public schools. I was utterly spoiled by the Scotts, but their kindness was a beacon in a rather bleak period.

# FIVE

MY MOVE FROM ALDRO TO Charterhouse brought new clothes, new friends, new rules, and new mores and customs—a metamorphosis for which my preparatory school had ill prepared me.

In Godalming High Street, Kinch & Lack, tailors, sold the school uniform—long grey flannel trousers, brown tweed jacket and grey pullover, shirts with cuff links and collar studs, and a tie. Weeks ahead of school term, I laid my new clothes over the back of a chair in my bedroom and stared at them, excited yet fearful of the future. From my brother I had gained some idea of the arcane hierarchy awaiting me—monitors and fags, cold showers, and beatings that were supposed to make men out of callow boys.

Charterhouse was then ranked in the top half dozen public schools—a gross misnomer since they were totally private and commanded high fees. However, once enrolled, one had gained access to an important rung on the English social ladder. It was like a silver spoon that helped pave a young man's way through many vicissitudes in life not accorded to less fortunate "lower orders." Although this rampant snobbery did not strike me as strange then, now it makes me shudder.

When not yet thirteen years old, I entered Weekites (founded half a century before by the Reverend Weekes), one of Charterhouse's twelve boarding houses. As one of the more modern houses, the five storey, red brick building was set on the side of the valley leading down to Godalming (known colloquially as Godge). It had concrete stairs with prison-like vertical iron supporting bars, and cavernous monastic dormitories with a dozen beds down each side. A hundred steps rose behind the house to the main school buildings and playing fields. A common punishment imposed by monitors on miscreant boys was to make them run up and down the steps.

The chapel's neo-Gothic spires stared haughtily over the rolling woods of rural Surrey. We were summoned there every morning for daily prayers, and being late for chapel earned an hour of steps-running. In chapel we were arranged by seniority, facing inwards along both sides of the aisle. Thus we could make our fellows opposite giggle, which would incur punishment by the monitors or masters (beaks) stationed in recesses behind the banks of pews. The headmaster was the last to arrive, dressed in black academic gown and carrying his mortarboard. He took his place in the "bishop's seat," from where he stared down the length of the chapel at the seven hundred assembled pupils. My brother once paraded the length of the aisle in view of the assembled school unaware that his trouser fly buttons were undone.

Every word in our vocabulary was shortened, and we had to learn by rote a totally unfamiliar slang from the "new-hops book" that we carried constantly during our first fortnight in the school. It contained the new language, school rules, privileges and customs, house colours, names of housemasters and monitors, captains of sports, and a horde of useless information designed to integrate us quickly into this bewildering and intimidating new world. New-hops were each assigned ᴊoy at least a year senior, who was responsible to see ᴊned the new-hops book from cover to cover. This we did in orᴀᴄᴛ to survive. We were tested on the book at the end of the first fortnight, and failure spelled punishment for both teacher and pupil. In it we also studied the various privileges—for example, monitors exclusively might walk with their hands in pockets, leave jacket buttons undone, and use the middle of the road rather than the pavement.

I was called Steele minor; my brother was Steele major. He was also in Weekites but he distanced himself from me, and did little to soften my newness. At evening convocation (Adsum) in the Common Room we boys stood, ranked as always by seniority, shoulder-to-shoulder round the big oak table that was used for Ping-Pong by day, and in the evenings for homework prep (banco). Senior boys studied in carrels, small cubbyholes built of plywood against the walls. Each carrel was an arm's span wide in each direction, and had a desk, stool, and cupboard. A curtain hung across the entrance for privacy. New-hops kept their books in metal lockers in the hall. The housemaster, Frank "Freddie" Ives, would enter ceremoniously through the library door trailed by house monitors, one of whom read out our names in alphabetical order, to which we answered an abbreviated "(Ad)Sum", Latin for "I am here." Many years later I could still repeat verbatim that deeply imprinted list of names.

In those first two weeks I began to acquire a survivor's upper lip, stiff but trembling and on perpetual verge of tears. Nights in the barn-like dormitory were lonely. I slept in an iron-framed bed alongside twenty other snivelling small boys. Our only privacy for a quiet sob was under the bedsheets. We stored our few personal treasures in a bedside locker.

One boy regularly peed his bed at night and had to sleep on a rubber under-sheet. Each morning the dormitory head, an outsized bully named Blume, would shout, "High tide or low tide, Davidson?" A "high" was greeted with derisive jeers as the shamefaced boy hung his sheet out of the window to dry.

We were introduced to competitions of lighting our farts to see who could kindle a flame.

For solace we indulged a newfound delight, and masturbated quietly under the bedclothes. I was disappointed at my output, having heard awe-inspiring stories of Blume and his mates at corps camp passing round a milk bottle that they claimed to have filled to the brim. I was convinced that I had the puniest cock ever bestowed on a boy. Also one of my testicles did not descend properly at birth, so I was known as One-balled Pete after I confessed my deficiency. However, it seemed to produce the ecstasy I craved and the wet dreams I didn't.

I rarely went to the swimming baths because we had to swim nude and I was very shy of my apparatus. A nearby girls' boarding school, Priorsfield, rented the baths for a couple of mornings a week. A friend told me that the girls also swam naked. He knew this because he had spied them by climbing a fence and peeping into the changing room. He unwisely repeated this trick once too often, got caught, and was subsequently expelled.

Throughout school, masturbation—wanking or tossing off—consumed most of our thoughts and much of our conversation. To us, wanking was synonymous with sin, to which the chaplain referred constantly in his sermons. A lot of it seemed to go on in the Bible, especially by Onan, whose nasty habits we could only guess at.

In summer I would ride my bicycle, three miles there and back, to Happy Valley, where older boys made assignations with Priorsfield girls. There I made a bower in head-high bracken and, staring at the scudding clouds, wanked to temporary blissful oblivion that was always marred by a guilty aftertaste of sin.

Any boy caught sharing this newfound delight with another boy in the showers was guilty of a major sin punishable by expulsion. A vicar friend of mine once confessed to me that he became the "school tart" at another public school, and was abused repeatedly in his heyday. Uncountable less fortunate public school boys' lives were scarred by similar first experiences of sex; others became overt homosexuals in adulthood.

I must have been a very unadventurous fellow—in fact a proper "weed"—because I was never beaten or buggered at school. Early on I became expert at flicking a tie or a wet towel with a sharp backward snap of the wrist. If accurately aimed, these left a painful welt on the bare skin of a potential molester.

Pubescent homosexuality thrived among the several hundred monastically cloistered adolescent boys. I became infatuated and fell utterly and unrequitedly in love with a cadet corps drummer boy. Thoughts of his peach-fuzz cheeks and rosy lips filled my every waking moment. Reading Plato's *Republic* assuaged some of my guilt and offered a ray of hope for the sinful. Robert Graves wrote, in *Goodbye to All That*, of his liaisons behind the squash courts at Charterhouse, which he evidently hated almost as much as trench warfare in France.

With each passing term, and the seniority that it brought, my bed moved nearer the dormitory door. This anticipated a rise to the single cubicles of the floor above. The monitors, Olympian gods who ruled our lives, had their own studies and slept in four-bedded rooms on the top floor from whence boys were summoned for beatings. These were carried out by the monitors for minor offences, by the housemaster for more serious ones, and by the headmaster for crimes just short of being sacked.

Privacy was absent in the lavatories ("rears") that we visited every morning after breakfast. Custom forbade closing the half doors of the six stalls that were ranged like a cattle shed, open to the sky. New-hops, therefore, had to perform for their first time in public under the watchful eye of the next boy waiting in the queue. The deed done, we had to report it to a senior but sluggish-bowelled boy who took roll call from a raised pedestal in cubicle number one. If we failed in this demeaning, constipating ritual, we silently suffered his derision. An unfavourable report to the matron was rewarded by a ritual dose of purgative.

At the end of the second week I fortunately passed the new-hops' exam and became a "running fag," a servant of the monitors' whims. When one of them stood at the door of the Common Room and yelled "fee-ag," we dropped anything we were doing and ran. The last one got the monitor's task, whether to carry a message to a friend in another house twenty minutes away, to clean his shoes or army boots, or to polish the brass of his khaki belt.

An elaborate ritual of privileges established the class structure and snobbery that permeated our lives and was reflected by the pejorative terms we bandied unashamedly then. Grammar School boys who had won scholarships to Charterhouse, and those with common accents other than middle-class BBC English, we called "oiks;" Jews were "Yids," and coloured people were "niggers." Now I sweat with shame to recall these names we used.

* * *

Sport was our measure of manliness; academic excellence stood low on the ladder of success. Those who studied were "swots," those who did not play games were "weeds." One passionate Weekite butterfly collector spent his afternoons chasing Purple Emperors with a net and bottles of cyanide instead of being on the cricket field; he—a weed—subsequently became a world-renowned lepidopterist.

I was determined to become skilled at some sport so I took up rackets, the mother game of squash, which originated in the exercise yards of Fleet debtor's prison. Ironically, it is perhaps the most difficult of all games to learn, but played well it is the most thrilling and graceful to watch. An expensive and élitist game on a par with Royal Tennis, rackets is played in a cavernous court of polished black walls three times the size of a squash court. A cleanly hit rackets ball zings like rifle fire and travels as fast as the ball in Basque pelota. The ball is made of green felt cloth, wound tightly with many yards of wet worsted that shrinks and hardens when dry. It was covered with white tape. Balls became quickly misshapen or blackened, so in a match thirty or forty balls might be discarded. Later Bill Hawes, the professional coach, would rewind them, press them back into shape, and re-cover them with white tape. Rackets were easily broken and we always had three or four available for a match.

The rackets courts lay a twenty minutes' walk over the hill from Weekites. Bill Hawes was a gentle, caring man, and I never heard him say an unkind or discouraging word. We worked hard to justify his teaching and to earn his praise. He influenced me more than any other person at Charterhouse because, not being on the school staff, I could safely share his confidence. Bill and his wife, Maisie, lived in a house on Peperharow Road behind the rackets courts. I could drop in there any time, and it became my haven from the hubbub of school.

Bill was of short and solid build, with broad shoulders and a slight stoop. He had black hair slicked back with Brylcreem. With long white flannel trousers hanging off his hips, he glided, rather than ran, around the court, and strokes flowed off his racquet with deceptive ease. He was one of the best rackets players in Britain and he had recently lost a challenge for the World Professional Championship to James Dear. His father, Walter, and his brother, Ronnie, were both excellent rackets professionals.

While waiting for a lesson, we boys would loaf around the small atrium to the court, where dank clothes hung from a line of pegs and the room reeked of sweaty bodies. Presses, each holding half a dozen rackets, leaned against the wall like soldiers standing at ease. A cast-iron fireplace with a coal fire stood beside Bill's workbench; there he strung racquets and re-covered balls. One quizzical eye was always half-closed against the curl of smoke from a cigarette that usually hung from the corner of his mouth.

I took up rackets along with Guy Warner, a serious, curly-haired Weekite, and we remained partners and firm friends throughout our time at Charterhouse. We spent countless hours practicing by beating a ball round the court and together made the school under-sixteen pair. Then we graduated to the senior school pair, where we were competent but never brilliant. Guy was the leader with his solid forehand. My backhand serve, learned from Walter Hawes, had plenty of cut so the ball died away in the corner, but my pizzazz led me often to fudge easy shots. I did not shine at any other sport except squash, where I was better than Guy. I gained much kudos from becoming proficient at rackets, especially when Guy and I started to perform well at the school competitions.

Rackets is an elegant game of strokes. The eye and timing compare to the sheer speed and fitness of squash. Many rackets players against whom we competed in matches were first class cricketers—Colin Cowdrey and Ted Dexter later each captained the England cricket team. In matches we wore long white flannel trousers, a white cotton vest that buttoned to the neck, and a cable-knit white pullover. Bill umpired from a box in one corner of the gallery, shouting "play" after every strike. He adjudicated on doubtful points and obstructions that were common in doubles matches with four players in such a confined space. If in danger of hitting an opponent—a potentially lethal accident—we called for a "let" to replay the rally.

The rackets master, Bob Arrowsmith, having been a capable cricketer, was reputed to know by heart *Wisden Cricketers' Almanack*. He walked with two sticks because of painful arthritis of his hips, which contributed to his miserable mien. When acting as referee, he would lean over the balcony and make loud uncomplimentary remarks, and groan when we played a bad shot. I once called up to the gallery asking him to shut up, an affront that took him many moons to forgive. However, my fellows lavished tremendous praise on me for this act of daring.

During term we played matches against other schools, both at home and away. Bill would hire a taxi and we would spend an exhilarating day away from the confines of Charterhouse. If we lost the match we would creep back to school, tails between our legs, dreading disgrace. During the holidays we played inter-school competitions in London at Queen's Club, a half-mile walk from Barons Court underground station, which was a great place to meet boys from other schools whom we had befriended in competition, and became a source of unbridled camaraderie. In the hope of getting good press reports, we learned to make friends with the correspondents of the *Times* and *Daily Telegraph*, who wrote most of their copy in the bar.

In our last year, Guy Warner and I were odds-on favourites to win the Public Schools Championship, but we floundered in the semi-finals to some comparative unknowns. We returned to school humiliated, and passed our torch to two juniors, Charles Swallow and Jeremy Carless, who subsequently won the championship. Charles went on to become the British amateur and world champion. His father, who was head of the plastics division of Imperial Chemical Industries, devised a new plastic ball that kept its shape and revolutionized the game by reducing the number of balls needed in a match.

Rod Tuck, my lifelong friend, also played rackets among the many sports at which he excelled more by athletic talent than style. In 1964 he represented Britain in modern pentathlon at the Summer Olympics in Tokyo, and in biathlon at the Winter Olympics in Innsbruck. Almost bald by the age of sixteen, Rod had a raunchy sense of humour and a mischievous, raucous belly laugh when the corners of his eyes would tighten into crows' feet. His father was a Captain in the Royal Navy, where Rod was headed. However, he flunked the entrance exam to Dartmouth College and joined the Royal Marines instead.

I idolized Rod, who was a year older than me, and I hung on his every word and action. As part of the Maniacs cricket team, we often cycled round the Surrey lanes in order to play matches on village greens with church, pub, and post office nearby. On Sundays, with a small crew of friends, we biked via unmotorable byways and country lanes to Frensham Ponds to go sailing. At a halfway pub we washed down our sandwiches with strong apple cider—a dangerously forbidden breach of school rules. Rod taught me to sail an eleven-foot Cadet class dinghy. In the school library we found photos of the great J class racing boats of the Thirties—*Endeavour, Velsheda, Britannia,* and *Shamrock*—and imagined ourselves crewing in the America's Cup beating into a gale in the English Channel.

Cecil Donne, a queer Old Carthusian, invited another boy, David Brundan, and me to his home in Cowes to crew on his yacht *Stiarna*. Cecil always wore a yachting cap and a blazer with the crest and buttons of the Royal Yacht Squadron, and he took an intense interest in Charterhouse boys who sailed at Frensham Ponds. At Cowes we met Uffa Fox, the racing boat designer, who crewed for Prince Philip in his designer craft the *Uffa King* (said quickly). Cecil never made overt advances to us but we soon realized we were there as our generous host's young companions, rather than to learn to sail.

In the cadet corps band, Rod played the big bass drum and I the tenor drum. The lead side drummer was an Indian Prince, Ranbir Singh of Ratlam. Our dodgy rhythm cheered flagging cadets marching home from mock battles on Farnham Common. We all perked up to a crescendo of drum beats when passing nearby Priorsfield School, where boy-starved girls hung out of upstairs windows waving ecstatically.

I became an officious cadet NCO and eventually rose to junior officer because I was good at shouting orders and crawling through undergrowth on exercises. Each summer at corps camp we were marched around by real army sergeant majors, who told us about prophylactics and warned us off the local whores. As we were quite ignorant of such fascinating wickedness, it made us feel very grown up. My only previous contact with such was when at the end of a haircut a barber had asked me, "Anything for the weekend, sir?" In our tent lines, boyhood pranks pitted one school against another with black-balling, a popular sport of ambushing a boy from another school and smearing his nethers liberally with black boot polish.

I passed the School Certificate O-Level exams before I was sixteen and moved into the science stream, since for many years I had set my sights on becoming a doctor. At Deudraeth Castle my father had given me some surgical instrument catalogues, which illustrated several gory operations. I pored over them with a friend and dreamed then of the day I would have my own shiny scalpel, scissors, and forceps. I was enthralled by Albert Schweitzer's *On the Edge of a Primaeval Forest* about his medical work in the African jungle. Rod needed science for the Royal Navy entrance exams, so we found ourselves in the same biology classes. The zoology teacher was Percy "Cheese" Chapman, who had adenoids that caused him to preface every sentence with a nervous, repetitive "ub, ub, ub." Oleg Polunin, who later discovered many rare flower species in the Himalayas, taught botany. While dissecting earthworms and dogfish that stank of formalin, we would idle away the time gossiping and drawing up lists of the prettiest boys in the school.

One Easter, biology camp was held at Lough Hyne, a tidal lake in southern Ireland. There were twelve of us under the supervision of the two biology masters. On arrival in Cork, I asked the bus driver when the bus would depart for Skibbereen. "To be sure," he replied, "it could be any toime." We pitched our tents round a cooking shack and got to work plotting the wild flowers in a square yard section nearby. We learned about seaweeds *Fucus serratus* and *Pelvetia canaliculata*, and downed draught Guinness in secret forays to a pub in Skibbereen, a village with as many pubs as houses and where they never asked our age. Tides filled and emptied Lough Hyne twice daily. Rod became the first to shoot the rapids on an ebb tide, in an old skiff we found and rigged with a canvas square sail. We all laughed maniacally at his bravery.

\* \* \*

With seniority, I eventually moved from the Weekites Common Room to a shared study. Then I became a monitor under Guy Warner, who was Head of House. Since I was allowed to walk with hands in pockets, I often did so. One day, sloppily climbing the indoor polished stone stairs wearing my bedroom slippers, I suddenly slipped in the runnel carved by countless boys' feet. Unable to remove my hands from my pockets, I fell on the point of my chin. Then I slipped from step to step and received a series of swift upper-cuts that left me dazed but still conscious, like a boxing nightmare.

The older and more independent my brother and I became, the more our relationship with our guardians deteriorated. Managing two rebellious teenagers was not easy for the Walshes, who tried their imperial best. The final straw for me was the Yellowlees incident, so with mutual relief we agreed to part. My brother was about to leave school and do his National Service in the Rifle Brigade; I still had three more years to do at Charterhouse.

I would thereafter make my holiday base with my father's sister, Janet Lack, in Barnet, Hertfordshire. She was always busy. She gardened furiously, learned to play the harp, made jewellery, embroidered, and looked after her demanding husband and four small children. Her austere house was always cold (nothing a pullover couldn't fix), and the geyser gas heater of the bath worked so slowly it produced no more than two inches of tepid water.

Charles Lack, my uncle, on return from the bacteriology laboratory he commanded at the Stanmore Orthopaedic Hospital, spent most of his free time sitting alone in an upstairs room deep in books, or fiddling in his workshop in the basement while listening to the radio. His political stripe was that of his friend J B Priestley and other far-left-leaning Shavians, and he tried to instill in me the concept of apprenticeship, for which I had little interest or patience.

Barnet seemed quite confined after spacious Munstead Grange. However, I was then sixteen and needed only a place to sleep and store my belongings. For the first time in years, I began to lose the envy I always felt for my peers with parents and a home of their own. Janet was loving, but unable to remain idle or to watch anyone else unoccupied, so it was not a restful house. If she was gardening on my return home she would thrust a rake into my hand even before we started talking. Charles was cool and oblivious to all around him.

I spent much time roaming London with a raffish school friend, Nigel Backsdale, who knew about women and regaled me with stories of his antics, outrageous beyond anything I could imagine or comprehend. I had a bad case of adolescent face pimples, so before every outing I went through a ritual in front of the bathroom mirror of dabbing each angry red zit with Eskamel, a skin-coloured foundation face cream. All this succeeded in doing was making me look like a clown whose makeup had smudged. We went to a smoky nightclub in a basement off

Oxford Street where Humphrey Lyttelton played jazz. We tramped the salacious parts of Soho looking in windows of adult porno bookshops and went to *risqué* films.

On one occasion I invited Amanda, an aristocrat with a double-barreled surname and a plummy voice, to the cinema to see *La Ronde*. I was nervous about what she would expect of me, so when the lights went down I sat stiffly immobile in order to avoid nudging her elbow. About halfway through the film I took courage and lunged round her shoulder with one arm.

"I hope you don't mind," I mumbled feebly.

"You can hold my hand if you like," she countered coldly.

Whether in passion or for punishment, she pressed the back of my sweaty hand against her suspender clip. This firmly indented the skin and was excruciatingly painful. However, I dared not move a muscle thereafter.

\* \* \*

With still a year to fill before joining the Royal Marines—my choice for National Service—I passed the Advanced Level School Certificate in biology, chemistry, and physics.

During one summer holiday, David Hume, a friend from Aldro School, and I bicycled round northern Italy on newly acquired touring bikes with racing drop-handlebars. We took a train to Nice and set off along the Riviera. For a month thereafter we camped in farmers' barns, stayed in youth hostels, or slept out under the stars, feeding ourselves on grapes, bread, and cheese. Exploring cathedrals and churches with my father had already stimulated my interest in architecture. We climbed the leaning tower of Pisa, trudged the museums and churches of Florence, and rode into the hills of Tuscany and visited San Gimignano and Montepulciano. We reached Siena, where we had a ringside place for the Palio horse race. We then turned north and cycled over the Apennines to Bologna and Padua, and passed through the Po Valley to Venice. Finally we crossed the Alps and caught the train from Zurich back to London. This was my first self-motivated adventure, and its successful completion gave me great pleasure and confidence.

In my last year at Charterhouse, having finished my exams but not being scholarship material, I took a course in art history based on all I had seen in Italy. A small group of boys would congregate in the studio of Ian Fleming-Williams, the art master, and delve into the art books in his tiny study. I also took music history classes with Bill Llewellyn, who taught me to appreciate Elgar, Glazunov, and Vivaldi. But I was still very unsettled and rootless, constantly dashing from place to place. My attempt to learn the violin was abysmal. I could not get down to practicing art or music and felt paralysed despite ample opportunity to draw, paint, or play an instrument. I tended to keep to myself because going out with friends, as an invited guest, was too painful seeing them with their parents and feeling my own loss.

However, a friendship that I struck up with Wilfrid Noyce, my Latin master, steered me in a new direction. Wilfrid did not play games and could not keep order in class. He was a Boy Scout leader and had just published *Michael Angelo: A poem in twelve parts with epilogue,* a biographical poem. All these things were enough for most boys to brand him as a weedy wimp. Little did we realize, or care, that he was considered one of Britain's best rock climbers of his day. His face was scarred and lopsided from falling off Scafell Buttress while climbing with the legendary rock ace, Menlove Edwards. In northern India during the war, Wilfrid made several small expeditions into the Himalaya, which laid the foundation for his being asked to join the 1953 British Mount Everest Expedition. However, none of us appreciated the implication of this prestigious invitation to this epic event. In early mornings before school, he would train for the Everest climb by running round the grounds in white tennis shoes and baggy shorts.

Over tea in his flat, Wilfrid introduced me to Geoffrey Winthrop Young's book, *Mountain Craft*. I read it avidly and tried walking uphill breathing in time with my footfall and swinging my legs over rough ground with a rhythmical, measured step. Young refers to ". . . that silence which is the fellowship of the hills." This phrase has surfaced often while sharing an inner wordless peace in company with a friend, when returning muscle-tired and footsore from a day in the mountains.

Wilfrid helped set up the high camp above the South Col of Everest from where Edmund Hillary and Sherpa Tenzing made their successful summit bid. Subsequently I would visit Wilfrid at his home in Peperharow Road to try to prize stories of this adventure out of him, and to report on my nascent climbing career, which he always encouraged. Ironically, after all the dangers he had survived, he was killed in 1962 when he slipped on an icy slope while descending an easy peak in the Russian Pamirs.

I was generally happy during my five teenage years at Charterhouse, where I made good friends and gained some stability in my life. But the monasticism, barbarity, philistine attitudes, and class élitism made me choose, eventually, a different schooling for my own children.

# SIX

A S AN ARMY CADET AT CHARTERHOUSE, I mounted guard at the Queen's coronation on 2 June 1953. A Welsh Guards sergeant major with a lion's roar, peak cap obscuring his eyes, and pacing stick under his arm, marshalled us at the St James's Park barracks before dawn. He then marched us to the Victoria Memorial opposite Buckingham Palace, where we took up our positions around the base of the plinth. We had a prime view of the procession of royal carriages and the military parade as it passed by us.

At daybreak in pouring rain before the procession got started, a murmur rippled through the patiently waiting crowd, the word "Everest" spreading from lip to lip. Then a cockney newspaper vendor held high the *Daily Express* with bold headlines—ALL THIS AND EVEREST TOO. Standing beside us awaiting orders to march as part of the mile-long column were a Gurkha regiment of laughing-eyed Nepali hillmen, jungle hats at a rakish angle and kukri knives slung from their belts. They spontaneously burst into cheers at the news that their countryman, Sherpa Tenzing Norgay, had reached the top of the world along with New Zealander Edmund Hillary. This added a touch of magic to an already magical—if moist—day.

The skirl of the bagpipes and marching drummers had bewitched me since I first played with lead soldiers—Scots Highlanders in kilts, mounted Hussars in busbies, and Royal Marine bandsmen with leopard skin aprons. A school friend knew a colonel of the 6th Inniskilling Dragoon Guards, who invited us to lunch at the Naval and Military Club in Piccadilly, evidently talent spotting. My romantic dreams of being a cavalryman evaporated when the moustachioed colonel told us the cost of the privilege of joining the regiment—for uniforms, mess bills, and polo ponies.

That same spring, when I was seventeen, my old friend Rod Tuck came down to Charterhouse smartly dressed in his Royal Marine uniform of dark blue tunic, red-striped trousers, and scarlet-and-white peaked cap.

"It's a great life, Pete," he said nonchalantly. "I'm at commando school at present. Then I go to the Special Boats Section. I join an aircraft carrier in a couple of months for a spell in Aden."

Rod invited me to join a bunch of his mates on a skiing holiday in the Alps. As soon as I returned after the holiday, I summarily enrolled in the Royal Marine Forces Volunteer Reserve. I chose to do my National Service immediately rather than accept an option open to medical students to defer it until after qualifying as a doctor. During the summer after I left Charterhouse, I went on an introductory course at Lympstone in Devon, where we swung on ropes through trees and marched over the moors by night.

In pubs in nearby Exmouth we got seriously tipsy on scrumpy, a heady half-and-half mixture of sweet and dry cider. This emboldened us to have our photographs taken in a shop where you could rent a full dress Royal Marine uniform splattered with gold braid, and a white pith helmet. Then we went on to commando school at Bickleigh. Before going "ashore" in Plymouth the company commander paraded us and lectured us sternly about catching diseases from girls who hung around the barracks. Meanwhile the sergeant stood behind him making obscene gestures. I felt very grown up.

* * *

Wilfrid Noyce had encouraged me to enroll in a course at the Eskdale Outward Bound Mountain School in the Lake District. The warden was his friend Eric Shipton, a distinguished pre-war Everester, who had recently been passed over as leader of the Everest expedition in favour of Colonel John Hunt. At the end of my last Charterhouse year I applied to Outward Bound and was accepted. Along with several other boys I travelled north from Euston by train, all of us full of nervous bravado anticipating the rigours ahead. In our carriage were two girls returning home to Cumberland. "If you can see the hills round here it's going to rain," one said, pointing to dark clouds that loomed over Coniston. "If you can't see them, it's raining."

At Ravenglass station we changed to a narrow gauge train, the *Eskdale Flyer*, known locally as "the Ratty." A miniature steam engine pulled a dozen open carriages along the length of the Esk Valley.

"Hey, see them cliffs," said one boy, looking up at a rocky outcrop. "Fall off them and yer'll never see yer muvver again. Bet yer can't get insurance."

The ninety boys on the course came from diverse social backgrounds—industrial factories, Borstal prisons, and private schools—a mix that was fundamental to the philosophy of Kurt Hahn, founder of Outward Bound. This was the first time that I had mixed in close proximity with boys from a different class to myself. During World War II Hahn observed that many fit and able young merchant sailors had drowned after shipwreck because of lack of basic survival skills and personal resolve. To counter this trend through practical education, he started a sea school at Aberdovey. His philosophy of character training through experience at sea and in the outdoors quickly caught on and spread to encompass mountains.

At Eskdale Green station, two instructors dressed casually in climbing breeches and checked shirts met us and escorted us on the half-mile walk up to the school. The main Outward Bound building was a baronial, red sandstone, Victorian mansion set on a high bank overlooking a small lake, surrounded by rhododendron bushes. Scattered around the grounds were an assortment of stables and outhouses that served as dormitories and storerooms. The elegant triangle of Harter Fell, clad in late autumn pastel shades of dead bracken and purple heather, rose above the distant rim of Eskdale.

Eric Shipton gave a welcoming talk to the boys. "Find your star and follow it," he exhorted us. "You may have riches, or brains, or physique, but character is your greatest possession." During the first week, several instructors encouraged us similarly to grapple with the upcoming challenges of the course.

As I was manifestly outgoing, I was appointed leader of Shackleton patrol; my sidekick quartermaster was Tony Bell, an apprentice bricklayer from Appleby-Frodingham steelworks in Scunthorpe. He was solidly built and broad-chested, but on exertion he developed a sonorous asthmatic wheeze. He often talked ruefully about his girlfriend, Margaret, a secretary at the steelworks back home.

"I've never been to the cinema alone," Tony once said. "Feels strange bein' 'ere not able to put an arm round 'er."

"D'you think you'll get married?" I asked.

"S'pose I might," he replied. "Lots o' people do."

"So they must," I said, "else you wouldn't be here."

"Rum business if I were," he said.

Utterly reliable, and with a laconic wit, Tony's loyalty was absolute—a quality I valued especially later when leading a rain-soaked, mutinous patrol over cloud-shrouded Lakeland fells, navigating by compass with only one small tarn for reference. Whenever I dithered he would say, in broad Lincolnshire dialect, "Git over thon gayte, mayte, or tha'll be layte mayte."

The first day we went on a shakedown hike with our instructor, David Ridgeway, one of the school's summer staff. Recently an officer in the Tank Corps, David was at Cambridge studying theology in the evangelical, muscular Christian mould. He was urbane and friendly and manifestly determined to make our course a rich experience.

And there was the warden, Eric Shipton, renowned of Everest. One day, when our patrol was practicing rock climbing in the grounds, he ambled up to watch and fell into conversation with a plumber-fitter from Grantham.

"And how do you spend your weekends, Terry?" he asked in a gentle, distant manner, his penetrating blue eyes staring out from under bristly overhanging eyebrows.

"The girlfriend, sir," shot back Terry's reply.

"Oh, it's a full time job, is it?" said Shipton casually, and moved on.

Eric Shipton, in company with fellow mountaineer, Bill Tilman, made a reputation in the 1930s for lightweight expedition travel, both in East Africa and in the Himalayas, where he was on four expeditions attempting Everest from the north side. During WWII he served as Consul General in Kashgar and later, at the opposite end of China, in Kunming. He was appointed leader of the 1953 Everest expedition. The team had grown in size from its original modest concept and at the last minute the Himalayan Committee thought that a more organized, military style of leadership was needed. So Shipton was usurped in favour of John Hunt, the excuse being that he was better suited to lead a small party. In fact, climbing Everest had become a matter of national importance in the year of the Queen's coronation, and the reputation of the British Empire was at stake. Several countries, France and Switzerland in particular, were poised in the wings for the next chance for permission from Nepal, which had just opened its borders to allow access to the south side of Everest.

To be deprived of leading the climb of Everest was a bitter pill for Eric Shipton, and along with the impending collapse of his marriage, accounted for his present sad mien. After the victorious heroes returned home, Shipton generously invited the entire Everest team to Eskdale for a relaxing weekend out of the limelight and razzamatazz. In high spirits they canoed the River Esk in flood and half the armada capsized. George Lowe, Edmund Hillary's New Zealand compatriot and climbing partner, while nearly drowning, lost his false teeth. Because Lowe was billed to lecture at the Festival Hall before the Queen the following week, the local radio station put out an emergency announcement. In response a local fisherman called the school. "I caught a pair of false teeth in my net five miles downstream," he said. "Might they belong to Mr Lowe?" The teeth were duly returned and Lowe gave his lecture on schedule.

* * *

Since I was used to boarding school, the discipline of Outward Bound was familiar to me, more than to those boys who had never left home before. Each morning, whatever the weather, we ran round the tarn, shed our clothes on the boathouse jetty, and dived in naked. This rule was only waived when an ice axe was needed to break the ice. Luckily this did not occur while I was there. One morning, as I towelled myself after climbing out of the gelid water, I introduced myself to a lone, white-haired gentleman dressing beside me.

"I'm Launcelot Fleming," he responded amiably.

"What's your job?" I asked.

"Actually, I'm a bishop," he replied.

Then Bishop of Portsmouth, Launcelot Fleming was a governor of the school. As a young man, after graduating from Cambridge, he went on a three-year expedition to Antarctica, an adventure that was the basis of his active interest in Outward Bound. Much later he became Bishop of Norwich and then Dean of Windsor. Subsequently we became close friends, often met in London to play squash, and adjourned to a pub afterwards. Launcelot's enthusiasm surpassed his skill. He was an inveterate but amiable cheat who repeatedly demanded time out to rest because of Horner's syndrome, which allowed only half his body to sweat.

During the first couple of weeks at the mountain school we learned the basic skills of rock climbing, canoeing, and map reading, and we were set various physical tests. Although not a skilled athlete, I managed the tests more than adequately.

In the next valley to the north, the hamlet of Wasdale Head boasted the deepest lake in England (Wastwater), the highest mountain (Scafell Pike), the smallest church (St Olaf's), and the biggest liar (Wilson Pharoah). Wilson, a former Cumberland-Westmorland wrestling champion, was landlord of the Wastwater Hotel, a tall, whitewashed stone building that was a landmark usually visible from the surrounding mountaintops. Wilson was a good-natured gentle giant, but he could be dangerous when aroused in his cups. On my first visit to the hotel, the bar window was boarded up after some cocky, loud-mouthed climber got cheeky with Wilson, who hurled him through the glass into the courtyard.

Beside the hotel, the dry-stone-walled barn, like all walls that checker the lower slopes of Lakeland fells, was laid without cement. An outside stairway led to a hayloft that by tradition had become a climbers' doss-house costing sixpence a night (the same price as a cup of tea in the bar). The traverse of the barn door involved delicate climbing without touching ground. It used to be a ritual of the Abraham brothers, famous Lakeland guides at the turn of the century. In an attempt at emulating our heroes, we would spend our spare moments spread-eagled over the lintel, strengthening our fingers and testing how small a hold we could stand on.

On our patrol's first two-day scheme we camped at the head of Wastwater in a downpour that created silver streams falling from every surrounding hillside. We dug trenches round our tents to divert water from porous groundsheets and soaked sleeping bags. We climbed over Red Pike and Pillar Rock and, returning by way of Windy Gap, we slid down the Yewbarrow screes back to Wasdale. Lake District valleys fan out like spokes from the hub of Scafell, and few roads cross the mountain range so the hills are unspoiled by wires, unlike north Wales where every valley is festooned with pylons and power lines.

We navigated our way back to Eskdale by compass and descended to the village of Boot, where the River Esk tumbles into a deep pool below Dalegarth Bridge. Following the example of Dick Marsh, our short, balding, and bespectacled chief instructor, we stripped to our underpants and jumped from the bridge twenty feet into a swirling pool. While being swept downstream by the current, we caught hold of a large boulder and pulled ourselves to the bank. One lad surfaced face-to-face with Dick's Boxer dog, Nim, who was paddling upstream. The surprised dog closed its jaws in fright, punctured the boy's cheek, and broke the underlying tooth.

Dick was a volcano of energy. When serving in India with the Royal Engineers during National Service, he and two friends who were also climbers planned a hare-brained attempt to climb Nanga Parbat, then one of the highest unclimbed peaks in the world. They signed up as sirdar, young Sherpa Tenzing Norgay, later to become famous with

Edmund Hillary as the first climbers of Mount Everest. Early in the trip Dick's two companions were buried in an avalanche while Dick and Tenzing were spared. They then spent two unavailing weeks searching in the avalanche debris for the missing men. Often marooned in their tents in bad weather, Dick got to know Tenzing well and was utterly won over by his charm and his outstandingly forceful character.

Our training course culminated in a five-day scheme. Our patrol, Shackleton, was directed to be off on our own following a map route over the hills and ending up in Wasdale where we would go climbing. We carried enough food for the duration of the scheme. As patrol leader, I had to set a good example, which was not easy with a group of ten boys from diverse backgrounds and with varying degrees of motivation.

We set off from Brotherilkeld Farm at the foot of Hardknott Pass, and followed Lingcove Beck to Throstlegarth Falls in Upper Eskdale. There we rested our aching shoulders that were unaccustomed to heavy packs. After a swim in Green Hole, we climbed over a pass on the shoulder of Bowfell. Low cloud hung over the hills, the wind bit deep, and a fine drizzle soaked us as we made our way to a rendezvous with Dick Marsh and Dave Ridgeway at Angle Tarn above Langstrath Beck. Those boys who had forgotten to pack their sleeping bags in plastic bags and place them in the bottom of their rucksacks were doomed to a damp, cold, sleepless night. Lakeland fells are more softly contoured than those of the north Wales that I knew from my childhood, and in foul weather they are often more interesting than under a cloudless sky.

The climax of our scheme was when Dick Marsh took my mate, Tony Bell, and me to climb on Raven Crag overlooking Borrowdale. On small outcrops of rock near the school we had practiced climbing, rope work, and belays, but this was our first experience of a full-length climb of nine pitches. Our chosen 500-foot gulley up the centre of Raven Crag was graded "Very Difficult" in the guidebook, with the final pitch

"Severe." I was soon soaked by water falling down the green slimy rock and, when I reached for a hold, water poured down my sleeve. But nothing could detract from my thrill of climbing on steep rock for the first time. The final pitch entailed traversing a mossy slab bent double under an overhanging rocky roof. My diary reads, " . . . I slid my left foot onto a hold an inch deep and three inches long, four feet away. I was then pinned against the rock face looking down between my feet into the wet chasm. I climbed over a boulder and emerged at the top to find my mate sitting placidly taking in the rope, my lifeline, apparently oblivious of my contortions. What a feeling of achievement!"

Halfway up the gulley we sat on a ledge and ate our sandwiches while looking out over Derwent Water, Skiddaw, and Saddleback, which lay in the distance. We were cold and envious of the sun that streamed above our heads.

The flavour of life's dramatic "first time" moments is soon blunted by familiarity, but Raven Crag Gulley opened a new chapter for me. Before the climb I could not imagine trusting myself totally to a rope; thereafter I dreamed constantly of my next encounter with rock. Tony forswore ever climbing again as he had not enjoyed the experience. After several more years laying bricks at Appleby-Frodingham steelworks, he bought a pub in Lincolnshire and settled into a quiet domestic life with Margaret. However, we kept in touch for many years afterwards.

At the end of the course I was very fit and ready for the five-mile cross-country run. Halfway up the first three miles of continuously climbing I was overcome by an inexplicable weariness. At the crest of the final hill where our route passed through a couple of farmyards I felt quite dizzy and dropped back from the leading pack. The next I remember was waking up in the school sick room with the matron anxiously hovering over me. Apparently I had collapsed beside the track and vomited a basinful of blood. On reflection, a few days before the run my stomach was quite upset but I had taken little notice.

Doctors came and consulted round my bed, and mumbled the word "ulcer." They prescribed a diet of ice cubes. I felt very weak for a few days and was kept at rest in the sick bay. I was bitterly disappointed to end the course on such a sour note while the other boys went off to finish their tasks. Nevertheless I proudly received an Honours Badge; the Warden's report read, "Peter's performance has been first rate. He was perhaps the most outstanding boy on the course." After the other boys left for home I stayed for several days recovering at Eskdale and got to know more intimately some of the instructors, especially Dick Marsh, Frank Dowlen, Roy Greenwood, and Vince Veevers.

That Outward Bound course boosted my self-confidence and steered my interest towards climbing mountains, which was to become a lifelong passion. However my illness—a bleeding stomach ulcer—upset all my future plans. On my return to the Royal Marines, aged nineteen, I went for a check-up into the Royal Navy Hospital in Plymouth and was turned down by the medical board. I had already postponed my entry into Cambridge, having passed the entrance exams and interview for Clare College, so I had time to spare.

Dick Marsh suggested I accompany him to India to research a biography of Tenzing, with whom he had kept in touch since their Nanga Parbat adventure. As one of the few people who knew the now-famous Sherpa personally, Dick had negotiated this coup with a publisher after Tenzing's Everest climb. I wandered round London with my head in the Himalayan clouds, intoxicated with the names that Everest conjured—Khumbu, Namche Bazar, Base Camp, Icefall. In a small street behind Marble Arch I visited Robert Lawrie's climbing shop that sold custom-made climbing boots, Meade mountain tents, and every piece of equipment that a Himalayan climber could need. Memorabilia of famous mountaineers decorated the walls, and I could sense the magic of distant peaks. Dick pursued the project with characteristic enthusiasm, and swept me along in his wake. We planned to go by ship to India, and then to trek with Tenzing into the hills around Darjeeling while collecting material for the book.

A telegram from Tenzing's agent shattered our dreams by announcing that he had sold out to a higher bidder in the publishing world. Caught up in the razzle-dazzle surrounding the climbing of Everest, it was hardly surprising that Tenzing no longer controlled his own destiny. Plans for an exciting year ahead crashed at my feet.

Dick was going to read theology at Ridley Hall, Cambridge, and had infected me mildly with evangelical leanings. He suggested I fill the time until I should go up to Clare College working on the farm of a community at Lee Abbey outside Linton in North Devon. I concurred, more from hero worship of him than for any religious conviction.

Lee Abbey was a spiritual holiday camp where people could think deep thoughts for a week. I was never comfortable with its Christian bonhomie but I enjoyed the outdoors work on the farm.

That spring I fell in love with Maud, a Dutch kitchen worker with whom I was united in adversity against the evangelical stance of the centre. She had spent the war years in a Japanese prison camp in Indonesia, where her guardian uncle caught animals for European zoos. Together we explored the steep cliffs and bays of the rugged North Devon coast and tramped over the Lorna Doone country of Exmoor with its wild, heather-strewn bogs and valleys where streams flooded with frequent heavy rains.

To assuage our disappointment over Tenzing's biography, Dick planned to take a small group of ex-Outward Bound boys to France to the Dauphiné Alps. It seemed an ideal chance to stay on and climb in different parts of Europe, so I wrote to the Master of Clare suggesting that I postpone going up to Cambridge for the summer Long Vac term to study organic chemistry, the fourth part of the First MB degree, which I had failed at Charterhouse. His curt refusal, implying that my place in the college would be in jeopardy, quickly put me in my place, and I concurred meekly.

Summer in Cambridge was leisurely, with tennis and cricket seemingly more important than organic chemistry. I punted on the River Cam, studied occasionally, and flirted with a French girl on the riverbank of Grantchester Meadows, Maud having returned to Holland.

At term's end I drove out to the Alps with Dick Marsh and others. Approaching the first snow-clad peaks from Grenoble, Dick erupted with a joy that infected all of us novice climbers. Under his tutelage we roped up for the first time on a glacier and learned to belay and cut steps in steep snow with an ice axe—a safe introduction to high mountains. We camped in empty valleys, crossed passes, and climbed several minor peaks.

Before returning to Cambridge I went back to Eskdale to instruct on a course at the Outward Bound Mountain School. Still with some time on my hands, I entered upon some wild notions for excitement. With my friend Jeremy Carless I roamed the London Docks and boarded several ships asking for a job as a deck hand. We narrowly missed the chance of heading into Antarctic waters on a whaler; I was interviewed by Sir Mortimer Wheeler about joining an archaeological dig in Jordan; I brushed with Roman Catholicism at Mount Alvernia's hospital in Ballinasloe, Ireland; and I took squash lessons from world champion Mahmoud Karim, who was coaching at a club in London.

Now, after several abortive hiccups, I was in earnest to pursue a career in medicine and I took the train to Cambridge to start the academic year.

# SEVEN

NEWLY ARRIVED AT CAMBRIDGE University, I wandered along the "Backs"—the gardens behind the colleges that overlook the River Cam—head-in-air drinking in the mediaeval atmosphere of the place. Clare College is an ancient establishment founded in 1326. Built beside the river, the Old Court is sandwiched between King's College Chapel and neighbouring Trinity Hall. The dining hall and chapel stand on one side of the quadrangle, undergraduate rooms sprout from staircases on the other three.

Clare Memorial Court, where many of my colleagues had their rooms, lies across the river in the shadow of the University Library. Because all the newcomer undergraduates could not be accommodated there, I was put into digs a little outside the town. I wore a yellow-on-black Clare College scarf as I rode my bike helter-skelter along King's Parade with a throng of other cyclists heading for nine o'clock lectures. A zigzag along Free School Lane brought me to Downing Street, where all the science faculties had their buildings.

I would often visit my new-made friends in other colleges for afternoon tea and crumpets, heady with my freedom after the confines of boarding school. Even after three undergraduate years in Cambridge, I still marvelled at my good fortune at being able to wander through the narrow alleys, across mediaeval courtyards, and under tall spires, ornate brick chimneys, and gargoyles.

One mid-morning shortly after I arrived I saw a student wandering through Clare Old Court in a dressing gown, towel over his shoulder and chewing on a toothbrush.

"Excuse me," I said, addressing the Senior Porter in grey suit and black bowler hat, "but what's he doing?"

"He's going for a bath. Sir." he said. (As in the army, the title "sir" had a decidedly pejorative tone.) "Undergraduate rooms don't have no plumbing or running water."

"And where are the toilets?" I asked

"Over in the corner there, sir. Through the arch, past the chapel doors, left down the stairs, left again into the basement. But mind yer 'ead on the ceiling."

A few days after I arrived, I was ambling through Old Court when a short, rotund gentleman with thinning, smoothed black hair emerged from the brass-handled door of the Master's Lodge.

"Good morning, Steele. How are you settling in?" asked Sir Henry Thirkill, who I had met only once before when, as a schoolboy, I had come to sit the College Entrance Exam.

"Fine, thank you, sir." I stammered in amazement at being recognized by the Master. Thirks, as he was commonly known, took pride in learning all his students' names by heart—a very disarming but admirable trait.

"I hope you'll enjoy your time here," he said. As he spoke his upper dentures sank and snapped back with a click on meeting the lower set. When he smiled, crow's feet radiated from the warty skin at the corners of his eyes.

Thirks interviewed all prospective Clare candidates himself, a task other colleges left to the Senior Tutor. Consequently Clare had a reputation for friendliness and for encouraging wide interest in sports, art, and music.

Medical students were allowed to defer the compulsory two years of military National Service until after qualifying. We came to the college straight from school, less mature than many of our fellow freshmen. Now barely more than twenty-one years old, some of them had fought in the Korean War and were already men-of-the-world with a couple of carousing years under their belts. Others were Commonwealth postgraduate fellows, or Mellon Scholars from the United States.

Clare Bridge, most elegant of all bridges that span the River Cam, leads to the Backs where wooded meadows and gardens flank the river colleges—Queen's, King's, Clare, Trinity Hall, Trinity, St John's—from Silver Street Bridge to Magdalene. While waiting for the bell to summon us to dine in Hall we gathered on the bridge, black academic gowns slung rakishly off our shoulders, gazing at the cows grazing in King's meadow. We could then study the form of punters on the raised deck at the back of the boat (obtuse Oxonians punt from the other end). The confident ones flung the quant pole high and forward, caught it single-handed, then leaned on it effortlessly at just the right angle to keep the punt driving straight ahead, with nary a drop in the lap of a swain reclining on cushions in the well. The less expert ones tacked aimlessly across the river, their quants getting stuck in the soft mud of the river bottom. Occasionally one would hang on tight as the punt slid gently from under his feet. Punting under Clare Bridge required raising the quant pole vertically to regain momentum; it then fell neatly into the hands of miscreants waiting on the bridge, and a sharp waggle could easily dismount an amateur punter.

Large stone balls balance on the balustrade of Clare.

"How many balls are there?" a second-year man asked me.

"Fourteen, it seems."

"Wrong. Thirteen and three quarters." He led me to the sixth ball on the King's side of the bridge. "Feel round the back."

A slice was absent from the ball. Nobody knows the reason, but, especially when smeared with honey, this jest caused much mirth among fellow students.

At dinner in Hall we stood, gowned, behind long wooden benches awaiting the procession of the Master and his high table retinue of college dons and fellows. The head butler banged a gong and a classics scholar then read the traditional grace of our foundress, Lady Clare: *Oculi omnium in te sperant Domine...* (The eyes of all wait upon Thee, O Lord.) That over, a hubbub of decibels rose as we were served dinner by the gyps, who were the college servants, in the manner, but not the quality, of a mediaeval feast.

On the farther side of Clare Bridge, a filigree wrought iron gate, spiked to prevent students climbing into college at night, led to an avenue of lime trees that crossed the Backs. From there the Gothic pinnacles of King's College Chapel (Rupert Brooke's "upturned sow") peep over the corner of the Jacobean facade of Clare, half obscured by a huge copper beech tree, in spring a deep plum colour that changes to tender green in summer and to rich gold in autumn. To the right, across the green sward of King's lawn, stands the neoclassical Gibbs' Building, forming one of the most spectacular compositions of all Cambridge.

The Avenue led past the riotous herbaceous border of Clare Garden, planned by my physiology tutor, Professor Nevill Wilmer. Weeping willows overhung a grassy bank where in summer, while pretending to study, we watched punts parading pretty girls. One misty autumn morning while crossing Clare Bridge, I heard wings beating from up-river. Three swans flew in V-formation low over the water; each bird took a separate span of the bridge and continued down-river, willows dipping in salute. The lily pond, enclosed by yew trees, had a bank of blue flowers, squashed under the combined weight of me and my May Ball dancing partner, a sporty girl from Newnham College. Across Queens' Road, in the shadow of the monstrous University Library tower, lay the modern Clare Memorial Court.

* * *

The Senior Tutor usually tried to accommodate first year men in college rooms in order to allow making new friends easier. Because of overcrowding, however, I was allocated lodgings (digs) in a row of red brick Victorian houses on Castle Street, just north of Magdalene Bridge. I rang the doorbell; it was answered by a wizened old lady wearing a pinafore apron and carpet slippers that were stretched out of shape by her bunions.

"I'm your new student," I said with some apprehension.

"Come in," she replied. "And take your muddy shoes off before you go upstairs. I'll show you your room."

I followed her into a dark and dismal hallway. A heavy magenta curtain barred the way into her back parlour from where wafted a rank aroma of frying pan grease and unwashed clothes. In almost total darkness she heaved her small, hunchbacked frame up the banister rail.

"This is your living room," she said, flinging open the door. "You sleep in the back."

A big bow window looked out on the tiny part-Saxon church of St Peter that stood on a grassy mound opposite. Its spire pointed above some elm trees to a moody autumn sky of billowing clouds penetrated by shafts of sunlight. The wallpaper of the room was a dreary brown with a curlicue pattern stuck on in place of a picture rail. A table sufficed for a desk and the room was chilly.

"How do I get heat?" I asked, looking at the empty cast-iron fire grate.

"Coal," she replied. "It's in the bunker in the basement. Costs a shilling a hod. And don't use too much 'cos it's scarce."

Once out of the semi-dark of the hall, my landlady looked even more like a termagant little witch. Grey hair was wound into a bun on the top of her head, her skin was deeply wrinkled and furrowed, and whiskers grew out of her nose and on her chin.

"You must tell me if you're going to be out in the evening," she said, "And no visitors in your rooms after ten, specially no ladies." She pattered off downstairs and disappeared behind the hall curtain beside which stood a man's muddy boots. I never saw any other sign of him, but I could smell the smoke of his cigarettes. My tiny back bedroom looked onto the mound of a ruined Norman castle where children playing on swings emphasized my solitude.

On the way back to my gloomy digs, in order to postpone having to greet my landlady, I would often call into the tailor's shop next door to chat with Alf Barnet. A cheery Cockney Jew with a trim black moustache and a balding pate, Alf always had a tape measure hanging round his neck like a badge of office.

"How're you today, guv?" he'd say.

One day, he said, "I've just got in the very material for that suit you've been talking about." He produced a roll of greenish, open-weave tweed.

"What sort is it?" I asked.

"Thornprufe. Good for town or country. Twenty-five quid. You can't beat that."

Alf measured me and in two days had made a snappy suit with waistcoat and fashionable baggy-bottomed trousers with wide turn-ups. I fancied myself striding across the Fens in it like a county squire. I whiled away many a happy hour watching Alf cutting his cloth, or chatting with his wife and young daughters—any excuse to delay returning to my digs and the spooky old crone awaiting me. She would often stand behind the hall curtain, watching me enter and climb the stairs to my room.

* * *

No one prepared me for my first visit to the Medical School dissecting hall. Random groups of freshmen wearing clean white laboratory coats and trying to look assured gathered in the hallway outside. Second- and third-year students oozed self-confidence and barged their way through the swing doors.

"What's the smell?" I asked a timid young man who stood beside me.

"I think it's formalin," he replied. "They store the bodies in it to stop them going bad."

"I hope mine's not bad, "I said. "When do we go in?"

"Any time you like."

"How do we know where to start?"

"They say there's a board inside with names on a list. It says which body you're on."

In the throng of freshmen, no one else seemed in a hurry to move. I stepped forward and pushed through the swing doors, boldly fingering in my pocket the dissecting instrument set I had used in biology classes at Charterhouse. Inside the vast mausoleum, a waxen corpse lay on each of the forty or fifty glass-topped metal tables, which were illuminated by huge roof skylights. Blackboards all round the walls were covered with diagrammatic scribblings.

Medical students milled around the room, inspecting the various bodies for the one to which they had been allocated and sizing up other members of their dissecting team.

"How do I get started?" I asked a senior student in a dirty white coat who was studying a list on a board near the door.

"Go and ask Ron," he said. "He's in charge of the dissecting room. He's in the coffee room over there."

He pointed to an open opaque glass door where lounged several older students, perhaps in their mid-twenties, tilting back on their chairs around a table littered with mugs and ash trays. They turned out to be demonstrators, postgraduate students of surgery from nearby Addenbrooke's Hospital, who were brushing up on anatomy and earning some pocket money besides. The walls of the coffee room were lined with bottles containing anatomical parts; one particularly large glass bottle contained an entire pickled baby. This hardly seemed the place for coffee and doughnuts.

"Ron," someone called into a neighbouring room, "a visitor for you."

Ron had tight curly hair and skin heavily pock-marked by acne that evidently made him self-conscious. As he spoke he stared at the floor with his head tilted towards one shoulder and his gaze averted to avoid eye contact.

"Come with me," he said. "I'll show you how to get started."

Having checked my name on the board, Ron led me across to a table, where lay the waxen body of a very old man with a growth of postmortem beard stubble and cotton wool in his eye sockets. I felt quite nauseated by the sight and smell of the dissecting room, and was both fascinated and yet at the same time appalled.

Several students had already begun cutting into the skin. Ron introduced me to my assigned partner, a student from Caius College, a neighbour to Clare. We were to dissect an arm, which task would occupy a full term. There were four other parts to be dissected—leg, abdomen, thorax, and (thankfully still attached) head and neck. This meant that there could be a full complement of sixteen people working on the same body.

"They rarely all come in together," said Ron, "so you should have plenty of space. Have you got a copy of Cunningham?"

"Yes." I said. "I got it secondhand."

"That's good," said Ron. "It'll soon get messy."

I had acquired my three volumes of *Cunningham's Manual of Practical Anatomy* from a former medical student who had changed to read classics after his first visit to the dissecting room. The once shiny pages smelled strongly of formaldehyde, and soon acquired a dull yellow stain from turning its pages with greasy fingers.

Over succeeding weeks we charted the course of every muscle, nerve, and blood vessel and identified each with the aid of *Cunningham*. Guffaws all round lightened the atmosphere. Black humour was mere bravado to lessen the tension of our macabre surroundings.

Ron took a small group of neophytes on a tour of the refrigeration room where bodies, each one numbered with a luggage label attached to its big toe, were stored on metal stretchers that slid on racks into the fridges. Some of them hung from hooks screwed into the skull in order to save storage space.

"Where do you get the bodies from, Ron?" I asked.

"Mostly they're paupers from almshouses around the county," he replied. "They usually haven't been claimed by relatives. Occasionally people bequeath their bodies for science to the medical school. A student was sent down last year for making a lampshade out of the skin of the body he was dissecting."

Ron pointed to the limp appendage to a male abdomen and said, "One girl from Girton came to me and said, 'But, Ron, I always thought there was a bone in it?'"

The student rabble in the hall next door were busy dissecting and gossiping the while. One third-year student recognized on a neighbouring table his staircase janitor, or gyp, who had recently been noticeably absent from college.

The bodies lost all human resemblance after a week of assault by students' scalpels. Once the initial horror had worn off we became quite blasé as they became less gruesome, if more smelly, owing to the form-aldehyde with which Albert, Ron's assistant, doused them. Wan, red-haired Albert looked as if any day he himself might appear on one of the tables. He walked around the dissecting room with a rolling motion and a vacant stare, answering simple questions in a broad Cambridge brogue. His job was to look after the huge lead-lined trunks in which the dismembered parts were stored, wrapped in formaldehyde-soaked cheesecloth.

Ron cared for his mother in a house on Midsummer Common, where each evening he would walk a big Alsatian dog, his closest companion. In second year, when we got to know him better, he would occasionally invite us into his inner sanctum for coffee.

"Watch the freshmen coming through the doors," he said with a wry smile. "D'you remember that first day yourself?"

I did—unforgettably.

I recalled how heads would peer diffidently round the half-open swing doors and withdraw after one glance. Several minutes later, when the students had gathered their wits (or had rushed off to gag in the toilet), one would reappear, step into the hall, approach the designated body, and touch it tentatively.

\* \* \*

Austere, cadaverous Professor Boyd and his teaching staff gave lec-tures in the Anatomy School auditorium, where three hundred students sat on rising banks of curved benches like a Greek theatre. Seats near the exit steps filled early, obliging latecomers to climb over a dozen fel-lows in order to find a place in the middle. A long table in front of the blackboard created a space where the professor paced ponderously up and down while delivering his lecture. Beside the lectern a complete, articulated skeleton hung from a hook screwed into its skull vault. One day a student seated in the front row tied a piece of fishing line to one hand of the skeleton. When the professor turned his back, the string was pulled and the skeletal hand rose in benediction; it returned to hang limply at the next turnaround. Laughter punctuated a notably dry lecture.

Anatomy comprised one third of our pre-clinical studies, but it occupied most of our time. I found physiology and pathology more interesting because they appeared to be related to real diseases that I might eventually treat one day. In the amphitheatre of the Physiology School, a gaunt building on the Downing Street site, Professor Bryan Matthews lectured us in neurophysiology where once stood his distinguished predecessors, Lord Adrian and Sir Joseph Barcroft.

The two physiology subjects I recall most clearly—high altitude, and thyroid goitre—were related to mountains. Professor Matthews lectured on the physiology of man at high altitudes, his forte being oxygen transport in the blood. He dropped magical phrases and names such as dreams are made of—alveolar gases at the summit of Everest, Norton and Somervell, atmospheric pressure at base camp, Hillary and Tenzing, closed circuit oxygen, acclimatization. Lectures on thyroid physiology told of retreating glaciers in aeons past leeching iodine out of the soil of high mountain valleys—in the Alps, Andes, Caucasus, and Himalayas—causing a goitrous thyroid swelling to trap any available iodine. That the disease of cretinism could be simply prevented by adding iodine to drinking water seemed true medicine to us. My newfound friends from the university mountaineering club, John Longland and Ted Maden, would join me to rehearse the lectures over coffee at a café opposite Downing College gates, relating them to our dreams of distant mountains.

In physiology practical classes we stimulated frogs' muscles and recorded twitches on a drum that carried smoked paper that became marked by the needle of the instrument. The experiments never worked out as they did for our teachers, some of whom had made world-changing discoveries.

I soon realized that I did not have the makings of a research scientist. Never did I get the hang of bacteriology because I disliked looking down microscopes; that was a reaction to the impressed enthusiasm of my uncle. Doddering, absent-minded Professor Dean, who had held the chair of pathology since the turn of the century, delivered such dry lectures that we dreamed throughout.

One sunny autumnal Saturday morning I was in the morphology laboratory on the top floor of the Anatomy School revising for an imminent exam. From the back of the hall where I was studying various animal bones, I heard a throaty chuckle resound from the front bench where Humphrey Hubert Huxley Knox-Macaulay, originally from Sierra Leone, was seated. In one hand he held a skull, in the other a picture of a huge gorilla sitting in the cleft of a tree, long arms crossed in his lap.

"Gee, man," he guffawed, "I could have sworn this was grandfather."

Sadly, I never saw Mac again after he left Cambridge, but I heard he had gone into politics—a dangerous game on his continent.

* * *

My college supervisors, allocated in each subject—anatomy, physiology, and pathology—were either senior faculty members who were also fellows of Clare, or postgraduate students studying for a higher degree. For an hour each week, in groups of four or five, we met them to discuss previously set work or to ask questions about problems—an intimate contact with teachers that was impossible in the hurly-burly of the dissecting room and the lecture halls.

I am now ashamed at how casually I took my Cambridge studies;

my priorities lay more among mountains than medicine. After failing organic chemistry, part IV of the first MB exam—for the third time— my tutor who oversaw my academic studies, Dr Michael Stoker, gave me an ultimatum: pass next time or be sent down. He was a brilliant virologist working on virus replication, and was subsequently made a Fellow of the Royal Society. His slicked-back hair, youthful looks, and jumpy, shy mannerisms disguised a titanic intellect, but he was not an easy person to get to know.

And so I buckled down and studied hard and was successful in the exam.

# EIGHT

ONE DAY WHILE I WAS DREAMILY admiring the gateway of neighbouring Trinity Hall, a slim figure dashed past me wearing a purple beret pulled down over one ear and with an army rucksack on his back. I caught a fleeting glimpse on his coat lapel of the badge of the Outward Bound Mountain School. He jumped on a bicycle and pedalled fast up Senate House Lane. I gave chase and caught up with him halfway down King's Parade.

"Hey, isn't that an Outward Bound badge?" I called out.

"Yes. Eskdale. Were you there too?"

"Yes."

"What course?"

"Thirty-five."

"I was on twenty-nine," he said. "I'm Bill Turrall. Come for tea this afternoon. E14 Trinity Hall Inner Court. I've got to dash now for a supervision. See you at four o'clock." He cycled off at speed.

Later that afternoon I knocked on the door of Bill's rooms. A lean, almost gaunt, person with an angular boyish face and a forward-thrusting jaw opened the door. Wavy black hair was shorn roughly above his protruding ears.

"Come in." He beamed a broad, friendly smile while crunching my hand. "Tea's made. D'you like crumpets?"

Bill's every movement was staccato, from lighting the gas fire to spearing the crumpets.

"So you're a climber," he said.

"Hardly," I replied, "but I did a couple of climbs on the five-day scheme at Eskdale."

"You'll have to join the CUMC," he said, referring to the Cambridge University Mountaineering Club. "It's a great way to learn. They climb in Derbyshire some weekends. There are meets in Wales, or the Lakes, or Scotland during vacations. There's a talk every Thursday."

Between crumpets and tea he dashed around the room with impetuous enthusiasm, gathering maps that he spread on the carpet. From his bookcase he pulled a copy of *The Night Climbers of Cambridge*. With his hands cutting expressive gestures to give dramatic emphasis, he read aloud a description of the first ascent of the corner pinnacles of King's College Chapel that we could see beyond the roofs of Trinity Hall and the mullioned balustrades of Clare.

"Let's go and scout some climbs," suggested Bill. "But we'd better be careful as you can get sent down for climbing on buildings."

A Siberian cold autumn wind blew across the Fens, and beech trees were turning golden brown. On open park spaces, fallen leaves made an ochre carpet that was crunchy underfoot. Halfway down Trinity Lane, Bill pointed to a row of revolving spikes set atop some railings that enclosed a corner of Trinity where a magnolia tree grew.

"Those spikes are meant to stop people climbing into college," he said. "But they don't. You can just pull up on them and balance on that ledge. A couple of easy moves get you to the windowsill."

We cycled across Garret Hostel Bridge and then along The Backs to the gates of King's. Just then emerged a crocodile of black top-hatted choristers wearing wide, starched Eton collars and short black gowns. After each evensong a choirmaster with a tasseled mortarboard and flowing gown escorted the boys back to their school across Queen's Road.

We craned our necks towards the southeast pinnacle of King's Chapel, two hundred feet above us.

"You can get a pinch hold on that lightning conductor," Bill said, pointing to a strip of metal running skyward. "Then you have to wriggle up with your back against the main buttress, and your feet pressing on that stone rib opposite. The book says those downward-pointing spikes fifty feet up make a good resting place. Apparently the rest of the lay-back to the top is a breeze once you've heaved yourself over them."

It all seemed so easy, so exciting. At the New Court of St John's College we mentally reconnoitered a route up the central gothic spire of the court known as the Wedding Cake. With our fantasies titillated, we returned to Bill's rooms in Trinity Hall for more tea and crumpets.

"Tell me about Outward Bound," he said. "Who was the warden on your course? Adam Arnold-Brown was mine."

"Eric Shipton," I replied. "We didn't see much of him. He was very retiring. I think he was smarting from being sacked as leader of the big Everest expedition."

"It was one of the greatest months of my life," Bill said.

"Same for me. But it was disappointing that I got sick and didn't finish my National Service. How about yours?"

"I was in the Parachute Brigade, mostly in Egypt," said Bill. "That was as close as I got to follow my father. Guy was twice wounded in action. He won the Military Cross in Ethiopia. He was one of Wingate's Chindits, an élite group of whom were parachuted into Burma to harass the Japanese from behind. But he never settled down and he drifted apart

from the family. For a while he lived in Canada and then in Tanganyika."
Bill would subsequently often mention Guy with sad longing as the father idol he wanted to revere and emulate, but the friend he never had.

My spontaneous and intense friendship with Bill Turrall had an un-
restrained, naive exuberance at a time of my life when everything was
new and exciting. He would frequently overtake me as he pedalled furiously along King's Parade to catch the start of a nine o'clock lecture.
He always wore a plum-coloured Parachute Regiment beret pulled over
one ear, a khaki camouflaged anorak, rubber-soled climbing boots, and
a rucksack full of books on his back. I envied his liberal, civilizing education reading classics compared with my chosen narrow scientific path.

Shortly after our first meeting, Bill Turrall and I went to a gathering
of the Cambridge University Mountaineering Club (CUMC). The club
was mustard keen, but had a tradition of encouraging and teaching novices. Mountaineers from Oxford and Cambridge then dominated climbing in Britain. Shortly thereafter they were supplanted by lads from the
Midlands, particularly plumbers Joe Brown and Don Whillans, and the
rough-tough Glaswegians of the Creag Dubh Club.

After club lectures on mountaineering topics, people could adjourn
to the rooms in King's College of Alfred Tissières, a patriarchal don and
an experienced alpine climber. There we met The Committee of undergraduates, whose doyens—Bob Downes, Eric Langmuir, Mike O'Hara,
Dick Sykes and John Peacock—were our heroes whom we wished to
emulate. We listened in awe as they recounted feats on the rock and ice
of classic Alpine routes and trials by wicked elements, and dangers on
the Walker Spur, Cassin Ridge, and Gervasutti Couloir.

Two of my CUMC friends were the sons of eminent pre-war
Everesters. John Longland, son of Jack, was a natural leader with several hard Welsh routes to his credit. Cocky and cheerful, with a deep
resounding voice, he chain-smoked, repeatedly flicking ash with nic-

otine-stained fingers. Bill Norton's father, Edward, had led the 1924 northern attempt on Everest from Tibet, reaching 28,124 ft (8575 m), then a world altitude record. Bill was tall and stooped, with an aquiline nose that dominated his angular, chiselled face, and the side of his nostrils twitched when he talked. He had enormous flailing feet, yet his fine hands painted superbly delicate watercolours. His faltering voice and shy manner belied a stoic toughness.

Another friend, Ted Maden, was a laconic, humorous, fair-haired northcountryman from Bacup. His chin protruded both in adversity and in argument when he would draw figures on the ground with his toe while gazing into space. Since he was very brainy, we tried to sit next to him in lectures so he could explain things we did not understand.

Every Thursday the inner conclave of the CUMC met for lunch at different coffee houses, and an invitation to join them was like getting the Masonic nod. It wasn't till the next year that I received this. Neophyte climbers would meet on random mornings at The Whim, a café on Trinity Street, where we planned feats of derring-do on alpine faces and ridges, interspersed with idle chatter.

We paid little attention to a pair of older graduates who often sat in a corner talking and scribbling on scraps of paper—they were James Watson and Francis Crick, who had recently unravelled the mysteries of DNA.

* * *

In the January dark of my first Cambridge winter, I became increasingly melancholy and sleepless. It started after a Medical Society lecture given by Dr Francis Camps, guru forensic pathologist who, over two decades, was prosecution witness in London's most notorious murder trials. He recounted ghoulish tales of gruesome crimes accompanied by bizarre and macabre photos to an audience, hungry for clinical stories. He talked casually of identifying criminals from blood spots, pubic hair, and semen. After seeing photos of the bodies found carved up under the floorboards of 10 Rillington Place, the toilets resounded with the retching of students. The horrors of the Anatomy School were nothing to this, and I had nightmares for a week.

"What did you think of the lecture?" I asked several of my fellows, not wanting to confess my own weakness.

Almost all the freshmen replied, "Couldn't sleep after it." Second- and third-year undergraduates, more in tune with black medical humour, were less distressed.

I began to lie awake in the night. To my dreary room on Castle Street came several well-meaning evangelical Christians from the college chapel, but their muscular religion only deepened my sense of gloom. Some clerical friends supported me but none of these holy men could lift my dark, hovering cloud.

"If you pray enough, and pull up your socks," they implied, "everything will be alright."

After earnest conversation they would kneel, leaning on a chair, and carry on a chatty exchange with their Saviour, as with a benign uncle on whom you dropped in for tea when the going gets tough. It seemed easy as pie. If only I asked to be saved and committed myself to the Lord (whatever that meant), all my problems would vanish.

Although I was then unaware of any specific problems, I realized, with the help of my friend Bill Turrall, that I had never truly grieved my parents' deaths nor faced the consequent adolescent turmoil. Adjusting to university life with all its freedoms, new friends, and wide horizons emphasized my loneliness. I dreaded the thought of returning to my dreary digs and my crone of a landlady, who was sure to be lying in wait for me behind the magenta curtains.

"I can't sleep or concentrate on my work," I told my tutor, Dr Michael Stoker, "and my rackets and squash have fallen off."

"You should consult a general practitioner," he advised.

So I made an appointment with a doctor at the top of Castle Street.

"Can't sleep, eh?" he said. "I'll give you some pills that should fix it."

He prescribed barbiturates, and for a few days I floated in a cloud with my feet hardly touching the ground. I became concerned about feeling unable to concentrate and returned to the doctor. "I'll switch you to liquid chloral hydrate," he said. "It tastes so disgusting it is unlikely to become addictive." When nothing seemed to alleviate my gloom he sent me to a psychiatrist at Addenbrooke's Hospital.

The doctor spent the entire interview writing down my every word as if taking evidence verbatim in court. He never raised his eyes from the paper to look at me, never sat back in his chair to talk with the empathy I yearned for. He whisked me off to Fulbourn Hospital outside Cambridge where I was admitted as a voluntary patient.

A rambling Victorian mansion set in flat marshy fenland housed the main hospital; the acute admission wards where I was admitted were two army huts in the grounds. Recalling details of the next three weeks is difficult because my subconscious successfully blanked them from my memory. The shame and horror of being in a hospital was so paralyzing that I never discussed it with anyone. A couple of interviews with a junior psychiatrist afforded me no reassurance that I would feel better soon, neither did he help me navigate the maze of emotions caused by my parents' deaths.

What I needed was a sympathetic ear, some gentle words of advice, and encouragement that things would get better. I perambulated the grounds of that grim establishment in the company of a fellow patient, an ex–merchant sailor, who had on his upper lip a mole with hairs growing out of the middle, and fingers stained dark brown with nicotine.

On return from bedlam, my tutor arranged for me to move into a room on W staircase of Clare Memorial Court, which lay across The

Backs from the main college in the shadow of the high tower of the new University Library. Being away from my lonely digs and surrounded by other undergraduates quickly put me back on my feet. Edward Platts, a fellow medical student, later to be best man at my wedding, continued to support me; he and Bill Turrall were the only people with whom I could discuss this awful episode, a silence I have maintained for most of my life.

Once roomed in college, everything took a turn for the better. I revived my interest in climbing, began to play rackets well again, and earned a place on the college squash team, one of the strongest in the university. My staircase neighbours were Francis Walker, an engineer, and Peter Barbor, a medical student and fellow squash player. Peter was graceful in every move; however, his fluent and dashing squash style was not aggressive enough to make him a ruthless winner. Francis was tall and gangly with a gentle Scots lilt in his voice. Having been a star schoolboy rugby football player at Edinburgh Academy, he always hoped—sadly unfulfilled—to get a blue. A wild one who got pissed regularly on a Saturday night along with his macho rugger friends, Francis impressed us by squiring one of the Professor of Engineering's daughters. Peter and I spent much time regretting our virginity and wondering what we should do about it. While walking our bikes back to college one evening, slightly tipsy, we agreed to send each other a telegram on first consummation. Nevertheless, it took a long time for telegrams to be exchanged.

Francis, Peter, and I took turns making breakfast, grocery shopping, and tidying our rooms so we would not anger our gyp, a college servant who was king of the staircase. Each of the eight suites leading off a staircase had a sitting room and separate bedroom. A lady "bedder" from the nether parts of Cambridge made our beds and pampered us and assisted the gyp.

Another neighbour was Hal Stahmer, an American postgraduate student from Columbia University in New York. He had just spent two years at a monastery in Tübingen studying religious philosophy under the German theologian, Martin Buber. Hal became our mentor since he seemed worldly wise and full of savvy, being several years older than any of us, yet only in his late twenties. His uproarious and irreverent laugh mocked our plummy English accents.

\* \* \*

The focus of our academic life was the dissecting room, where we medical students frittered away hours while trying to learn anatomy. We became mildly hysterical, closeted in that stinking hall on a summer afternoon when other students were playing cricket or lazing beside the River Cam. To pass the time we told vulgar stories at which we laughed immoderately.

One afternoon when all the demonstrators were absent at a departmental meeting, John Longland and I attempted to traverse an entire circuit of the dissecting room without putting foot to ground. Blackboards along two walls gave handholds so we could step lightly on a skirting just above floor level. At the far end of the hall we easily crossed the lids of the coffin-like boxes where anatomical "parts" were stored. The final tricky manoeuvre was near the washbasins outside Ron's coffee room. We swung round the main door, made a tricky stretch to the first basin and straddled the plumbing, careful not to pull the pipes from the wall. Students, bored with their dissections, applauded the hour-long climb. Ron silently abetted us on the sidelines until Dr Wright, our supervisor, returned prematurely, which caused a flurry of embarrassment and apology.

Our mild pranks compared palely with the student revolutions occurring in Paris and Hungary at that time. The political climate in Cambridge was stable, if boring. We pursued our studies in peace, imagining, with disappointment, that the action was always elsewhere.

The porters' lodge gateway to Clare Memorial Court, as in most university colleges, was locked at eleven o'clock each night. Iron railings, revolving spikes, jagged pieces of broken glass set in concrete, and barbed wire guarded all other access to the court. The night porter, with only one entrance to watch, could control the comings and goings of undergraduates from the lodge. The only exceptions to this surveillance were ground-floor occupants who had learned to unscrew the wooden blocks that prevented the window being opened more than a couple of inches—or skilful climbers.

I discovered a way into college by an easy climb up the outside wall of my staircase, where every alternate corner quoin projected half an inch. Ample finger- and toeholds led to the upper floor window of a large and muscular fellow medical student, Drummond Rennie, whose first-class brain hid behind a determined, prognathous visage. The only difficult manoeuvre to reach his room was a swing across onto the windowsill using an undercut mullion for balance. I could then open the window provided Drummond had not locked it from the inside. He became inspired with climbing following my entering his window late one night and catching him *in flagrante*. Subsequently, in order to teach him to rope down, or abseil, out of his window, I attached my climbing rope to the radiator in his bedroom.

"Stand securely on the sill," I ordered. "Pass the rope forward between your legs. Now take it across the front of your chest and over your left shoulder. Grip the trailing rope with your right hand. Now lean outwards. When you're horizontal, start walking down the wall backwards. Just gently grip the rope with your fingers to control your slide. Friction will take care of the rest . . ."

A crash shattered the still night air, which was orchestrated by the tinkle of glass from a ground floor window and loud cursing. The doubled rope stretched taut over the sill. I looked over to see Drummond hanging from the rope, gyrating in space, legs flailing in search of a footing, and in danger of being emasculated. I untied the climbing rope from the radiator and lowered him to the herbaceous border below, from where he hurled abuse at me in between apologizing to the room's astonished occupant.

The commotion brought to the scene a college porter doing his night inspection round.

"Oy, surrs," came a voice. It was that of Jock Scobie, a shiny-pated, six-foot-plus-tall, ex-Glasgow police sergeant. "Wha's goin' on here?"

"We're just practicing, Jock." I replied feebly and guiltily, because Jock was a gentle giant who had become a good friend.

"Ye'll pay for the window then," he said. "And next time ye'll be in deep trouble."

This was a small price for a crime that could have led to our rapid dispatch from the university. Jock rode off into the dark on his outsize iron-frame bicycle in search of other miscreants.

Drummond never did join the mountaineering club, but years later he became an expert clinical high altitude physiologist with some big climbs to his credit, both in the Andes and the Himalaya.

My climbing friends and I soon realized that the thrills of night climbing were not worth the penalty of being expelled. We satisfied ourselves with Sunday morning visits to the southeast pillar of the quadrangle colonnade of Trinity College Library. Designed by Sir Christopher Wren, it stands above an open cloister overlooking gentle lawns that slope towards the River Cam, in spring flanked by weeping willows and banks of daffodils and crocuses. Here generations of Cambridge mountaineers in rubber-soled tennis shoes had honed their skills by traversing the outward sloping moulding at the base of the sturdy L-shaped cornerstone pillars without putting a foot to the ground. These pillars were set half a metre above the flagstones and a horizontal distance of about 15 metres. We considered the risk of being caught at this innocent exercise acceptable, but while executing the traverse we posted a lookout for the billowing gown and tasselled mortarboard of the law-keeping Proctor who patrolled the university with two henchmen ("bulldogs") dressed in black morning coats and top hats.

The climb starts in a deep-cut corner and is accomplished thus: stand up gingerly on the polished moulding, reach round the pillar with the right hand and insert fingernails into a vertical crack, pull sideways while standing on tiptoes. Then shuffle round the next corner facing the grass of Neville courtyard. A few easy moves around the inner side of the pillar bring you to the crux (here imagine you are a few thousand metres above one of the mighty glaciers of the Alps on the crucial pitch of a classic route that could one day put your name beside the Immortals). Stand with one foot on either side of the corner block, take a friction finger hold on the smooth stone and, with the right hand extended, fall across into the angle without dislodging your footing or buckling. Insert a finger into a tiny hole in the masonry and pull yourself up into a standing position. Hey, presto! The traverse is complete.

One sunny Sunday morning we were engrossed in the traverse and our sentinel, bored with his duties, was practicing on the twin pillar opposite. A guttural European voice behind me said softly, "Longland didn't do it like that. He always used his chin." An elderly bearded gentleman in carpet slippers and supporting his stooped frame with a cane peered at me from behind thick black spectacles. This retired professor of mathematics was well known to all who meandered the great courtyards of Trinity. I thanked him for his advice. Then we listened to him recount tales of climbers he had known over the years. It was like a compendium of a mountaineering history.

* * *

A small group of us, now growing in confidence, planned some winter snow and ice climbing in Scotland for the Christmas vacation. I drove north to Boston Spa, near Leeds, to pick up Josephine Scarr, doyenne of the university women's mountaineering club, the Magogs. The CUMC was then a male preserve, so for Jo, more talented than most men, it was particularly frustrating having to depend on them for leaders. The ultimate insult was for those "misogynists at heart" (her words) to name her club after small hilly bumps on the flat Cambridge horizon—the Magogs. Within a few years she was climbing hard rock, leading routes in the Alps, and co-leader of an all-women expedition to the Himalayas.

After vying with juggernaut lorries on the Great North Road, it was a pleasure to breathe the fresh air of the undulating Yorkshire Dales. We picked up Peter Thursfield at the Scotch Corner roundabout, and Sandy Wright from his home outside Glasgow. Then we headed for the Scottish Highlands, purple with heather, golden bracken against grey rocks, blue sky and sea beyond. People are scarce in the lonely crofts and hamlets scattered over the two hundred wild miles from the Clyde to Cape Wrath.

Beyond Loch Lomond the road wound among peaty bogs and lochans of Rannoch Moor. On that cold, stormy midwinter day the moor was a desolate place with surrounding primaeval humpback hills, recently snow-dusted, rolling towards the horizon. Suddenly on the left rose the majestic triangle of Buachaille Etive Mòr, standing guard at the portal to Glencoe. Despite our slim experience, the exciting prospect of winter climbing using ice axes and crampons was intense.

We stayed in the youth hostel in Glencoe and, mostly in foul weather, made forays into the mountains round the glen. We were nearly blown off the ridge of Sgùrr Dearg above Ballachulish, and we climbed Aonach Dubh in a hailstorm that covered the rocks with icy verglas. At the end of an adventurous week, brimming with confidence, we planned to climb Forked Gulley on Stob Coire nan Lochan. Jo and I tied onto one brand new, white nylon rope, Sandy and Peter onto the other. We kicked steps in the steep crusty snow and, where the gulley forked, alternated in cutting steps with my ice axe. With immaculate balance Jo followed easily.

As we crested the ice pitch we heard a *whoosh* below and saw Sandy and Peter catapulting down the gulley, creating their own avalanche. Sandy had been adjusting his new goggles when his stance gave way and he hurtled past Peter, pulling him off his stance. With pride bruised, but little else, they climbed soberly up in our steps till we all reached the top and celebrated with sherry-soaked Christmas cake. We gazed at the mantle of snow up which we had climbed with renewed respect for the Scottish conditions that can change from sunshine to savage blizzard in the blink of an eye.

On New Year's Eve we drove to Fort William.

"What are we going to do for Hogmanay?" said Sandy.

"How about the Ben?" I suggested, looking up at Ben Nevis looming over us.

No one dissented, so in gathering darkness we climbed the track. Four hours later, in a snowstorm, we pitched our tents near the triangulation survey cairn on the summit plateau of the highest mountain in Britain. The wind howled throughout the night and we had to go outside to weigh down the floor flaps of the tent with stones and snow, and to adjust the guy ropes repeatedly. We huddled in our sleeping bags, unable to cook because of a buffeting wind. We learned the meaning of the jingle, "First it friz and then it snew, then it frizzed and then it blew, then came on a shower of rain (hail) and then it friz and snew again."

On a clear dawn, mist swirled deep in the corrie of Observatory Gully only a few paces away from our tents. On return to Fort William a headline in the *Daily Mail* read, "Climbers brave the Ben to welcome 1956" and followed with a dramatic account of our adventure of which we had spoken in the grocery store and must have been passed from mouth to mouth.

We returned to Cambridge confident that we had climbed one step nearer becoming mountaineers—a pinnacle we yearned for. I determined to catch up on work, but my mind was elsewhere. So was Bill Turrall's. We met often and I increasingly admired his enthusiasm, constancy, and integrity. He was deeply religious, did not swear or drink, and never pushed his evangelical views on his friends. I could not imagine him ever being mean or unkind.

# NINE

ONE WINTER SUNDAY BILL TURRALL and I pedalled our bikes, heads bowed against the wind, across the fens towards the village of Coton for lunch at the pub. Skeletal, leafless trees were silhouetted against a wide East Anglian sky, where scudded high cumulus from the Baltic Sea, pushed along by winds from Siberia. Cambridgeshire was bone-chillingly damp, its furrowed loamy soil awaited spring seeding, and crows pecked at shrivelled berries in gaunt hedgerows.

At the Coton pub we met by chance Andrew Millewski, a South African postgraduate research mathematician. It turned out that he was a fellow of his college and also a mountaineer.

"Where do you climb at home?" I asked.

"The Drakensberg," he replied in a twangy accent tinged with Afrikaans. "It forms the border between Basutoland and Natal. That's my home."

"What are your plans for the summer?"

"Nothing special. I'd like to climb in Europe."

"Why don't we all go to the Pyrenees," suggested Bill. "The mountains aren't as serious as the Alps."

"Great idea," said Andrew. "We won't have to depend on the club leaders. It'll be our own alpine expedition."

We planned for an August start since I had to return for the Long Vac Term to dissect a leg and to finish part IV of the First MB exam. After cheese rolls and pickled onions washed down with a pint of shandy, we were already halfway there.

The storm clouds having cleared, we cycled on through country lanes to The Mill pub at Grantchester. In the tradition of Rupert Brooke, we ordered afternoon tea, with the church clock standing at nearly ten to three. We sat in the garden under a pear tree beside the River Cam, which meandered into the distance through flat meadows. There we met Tony Delafield, a strong young man with fiery red curly hair and thick spectacles. He came on board with barely a murmur.

We cycled back to Cambridge, intoxicated with excitement, and called on Ted Maden. As the strongest of our embryonic climbing group, he deserved a place in the adventure afoot. He agreed to join us, so now we were five—an unwieldy number for climbing ropes since people usually climbed in pairs. Nevertheless the idea was launched. We invited John Longland, but he had plans for the Alps. Our philosophy for our Pyrenean expedition mimicked that of our heroes, Eric Shipton (who claimed that "an expedition that cannot be planned on the back of an envelope is too complicated") and Bill Tilman (who called an expedition "a party with too many people in it").

During term, the mountaineering club organized day trips to Derbyshire to climb on gritstone outcrops, a series of cliffs about one hundred feet high. A bus left the Senate House at seven of a dark morning. At halfway through the four-hour journey it stopped at the Blue Boar transport café on the A6. Beside a raucous jukebox we sleepily ate a breakfast of greasy fried eggs and bacon with baked beans, washed down with strong tea laced with condensed milk and sugar. Flat fens gave way to rolling hills as we approached Derbyshire, where a jagged horizon of gritstone stuck out like teeth from deep dales.

The gritstone edges of Froggatt, Stanage, and Curbar lay beyond the gentle hillsides above Chatsworth under sky more often raincloud-laden than blue. Grazing sheep, lone denizens of rugged moors around High Peak, seemed oblivious to the millions of people living in the nearby smog-choked cities of Sheffield, Manchester, and Stoke-on-Trent. Gritstone climbs were short—a couple of fifty-foot pitches at most—but with all grades of difficulty, they taught us the techniques of hard, gymnastic rock climbing. The guidebook catalogued a hundred or more climbs along a mile of gritstone edge, so there was plenty of room for our busload to climb our hearts out. A pair of cheap black Woolworth's gym shoes that were fashionable for hard, short rock climbs gripped the rough rock and, protected by a top-rope, we could perform unaccustomed feats without dangers of exposure.

In awe and envy we watched experienced "tigers" of the club drift gracefully up steep rock, swing out under overhanging roofs and pull up on hands jammed into narrow cracks. Bob Downes, president of the club and my neighbour in college, was short and puckish, with tight curly hair, pointy elf-like ears, and a scarred cheek. He stood on a tiny toehold quizzically surveying the rock above him. Then with confident grace he apparently floated up a stretch of difficult rock.

By evening our fingers were rubbed raw and we collapsed into the bus for the journey back to Cambridge. Two hundred miles each way seemed long for a single day's climbing, but it was worth it for the confidence we gained, which allowed us to contemplate ambitious plans for longer, harder climbs in far-off ranges. We thought we were indestructible.

* * *

In the Amateur Rackets Championship at Queen's Club in the Easter vacation, I drew in the first round the reigning world champion, Geoffrey Atkins. I had played against him before in a doubles match, and knew the artistry of his faultless strokes. In the first game, with my strong backhand service learned from Bill Hawes's father, Walter, I led by twelve points to nothing before Geoffrey was truly awake. This gap spurred him to cut me down like a scythe mowing hay. With unfailing accuracy he drove the ball down the wall time and again just above the board to die in the corner until I was demolished. However, the experience of playing against someone of Atkins's calibre was a thrill and a privilege.

In the Amateur Doubles competition my partner Jeremy Barron and I drew John Thompson and Richard Gracey, the eventual finalists. Thompson, a master at Marlborough College, and David Milford, a former World Champion, had once played against Guy Warner and myself at Charterhouse in a hard fought match where, even in defeat, we felt we had acquitted ourselves with honour. Gracey was one of the outstanding schoolboy stylists of our contemporaries.

I left Queen's Club—long white flannels, club bar, and green lawns—and raced up to Wales to join my scruffy climbing friends for the CUMC Easter meet. It was held at Helyg, a Climbers' Club hut in the lee of shapely Tryfan between Capel Curig and Llyn Ogwen. The small stone farmhouse had a communal kitchen, a dining area with rough wood tables and benches, and a bunkhouse where bodies could be stacked to the roof. I slept on the folded-down back seat of my Standard station wagon, surrounded by my ragbag of climbing gear. Some Magogs joined us for this meet, one in particular looking seraphic by candlelight as we read poems from General Wavell's *Other Men's Flowers*. Many of my fellow climbers, now a tight-knit group of friends, thought similarly, but our shared passion for the hills sublimated lustful thoughts.

During my childhood at school in Wales I came to love its varied scenery. Returning there as an adult, I found the shapes of the mountains were familiar, like encountering old friends after an absence. Curly bracken shoots smelled sweet in spring and fronds shredded through my fingers were more acrid; in autumn, mellow browns and pastel ochre shades clothed the rolling hillsides. We used to dance from boulder to boulder in rocky streams and to swing over pools on branches of dwarf oak trees.

During the meet at Helyg we climbed routes on the Idwal Slabs and scrambled up the Devil's Kitchen. John Longland and I navigated over fog-shrouded Glyder Fawr and descended to the valley by the nose of Tryfan. We strode over the Carneddau covered with a sprinkling of snow and rime ice that clung to the lee of grass stalks like prayer flags. If the weather was foul we escaped to some small cliffs above Tremadog which were often sunbathed and clear.

One day when Snowdon was shrouded in cloud and rain, George Fraser and Jim Lee decided to climb Cnicht, an elegant cone-shaped mountain near Blaenau Ffestiniog. Bill Turrall and I tagged along, eager to learn anything we could from the maestros. We found a derelict mine shaft adit with rail tracks leading to the end of a huge tip that emptied high above the valley. A dozen abandoned, rusty ore cars lay scattered pell-mell, their wheels still intact.

"Let's see if we can get them back on the rails," said George.

We righted the cars, using iron bars and wooden beams as levers. Then we pushed them to the end of the tip and with a final shove sent them hurtling over the edge. Several tons of metal cartwheeled slowly and gracefully through the air before crashing on the mountainside below. An uproar resounded throughout the still valley as the cars bounced off the rocks. Wheels broke off axles in slow motion and scattered into the air amid a shower of sparks. Half a dozen more cars followed. Then we hooligans dashed off down the mountain, yelling in jubilation.

Each evening we drove round to the Pen-y-Gwryd Hotel – PyG - for a glass of Worthington 'E'. The PyG stands in the shadow of Snowdon, which one can see on rare clear days. One fork in the road goes over Pen-y-Pass to the Llanberis Valley, the other heads towards Beddgelert and Porthmadog. Chris Briggs, a northcountryman, bought the PyG in the early 1950s and turned it into a climbers' mecca. Though not a climber himself, Chris became expert in organizing mountain rescues at a time, before helicopters came on the scene, when arduous ground searches were the rule. The 1953 Everest party trained out of the PyG, and subsequently the victorious climbers signed their names on the ceiling of a small bar—now known as the Everest Room. Chris held court in the inner sanctum bar of the PyG where privileged invitees drank beer from tankards embossed with the names of Everest climbers. The atmosphere was always friendly, if somewhat obsequious.

Back in Cambridge, the Long Vacation Term dragged out in a balmy haze of unusually hot summer sunshine. Tennis rackets took the place of books in bicycle baskets, and pretty foreign girls from the language schools lounged in punts. A relaxed tempo contrasted with the intensity of the rest of the academic year. During the extra term, medical students were meant to catch up on biochemistry and pathology courses, and to complete at least one anatomy dissection. Like naughty schoolboys kept in after class, we resented the undergraduates studying arts subjects who were lying in grassy fields beside the River Cam or basking on some Mediterranean beach. Worse still, our climbing friends were probably chalking up new routes on mountains in Scotland or the Alps.

In the dissecting room of the Anatomy School, adversity forged camaraderie; and the atmosphere would have been festive but for the formalin stench of corpses fighting decomposition. Along with sixteen other students, I worked on a body with Jonathan Miller, a tall and gawky man with curly red hair, whose jacket and trousers were too short for his loose limbs. His career in the Cambridge Footlights Revue production of *Beyond the Fringe* was soon to be launched in London. Jonathan's success eclipsed his avocation in medicine, but being a polymath he went on to other successes in the arts and literature. He clowned through that long hot summer while dissecting a leg, buffoonery disguising his gigantic intellect.

By dissection we exposed and identified every anatomical structure layer by layer, at each stage having to pass a viva voce exam before digging into a deeper plane. Vivas were conducted by demonstrators who were either senior lecturers and research fellows, or budding surgeons relearning anatomy for the Primary Fellowship Exams of the Royal College of Surgeons.

We tried to get vivas from young demonstrators, in the belief that their own anatomical knowledge was shaky so they would be more sympathetic to gaps in ours. Nevertheless, one day my dissecting partner and I thought we were ready to move on to the next chapter of Cunningham. Since no apprentice surgeons were available, I approached Dr Millen, a senior fellow of Clare and my own anatomy supervisor. His gentle manner had earned him the sobriquet of "a steel hand in a velvet glove."

"Please, sir, will you take our viva?"

"Are ye sure ye're ready for it?" he asked in his soft Northern Ireland brogue, scrutinizing a tangled mass of tissue around the shoulder that we had tried to tidy by cutting away anything superfluous. Dr Millen gave away nothing as he probed deeply with a pair of forceps.

"What muscles does the circumflex nerve supply?" he asked.

"We haven't got to that part yet, sir. We're only on the brachial plexus."

He continued his meticulously polite inquisition with questions that revealed in us a deep sump of ignorance.

"It's like a punnet of strawberries, Steele," he said, handing back our unsigned viva cards. "Pretty on top, but if ye delve it's rotten right through."

Several years later I became a demonstrator myself, drank coffee with Ron, and swaggered round those very halls, giving searching vivas to students who appeared to know considerably more than I did. Albert, Ron's previous assistant, had since passed on, and thankfully had avoided the glass-topped tables.

* * *

The term rolled by and then the keenly awaited moment arrived for our climbing expedition to head off to the Pyrenees. Our adventure started outside Bill Turrall's home in Holland Park Gardens. He had mislaid his keys so he shinned up a drainpipe and climbed over the third floor balcony balustrade of his mother's flat. He disappeared through the French windows just as the landlord appeared.

"Come down from there," he ordered, "else I'll call the police."

"I'm just getting into my mother's flat," said Bill. "I left my keys inside and there's no one there to let me in."

We mollified the fuming landlord and hurriedly crammed our climbing gear into my small car. We crossed the English Channel by ferry and collected Andrew Millewski from his sister's home on the outskirts of Paris. As we drove southwest towards the Pyrenees, poplar-lined avenues cast mesmeric shadows across the road leading towards Bordeaux. A tang of fresh baguettes and Gauloises scented every village shop. At Lourdes we rubbed shoulders with throngs of pilgrims visiting the grotto of Saint Bernadette, where racks of crutches hung from the walls—purported to be evidence of miracles fulfilled there. But our inspiration lay yonder among the snow-capped peaks that stretched across the southern horizon straddling the narrow neck of Basque country between France and Spain.

At Gavarnie village, coachloads of pilgrims, enjoying a day of re-spite from their devotions at Lourdes, had come to gaze in awe at the surrounding mountains. The air was rank with the dung of dozens of mules and donkeys. Garlic-sweaty muleteers wearing black Basque be-rets harangued tourists to ride along the well-trodden trail towards the sombre cliffs of the Cirque de Gavarnie that barred the head of the val-ley.

The Cirque is a natural amphitheatre—part vertical, part ter-raced—1,000 metres high and five kilometres  in circumference. A waterfall, the Grande Cascade, drops clear for 500 metres dividing the Cirque in two. To the left, Le Marboré, the highest peak in the region at 3,250 metres is flanked by the Pic Occidental d'Astazou. On the right rise the vertical walls of the Mur de la Cascade separated by three sloping, tiered terraces. Peaks of La Tour du Marboré, Le Casque du Marboré, and La Brèche de Roland form a jagged horizon.

A dusky, weather-beaten muleteer tried to persuade us to include his scrawny beast in our *équipage* but, realizing we were unlikely takers, he tried to offer himself for a fee as an invaluable member of our *équipe*. Instead, Bill and I set off on our own carrying huge packs that did not bother us since we were both very fit. A kilometre outside Gavarnie we quit the main track and struck across an open meadow, leaving behind the cavalcade of obese tourists, children on school outings, and soldiers escaping the tedium of military barracks in Tarbes.

We set up our Meade mountain tents beside a stream in a secluded stand of pine. Next morning our camp resounded with the bells of cows grazing beside our campfire. We were fatigued after the long journey through France, so we lazed over breakfast admiring the panoramic view of a coliseum of big peaks around us. The arrival of our friends Ted Maden and Andrew Millewski at a rendezvous in the post office spurred us into action. We followed through the woods a trail that led to a log bridge over the river, and some rock steps reached the mule path below the Hotel du Cirque. There we sat on the terrace and drank fizzy pop alongside tourists now thankful to have dismounted from their donkeys.

We looked very amateur, kitted out with climbing gear bought mostly at army surplus stores. I wore a baggy khaki anorak and thread-bare tweed breeches made from my grandfather's knickerbockers. Our Vibram-soled boots gripped well on dry rock, but if wet or icy, old-fashioned clinker nails were better. Hard helmets had not then come into fashion so I strapped my climbing goggles round the crown of my hat, hoping to look like a professional guide. Nylon ropes, such as we had brought with us, were then so expensive in Europe that British climbers could pay for an alpine holiday by selling their nearly new ropes before heading home. To avoid nylon burning on nylon by friction in case of a fall, we tied several turns of hemp line round our waists as a harness. The gates of our army surplus steel karabiners were liable to open under strain.

The patron of the Hotel du Cirque, Pierre Vergez, noticed our climbing ropes and came over to talk to us. He was short in stature, with bulging muscles, spade-shaped hands, and knobbly knuckles. A tonsure framed his balding head. As he recalled some of his climbing adventures on the walls towering above us, a warm mischievous smile spread across his face made ruddy by the sun, wind, and wine. He knew this central part of the Pyrenees better than any living man. He had hunted chamois in their spring hideouts on high alpine pastures, and he guarded jealously the secret of places where edelweiss and gentian grew. He had climbed every wall of the Cirque (three times on the Mur de la Cascade at night to bring down injured climbers) and had taken part in countless mountain searches and rescues.

"We want to climb the walls of the Cirque," we told him, "but we're not very experienced. Do you think that's wise?'

"Of course, montagnards," he replied. "Try the ordinary route first and then one of the more difficult ones, like the one I did years ago with my friend Castagnez, now known as the Castagnez-Vergez."

To be called "montagnard" immediately set us apart from the tourists. They just gaped at Pierre's beloved mountains whose secrets he kept for those prepared to toil up their slopes, to crest their high ridges, and to look from their summits into distant valleys.

By dark we returned to camp, brimful of ideas. We planned to climb the Pic Occidental d'Astazou next day, but in the event we were turned back by sleet and mist halfway up the rocky north arete. So we scrambled up to the Brèche de Roland, a huge gash in the upper tier of the rock walls forming the border with Spain like the portal to a distant kingdom. Legend tells that the mediaeval crusader, Roland, created the cleft in the final tier of rock by trying to shatter his faithful sword, Durandal, to prevent it falling into the hands of Moorish infidels. We looked southwestwards through a purple haze into the canyons of the Spanish Pyrenees and the barren Sierras beyond; behind us lay the pine-forested alpine valleys of France—a dramatic geographical contrast. Using our headlamps we climbed down to the mouth of the Grotte Casteret where begins a vast limestone cave system, but the tunnel was soon blocked with ice that never saw the light or warmth of day.

Now on our second day and confident for bigger things, we climbed an alp leading to the Marboré, our first big mountain. We tramped ankle-deep through brilliant red-flowered azaleas. Gentian and scattered tufts of saxifrage grew on sandy grey rocks. With the sun at its zenith we kicked steps across the soft snow of a steep couloir that led to the summit. We basked in sunshine and ate our lunch of chocolate, Kendal mint cake, baguettes, and pilchards. Clouds boiled in the cauldron of the Cirque below us.

"Ted must have left the pressure cooker on," remarked Bill, looking down at our camp where Ted was nursing an upset stomach.

Three hours later we descended to an avalanche scar that crossed our early morning upward tracks. Sobered by our folly, we hurried across the couloir. Down the mountain we raced, straight to the hotel cellar to recount our adventures to Pierre Vergez. He discarded his blue-and-white striped apron, called to his wife to bring a bottle of wine, and signalled us to draw chairs around the big kitchen table. Margaret Vergez, a tiny figure dressed in black with white lace at her wrists and a black shawl round her shoulders, appeared with a goatskin gourd of red Bordeaux wine mixed with champagne. As we squirted it into our mouths our exploits grew. Pierre listened patiently to every detail as though he had been there with us.

Next day Bill and Ted, who was feeling better, went off to complete the arete on the Pic Occidental d'Astazou. Andrew and I attempted the voie normale on the Mur de la Cascade but were forced to abandon it after getting soaked traversing under a waterfall below the final pitch.

"How about exploring the Cauterets valley," said Ted after we returned to camp. "I'd like to walk there across the mountains. Who'll come with me?"

I agreed to go and we set off in a downpour under sinister, anvil-shaped clouds. Thunder rumbled in the distance and lightning stabbed the valley. Bill and Andrew drove round to Pont d'Espagne having stocked up with provisions in Cauterets. There they met Tony Delafield, who had hitch-hiked through France after finishing his exams. We camped in a meadow close beside a stream. Around the campfire after dinner we skimmed our metal plates up-river; they would then float down into a dam of stones we had built beside us. The first plate to reach the pool was the winner. The dishes washed poorly but this aimless pastime entertained us for hours.

Near our camp we joined some French parachutists who were teaching recruits to climb a small rock cliff. A few days before, the sergeant, a French Foreign Legion veteran of Dien Bien Phu in Vietnam, had parachuted onto the Vignemale glacier with his platoon. The soldiers offered us food and wine, adding, *"C'est l'état qui paie."* (It's the state who pays.)

Profuse wild azaleas filled our memories of the Vallée du Marcadu where a mule track led up a pine-clad valley and over the mountains into Spain, one of many trading routes that criss-cross the Pyrenees. From the top of a small peak on the frontier ridge we looked into the barren canyon lands of northern Spain. To the east lay the Vallée de Gaube leading towards the Vignemale, its precipitous, smooth granite north face rising a thousand metres out of the flat grassland. We climbed the main peak by the easy backside route from the Baysellance hut over the Petit Vignemale with the Face Nord always in view, a beckoning challenge.

At the top the party split. Ted Maden and Tony Delafield descended the Arete de Gaube, while Bill Turrall and I returned by the Glacier de Vignemale. Alert to the perils of glaciers, we trod carefully, watching for hidden crevasses. After a seventeen-hour day we plodded robot-like towards the haven of our camp, the music of bubbling streams unheard, alpine flowers unseen, and grazing mountain cows unheeded.

We returned to Gavarnie for the final climb of this, our first season—the Voie Normale on the Mur de la Cascade. The guidebook description talks of "vertical rock and fantastic overhangs where during storms one can be half drowned by waterfalls or caught up by stonefalls." Though fearful to the lily-livered, our burgeoning confidence left us undismayed. After eight hours climbing we sat on moss among alpine violets and gentian; to our right was the Marboré, below us lay the Cirque and the hotel of our friend Pierre Vergez.

During this, our first climbing expedition, we had gained confidence of leading on steep rock, of belaying and handling the rope safely, and of trusting our map and compass. Our fingers were rubbed rough by rock, eyes replete with beauty, feet hardened with miles tramped, and hearts warmed with a new love—the Pyrenees.

\* \* \*

To reach La Bérarde in the Dauphiné Alps in order to join the CUMC meet, our party split up. Ted decided to hitch-hike; Bill visited Andorra en route; Tony, Andrew, and I drove a winding route through the Massif Central towards Grenoble.

At La Bérarde, neophytes were grouped with climbers who had experience of daunting alpine routes; Tony and I joined Bob Downes's party, Bill went with Geoff Sutton, and Ted with Eric Langmuir. We all set off in different directions to climb on Les Bans, Mont Pelvoux, and the Barre des Écrins, which two years before, with Dick Marsh, I had approached from Ailefroide on the opposite side of the range. This was more serious climbing than we were used to, but our adventures in the Pyrenees had made us feel reasonably competent. We were now familiar with the techniques of wearing crampons, of hammering steel pitons for belay protection, and of moving, roped together, carrying coils to allow for speed on rotten rock and snow.

We began to think ourselves invincible until suddenly unpleasant things began to happen, as they will to the overconfident and imprudent. Tony fell thirty feet while leading on the Écrins, but he was held by his second, who a few minutes earlier had banged in a piton for extra belay protection. I heard a shout, "Rock below!" from the party above, and saw a boulder bounding down the snow slope towards me. I ducked into the snow and the rock crashed onto my pack, knocking the wind out of me and nearly me off the mountain. Sixteen hours later we got back to camp and met Bill, who told us that Ted had survived a fall of one hundred feet when a granite corner gave way, but Eric Langmuir had held him one-handed. These humbling and sobering experiences alerted us to the unforgiving nature of the mountains where respect and caution are necessary to safeguard a long career.

For our final Dauphiné climb Bill and I chose the Aiguille Dibona, a prominent needle pointing skywards on the southwest flank of La Mèije.

The rock of the Dibona was firm, warm, and sound, and continuously exposed right to the summit. After nearly a month of strenuous climbing, Bill and I moved confidently and my pleasure was heightened by his company, the most considerate and unselfish person I had ever met.

We returned early to the crowded alpine bunks and at midnight a party of French schoolgirls invaded the refuge. I woke next morning to find a girl insinuated between Bill and myself.

*"Votre grand-père était-il une sauterelle?"* (Was your grandfather a grasshopper?) she asked indignantly after enduring a disturbed night.

# TEN

BACK AT CAMBRIDGE FOR MY second year, I quickly forgot the low points of the previous year and the agonies of being a callow undergraduate freshman—a new boy. My tutor, Dr Stoker, had given me an ultimatum to pass the organic chemistry Part IV of the first MB next time, so now I had to concentrate on serious study. I had a mental block with organic chemistry; for me it was like trying to read music or, later, electrocardiograms. I drew a chart like a map of the London Underground on a single huge sheet of paper. Arrows radiated out from the focal point—benzene—navigated round equations, and reagents led from reaction to reaction. My map, once memorized, enabled me to satisfy the examiners even though I never really understood the subject.

My anatomy supervisor, John Withycombe, was a surgeon at Addenbrooke's Hospital. He was also a talented watercolourist, and he lent me the drawings and diagrams he made during his surgical apprenticeship—pop-up leaves showed layers of the abdominal wall overlying an inguinal hernia, and a convoluted map of the brachial plexus looked like a family tree. I copied them with crayons into small sketchbooks that I carried constantly in my back pocket.

John applied the boring details of anatomy to practical surgery, which reinforced my wish to become a surgeon. I certainly had the long fingers suited to surgery. However, I was nearly turned off by well-meaning friends and relatives who continually eulogized my father's skill. Now that I had become more analytical of his death, I felt cheated and let down and was less keen to follow in his footsteps.

Through shared travails with organic chemistry I became close friends with Edward Platts who was in Fitzwilliam House. Situated at the south end of Trumpington Street, "Fitzbilly" was not yet recognized fully as a college. It was snobbishly considered inferior to the élitist riverbank colleges like Clare. Most Oxford and Cambridge entrants came from the ranks of public schools, as did Edward, and considered themselves superior to grammar school boys on scholarships—a ridiculously anachronistic hierarchy.

Crinkled sandy hair and high-coloured cheeks gave Edward a Bertie Woosterish manner that was endorsed by an amber cigarette holder and a silver-embossed case. To reach the upholstered leather driver's seat of his vintage Rolls Royce, he had to climb over the brake handle; the instrument panel was of veneered walnut. We envied Edward's sophistication and his gentle, soft voice laced with piercing wit. He attracted many friends, especially my fellow Clare medical students—Simon Dean, Andrew Elkington, Peter Barbor, and John Sheldon.

Edward invited me for Christmas to his home in Haxby, north of York, a Queen Anne house built of variegated brick with a spacious garden and tennis court. His father, Frank, was a solid man of few words. As a general practitioner he was idolized by his patients, most of whom lived in a working-class neighbourhood of York. Every morning after a cold shower Frank would run the length of the house stark naked, shaking his hairy torso like a wet puppy—a signal that it was time to get up.

Edward's mother, Mavis, was the antithesis of Frank. Her living room decor was in chintz and silk, diaphanous lace curtains draped elegant bay windows, and a rare collection of long-stemmed glass bells with glass clappers stood on a Chippendale table near the doorway and in a nearby display cabinet. Everything about Mavis was dainty and feminine—her coiffure and makeup, manicured hands, and shapely ankles. Edward most resembled his mother. He rarely spoke about his twin brother, who had died suddenly and inexplicably while doing National Service in the Tank Corps. His loss forged a strong bond between us.

I appreciated profoundly the warm home life of the Platts family, then and in subsequent years, and it seemed to make up for the family life I was missing. Christmas was a busy social round of their hunting, shooting, and fishing friends scattered in comfortable houses round North Yorkshire. Each Christmas Eve we went to York Minster for the full midnight carol service. There I fell unrequitedly in love with Edward's cousin, ten years older than myself, and entertained fantasies of walking down the vast gothic aisle with her after our nuptials. On Boxing Day we beat the undergrowth of the grounds of Castle Howard, in the barbaric sport of putting up pheasants for hidden waiting guns.

\* \* \*

I had arrived at Cambridge with a reputation as a good schoolboy rackets player but, because of my setback, I never got into stride during my first year. Now that was behind me, I started to play seriously again and became a contender for a place in the university pair. At Portugal Place I thrashed a ball around the dank, dark rackets court until I could drive it just above the tin and deep into the corners. I practiced my strong backhand serve, cutting the ball into the forehand court, and sprinting for balls dropped short near the front wall. The university rackets professional, Peter Gray, who was related to the famous racquet firm, Grays of Cambridge, had a paunch and smoked constantly. He was well past his athletic best so we got little coaching. Peter was amiable, but Portugal Place never had the camaraderie that developed round the coal fire in Bill Hawes's workshop at Charterhouse.

I did well in trials for the annual university match against Oxford in which "blues" were awarded. I awaited nervously the day when the pairs would be posted on a notice board in the window of Ryder & Amies, the university tailor. Each university sports club had its own board in the windows facing King's Parade and Great St Mary's Lane. When major sports teams like rugby, cricket, or rowing were announced, a throng four or five deep awaited the notice announcing who had been awarded a blue. Rackets, a minor sport, got no such attention and merited only a half-blue.

On the day of posting I eagerly peered through the Ryder & Amies plate glass window. There stood my name, chosen to play in the first pair against Oxford along with the captain, Roger Newman. Immediately I marched in and ordered a short-sleeved vest with light blue silk ribbon at the neck, and a white cable-knit pullover with CURC embroidered above light blue crossed racquets. I laid my new clothes over a chair so I could admire them from my bed, and on each awakening I pinched myself to be sure it was no dream.

Along with getting my half-blue I was elected to the Hawks' Club, haven of the university athletic élite. Tall windows of the clubhouse overlooked a small park opposite Trinity College. A genteel hush pervaded the room where gentlemen lounged in leather chairs. Ackerman sporting prints and "Spy" cartoons hung on the walls, and newspapers lay on a large oak table. Downstairs in the dining room, which smelled of mulligatawny soup, conversation revolved exclusively around sport. Even though I was no outstanding athlete—above average at several sports, excellent at none—I wore my maroon-and-gold striped Hawks' Club tie with pride.

In training for the university match, we played against Colin Cowdrey and Ted Dexter, both renowned cricketers. On the big day of the university doubles match at Queen's Club, however, we were trounced four games to nil by the Oxford pair Michael Coulman and Roddy Bloomfield. In the singles Coulman beat me but, as reported in the *Times*, " . . . not without overcoming some fine resistance." Just to have gone that far was a boost to my self-confidence.

I made the Clare College "Cuppers" squash team for the final of the university league competition against Trinity. We had two blues, Peter Harris and Leo Melville, a South African; and two university second team "Ganders," Fred Gardiner from Yale, and Guy Grose. Mine was the crucial deciding match, which went to two games each, and to 8—8 in the final game. I won by belting the ball hard down the side walls, as one does in rackets. As a result I was elected to the Clare Falcons Club, another fillip to my wilted self-esteem. My squash and rackets companions were sophisticated and worldly, but I felt more at ease with my scruffy climbing friends.

Chastened by my tutor's threat I got down to serious study and passed Part IV of the First MB. As the work became more relevant to medicine, I enjoyed it more and worked harder, realizing that one day I might actually become a doctor.

* * *

1956 was a busy mountaineering year. I was not a natural climber like Ted Maden or Bill Turrall, but I could hold my own with them on any route. Although supposedly a non-competitive sport, we scattered all over Britain and Europe notching up successes on increasingly difficult climbs.

At Easter I headed north with my CUMC friend George Fraser to rendezvous on the west coast of Scotland with Mike O'Hara and his girlfriend, Marjorie, Eric Langmuir's sister. George's shyness and aloof manner insulated and isolated him from other people. Unkempt curly reddish hair and thick granny glasses perched on his Roman nose emphasized his social awkwardness in London, where he served out time in an engineering office between dashes to the hills. Once in the mountains, however, his spirit was set free and soared, and self-reliance and courage gave him confidence. I slowly got behind this barrier and found warm sympathy and humour.

From Fort William the road to Skye winds through Glen Garry, over the moor tops and down Glen Shiel, past the Five Sisters of Kintail to the head of Loch Duich, where stands Eilean Donan castle. The highland scenery became more spectacular the further north we travelled into Wester Ross. We crossed Loch Carron by the Strome Ferry to reach Glen Torridon, and then followed Loch Maree to Gairloch where we met Mike and Marjorie.

Our ultimate destination was Carnmore, a roadless area of moor and mountain northeast of Loch Maree, and the shooting estate of the Whitbread beer family. Mike had visited Carnmore previously and had discovered much clean, unclimbed granite. His then companion, Bob Kendell, noted, ". . . climbers tend to be unpopular in the shooting season, and that is a dangerous season to be unpopular." How did anyone (we anarchists reasoned) have the right to keep such a paradise private for murdering deer, when all we wanted was to explore its unique, unclimbed cliffs? Laws of trespass and private property did not feature in our thinking; they just made the expedition more of a challenge. However, we were there in spring, well clear of the stalking season.

We left the car at Poolewe and set off carrying heavy packs to walk the twelve miles to the head of Fionn Loch, where Mike had previously slept in a bothy hut that lay under magnificent Carnmore Crag. Being a Cambridge postgraduate geology student, Mike conveniently chose the far northwest corner of Scotland for his doctoral study. His wild appearance, strident voice, and maniacal laugh disguised a sharp intellect. An impetuous drive made him a natural leader. Marjorie, newly graduated in medicine from Edinburgh, exuded warmth and friendliness.

I strode across the heather wearing the kilt of Grandfather Steele, who had been a chaplain to the Black Watch in France during the First World War. I used to believe Grandfather's stories implicitly until I discovered he was born in Cork, and only much later did he move from the south of Ireland to Scotland. There he married my grandmother, whose tenuous links with the Fraser clan supposedly allowed me to wear the Hunting Fraser tartan. I wore the kilt only when unlikely to bump into a proper Scot, because of my plummy English accent. (However, I could offer a passable rendering of Robbie Burns's poem *To a Mouse.*)

A low, drystone-wall bothy, situated at the foot of Carnmore Crag, had a single door and no windows. A floor of dry bog peat provided not only a comfortable bed but also ready fuel. To stoke the fire we just reached from our sleeping bags into a dark corner and gathered a handful of peat. A pall of acrid peat smoke irritated our eyes as soon as we stood up.

Next day a red smudge of dawn tinged Fionn Loch before the morning breeze scalloped it's tranquil surface. This remote, uninhabited corner of the Western Highlands would be ours alone for the week. Each day we climbed ourselves to exhaustion, finding long new routes on warm, dry rock under a cloudless sky. From our belay stances we looked offshore towards Skye. Purple heather mingled with golden brown of drought-scorched moor. The final day was a fitting climax. Mike and George made the first ascent of the near vertical, thousand-foot nose of Fionn Buttress on Carnmore Crag, which rose almost from our back door; Marjorie and I did a new unclimbed route nearby which we named Shark's Tooth after a large rock we found at the foot of the climb.

The only blight on a perfect week was the dehydrated food, a prototype supplied by the Ministry of Agriculture to Mike for testing. It looked like rabbit droppings, and made us fart so odiously that we had to leave the bothy door open at night, regardless of frost that rimed our sleeping bags.

Eventually we parted to go our several ways. Mike and Marjorie headed south in search of other rock to climb, while George and I walked north to the reputedly haunted bothy of Shenavalt. We traversed An Teallach and from the summit had expansive views across to the Summer Isles. At Dundonnell we hitch-hiked back to Poolewe. Desperate for a Mars Bar, I made straight for the post office, the only shop in the village. There in the window lay a boxful of my craving, but being Sunday—the Wee Free Sabbath—it just mocked my greed by being firmly closed.

That week in Carnmore was our climbing apogee—Scotland's wilderness at its most beautiful, days filled with laughter, and intense bonds of friendship forged on sound steep rock beyond compare.

I had to hurry to Edinburgh for an interview with the dean of the medical school where I had applied to do my clinical studies. I urgently needed to wash and shave so, still wearing Grandfather's kilt, I asked the grandly-uniformed doorman on the steps of the Princes Street Hotel if I could rent a room for a bath. He scrutinized me from a lordly height and said in a scathing, steely burr, "But ye're no a true Scotsman, laddie."

This was almost as deflating as my interview with the dean.

"Why d'ye want to study so far away from home, Mr Steele?" he asked, eyeing me cannily over half-glasses perched on his nose. "Are ye sure it's nothing to do wi' the hills?"

"My grandfather was a minister in Inverness," I replied. "He taught me to love the Highlands." It didn't sound very convincing, even to myself.

"But he'd no approve of ye dashing off to Glencoe every Friday evening and returning exhausted on Monday morning, would he?" he asked rhetorically, piercing me with a suspicious eye. "He wouldn't want ye climbing when ye should be studying, would he?"

"My friends tell me Edinburgh is one of the best medical schools, sir," I said.

"Ye're correct there," he said. "But we've had climbers in our school before, and they were never in class."

On leaving his office, a sinking feeling told me that I had failed to impress on the dean that Edinburgh University Medical School would be lucky to have me. A few days later I received a curt letter of rejection. It was a painful blow to my pride but a salutary experience.

Back in Cambridge I had to finish my second year exams before embarking on a busy summer climbing schedule. The written exams were held in the mausoleum-like examination halls off Mill Lane. After each paper we went to The Mill pub nearby, ordered a pint of beer, and sat on the wall over a weir that shoots into a pool above Silver Street Bridge. This was a favourite summer student hangout where punts came and went from Scudamore's boathouse below The Dolphin pub. Frequently some inexperienced punter showing off to his girlfriend would get broadside to the weir current and topple into the water to the cheers of a maudlin audience.

Opposite stood Newnham Grange, an elegant Georgian house once owned by the Wedgwood family. Gwen Raverat, granddaughter to Charles Darwin, lived next door and wrote *Period Piece*, a charming Victorian memoir of childhood. By then badly crippled with arthritis, she was often seen sketching the Backs from her wheelchair parked beside Clare garden.

I gained a third-class result in my exams. I was capable of better, but arrogantly I thought I should keep my academic energy for the final year tripos and then magically pull a second-class out of the bag.

To round off the term I went to the May Ball with an athletic undergraduate who, in the early hours of the morning, pummelled me into the mauve rock plants beside the Clare garden lily pond. A year later the plants were just recovering, and I had moved on.

I set off to Wales for a CUMC meet at Ynws Ettws, a Climbers' Club hut in the Llanberis Valley. The leaders were Roger Chorley, Bob Downes, and John Peacock, along with Oxford climbers Hamish Nicol and Tom Bourdillon, recently returned from Everest. John Longland and I spent a day traversing the Snowdon Horseshoe. We finished on the steep dank cliffs of Lliwedd, where Menlove Edwards, doyen of pre-war rock climbers, had done many delicate climbs using clinker nailed boots. We closed a halcyon day with a swim in Llyn Llydaw and returned to the PyG for a glass of Worthington E.

I drove via Wasdale in the Lake District to Scotland and met Bill Marks in the youth hostel in Glencoe. In fine weather we climbed Crowberry Ridge on the Buachaille Etive Mòr and then moved northwards. Bill, an officer in the Royal Engineers, was on a scholarship at Cambridge while still on full regular army salary. I envied his suave good looks and relaxed, confident manner. Square-built and muscular, he was a fanatical rugby player.

On the way to Skye we camped in Glen Shiel and walked through heavy Scots pine forest to Loch Affric, where we camped in a disused cottage. The delectable teenage daughter of a Canadian family staying at a posh fishing lodge nearby gave us five fresh brown trout. A couple more days took us over Sgùrr na Lapaich and Càrn Eige, and then we descended to the Falls of Glomach. Some of my most enjoyable memories of the highlands are of simply ambling, which made me appreciate the subtle beauty of the mountains and mellowed my fanatical urge to climb steep rock.

On Skye we stayed at the youth hostel in Glen Brittle and forayed into Coire Lagan, climbing Cioch Buttress by several severe routes on steep slabs of gabbro, a pumice-like feldspar rock to which cheap black gym shoes, even when wet, clung like limpets. However, after several days of perfect weather, our fingertips were raw so we had to tape them and retreat to the beach of Loch Brittle to allow them to heal.

After a rest, Bill and I hired a boat to take us round to Coruisk on Loch Scavaig. Rain poured into our bivouac so we started up the Cuillin Ridge with little enthusiasm. The rock was so slippery we abandoned the ridge at halfway. We ran down the massive screes of Sgùrr Alasdair and headed for the bar of the Sligachan Hotel. It was a wet end to a busy Easter.

I returned to Cambridge for the summer Long Vac Term in order to dissect an abdomen. In idle moments I punted on the Cam with a French girl studying English, but despite this pleasant diversion I itched to reach the Alps before losing my Scottish fitness. In mid-July George Fraser, Mike O'Hara, Bob Kendell, and I set off in my little Standard car across Europe towards the Bregalia in the Italian Alps. We packed the roof rack with climbing and camping gear and were tempted to drive through Paris with crampons strapped to the bumpers to discourage wild French drivers from coming too close. Mike was in manic mood planning routes for us, and I became nervous when he kept asking how strong was our death-wish.

We walked from Promontogno up the Val Bondasca to the Sciora hut lying in a cirque of jagged rock spires under the Piz Badile—our goal. While warming up next day on the Punta Innominata, a storm broke. Flashes and explosions of thunder seared the sky and lightning flashes bounced off the very face down which we abseiled. In terror we waited on small stances while the last man climbed down to the abseil point. There we placed a sling through which passed the rope. On the last abseil the rope got stuck and Mike had to climb up to free it, still with lightning all around.

Next morning looked settled so George and Mike grasped the window of clear weather and headed for the Flatiron Ridge of Piz Gemelli. Bob and I had more modest aims on the North Ridge of Piz Badile. This was by far my most serious alpine attempt so far. Our route lay on the right-hand skyline of the Badile's huge scalloped face; it was four thousand feet long, steep, inescapable, and continuously difficult. At the very top, as we traversed the blank open face of the mountain, I had my first and only attack of a paralysing fear of heights, which gripped me in the pit of my stomach like that empty feeling one sometimes gets looking from the top of a very high building. Bob's calm reassurance dispelled the overpowering draw to jump off the face.

We reached the summit twelve hours after setting foot on the mountain. As darkness fell, storm clouds rolled into the lower valleys. We had been warned of a dangerous abseil off the back of the mountain. At the top of a steep couloir, a pair of Italian climbers suggested we tie our ropes together to speed our abseil. Foolishly we agreed. One of them grabbed our rope and shook it into a spaghetti-like tangle, which took a precious half hour of failing light to unravel. I vowed never again to let a stranger touch my climbing rope.

The rock on both sides of the couloir was rotten and fragmented, and in pitch dark no one could see what they were grabbing. Showers of rock screamed down the chute and we just hugged the underside of any overhang we encountered. Eventually we emerged from the fissure and fled from the Italians to the relative safety of the glacier and the Rifugio Gianetti, which glinted in the distance. A few minutes after we arrived at the hut Mike and George stumbled in, exhausted but triumphant after completing the Flatiron. We celebrated our combined successes with pasta, *biftek* and rough *vino rosso* while a storm lashed down outside.

Next morning in a whiteout we crossed the Passo di Bondo deep in new snow to regain the Sciora hut.

We moved across northern Italy to Courmayeur, in the shadow of Mont Blanc, our next goal. We had ambitious plans to climb the Route Major, a serious climb up the Brenva face. During some very difficult warm-up climbing in deteriorating weather we got halfway up the Aiguille Noire de Peuterey, and escaped by descending the Welzenbach route. At the Rifugio Torino we met Ted Maden and Bill Turrall, who both had ambitious climbs in mind. However, because of doubtful weather, we decided to join forces and try one of the classic routes on the Brenva face. After supper we left the refuge at 8:00 p.m. and dropped down to the upper Géant Glacier in order to make the most of the frozen snow before the sun would soften it. Our boots crunched on moonlit snow and we spied a light flickering from a bivouac halfway up the vertical east face of the Grand Capucin.

We crossed a bergschrund (a glacial crevasse) and climbed steeply to the tiny Rifugio-bivacco Alberica-Borgna that precariously straddles the Col de la Fourche. It is built on iron struts driven into the mountain and overhangs an amphitheatre on the south side of Mont Blanc. The half dozen bunks were already full of snoring climbers. Bill cooked an unappetizing but nutritious brew of pemmican and porridge over a Primus stove set in the middle of the floor. On a small platform outside the hut, George was anxiously watching clouds roll up the valley from Italy when a figure emerged from inside.

"I haf no fear," said the dauntless Münicher after one cursory glance. Then he returned to bed.

While the Germans still slept, we left the hut at 11.30 p.m. after a very short sleep, and descended to the Brenva glacier. Bill described the magical scene in his diary, " . . . Above us the great Brenva face loomed in the moonlight, unearthly somehow, colossal. The silence, the remoteness, the cold moonlit sky, that strange radiance on the snow high up there—I wanted to talk in a whisper."

As we cramponed towards the face, an avalanche swept the entire Route Major and the Pear Buttress, our intended destination. We held a council. Mike and Ted felt that the face was unsafe; Bob was sick to his stomach; George thought the Old Brenva, the classic route of the face, would go; Bill and I had utter confidence in George as leader. So by moonlight the three of us cramponed up mixed snow and rock to reach the knife-edge snow ridge above. Both sides of the ridge dropped steeply into a dark abyss, and it required courage to stand upright and rely only on our crampons. A pink dawn glow from the eastern sky tinged the seracs and the summit above us; we cast our own brilliant blue shadows against the white snow of the ridge. The valleys of Italy still slumbered.

"It feels like we're on a great climb, Pete," Bill whispered to me. We were both overawed by the scale, the danger, the beauty of the mountain. George moved fast and confidently despite the altitude that caused us all to feel tired and sick with pounding headaches and laboured breathing. When the rising sun struck our slope we stopped for a bite of food, our first proper halt for nearly six hours. Bill hunted in his rucksack for the glacier cream and realized he had given it to Ted before we parted company. That left toothpaste or condensed milk to bar the sun's ultraviolet rays. We chose the latter, aptly named *Lait concentré sucré MontBlanc*. As we sweated, it melted down our dirty faces so we continuously had to lick away a dribble of sticky sweet milk.

The wind rose, filling the footsteps of the leader with spindrift snow. We were in danger of setting off a wind-slab avalanche. Passing under beautiful ice tower seracs, we hurried for fear a huge chunk might break off. George cut ice steps through a breach. We were rejoicing at the sight of the summit above us when my world suddenly disappeared.

Falling through air, I felt the rope jerk tight round my waist and I was brought to a halt. From the dark depths of a crevasse, I could see sky above me. Fortunately I had landed on a snow ledge from where a short ramp allowed me to climb out easily. I was surprised rather than shaken.

On the summit Bill announced, "Hey! It's my birthday." We hurriedly toasted him with our water bottles, gnawed some chocolate, and fled towards the Vallot hut 1,300 feet below us. Exhausted, we rested while brewing porridge and coffee. Then followed a gruelling descent, at first by snow ridges to the Dome Glacier and then by plodding over loose, trackless moraine to the valley—and azaleas, soft turf, trees, and musical streams. It had been a climactic expedition, done with style and speed, in just under twelve hours. We were very proud.

# ELEVEN

FTER OUR EPIC CLIMB OF MONT BLANC, Bill Turrall and I joined the Cambridge University Mountaineering Club alpine meet in Arolla, Switzerland. For the first week of August the club had hired a Swiss guide to instruct us in the finer techniques of mountaineering. We believed this would build on experience we had so far acquired mainly through mistakes. We practiced step-cutting with ice axes, moving together on loose rock, avalanche safety, and crevasse rescue. The guide was a stickler for the 2:00 a.m. alpine start, but one day we pleaded for a lie in, to which he reluctantly agreed. We understood his preference the next day as we trudged back to the hut at noon, knee-deep in soft snow, the crust having melted with the sun's heat.

In the second week Bill Turrall and I, with half a dozen other CUMC climbers, traversed Mont Collon, Le Mitre, and L'Évêque in perfect weather. When storms hit the Alps, Bill and I scurried back to the Pyrenees and Gavarnie, our mountain "home from home." Bill Marks and Mark James joined us there. We all climbed to about the same standard, our enthusiasm was unlimited, we were very fit, and we felt unbounded confidence—not necessarily a good thing for mountaineers.

Straightway we went to the Hotel du Cirque. In the cellar, Pierre Vergez plied us with vintage Bordeaux, kissing his bunched fingertips as a sign of the quality of the wine and of his happiness to see us again. Madame embraced us and kissed us on both cheeks. We studied the walls of the Cirque de Gavarnie with Pierre and nurtured our ambitious plans.

Next day we set off to climb the Cirque from bottom to top by way of the three walls. After romping up the Mur de la Cascade, we crossed easy snow of the first terrace to the foot of Le Grand Dièdre, a large sloping slab, shaped like an open book. The vertical wall of the third tier made a fine climax to a classic mountaineering route that had taken us seventeen continuous hours from bottom to top; the descent took us just three hours. We were exhilarated by our comradeship and mutual trust, united as we were by the rope. Bill Turrall, a natural maestro with unquenchable drive, was nimble, strong, and wiry. I see him now, poised on tiny holds, lower jaw stuck out towards the rock, purple beret pulled over one ear. Bill Marks, square-built of solid muscle, smoked steadily with little apparent effect on his stamina. Mark James, who was engaged to be married, cautiously balanced our impetuous drive with droll humour.

In top form and full of confidence, next we chose the Voie Castagnez-Vergez. First climbed by Pierre and his friend Castagnez when in their prime, it scales a vertical rock wall between two waterfalls.

In the dim light of chilly dawn, still munching the remnants of our breakfast, we left camp in single file with headlamps shining like miners going on shift. The sun touched the crest of the Marboré as we passed the hotel that was nestled in the shadow. Everyone was fast asleep; not even a donkey neighed. We tiptoed past the hotel, hoping not to waken the Vergez family. However, our boots crunched unavoidably on the gravel. An upstairs shutter opened, and Pierre's face appeared framed in the blackness of the window.

"*Attendez un moment, mes amis,*" he called. "*J'ai une idée.*" (Wait a moment, my friends. I have an idea.)

We shuffled to warm our feet in the frosty morning. Pierre descended to the terrace still in his nightshirt, a shotgun over the crook of his arm and binoculars round his neck. He looked more like a hunter than a mountaineer.

"Listen a moment, my friends," he said. "You may have difficulty finding your way up the rock face. I will watch you through my binoculars. If you go off the route to the right I will fire two *coups de fusil*; if to the left, one shot. *Bonne chance, mes amis.*"

We walked for an hour to the foot of the Mur de la Cascade. Then we climbed in fading darkness on firm granite with the ecstasy of walking in space and the sleeping world at our feet. The sun hit the rock and warmed our fingers.

"Hold tight, Pete," Bill Turrall called from the end of a rope's length. "I'm stuck. I may fall off."

His face was contorted, working out his next upwards move as he stood on a toe-hold high above me with sky showing between him and the rock. His feet and ankles trembled with the strain, and tremble turned to violent shaking. The still air was suddenly rent by two shots that echoed off the walls. More than a mile away we could just make out Pierre on the balcony of his hotel. At this signal order, Bill stepped down and moved to the left along a narrow, sloping ledge where the steepness of the rock eased. He belayed his rope round a projecting rock flake.

"I'm tying on," Bill called. "This way, Pete. Climb."

"Climbing," I shouted back. I moved up to join him, impressed by his skillful lead on a pitch that was more severe than any we had yet done.

Ten hours later we knocked at the door of Pierre's cellar long after the last donkey-sore pilgrim had departed. Pierre wrung our hands and beamed with pleasure as though he had done the climb himself. To celebrate he brought a bottle from a cache in the back of the cellar while Madame Vergez prepared fresh artichokes.

"That must be the first alpine climb directed by gunfire, *montagnards!*" said Pierre.

* * *

With that climb under our belts, the long steep North Face of the Vignemale beckoned. So we drove round to the Cauterets valley while the weather, and our luck, held. The sun cast long shadows across the massive North Face as we bivouaced under a huge boulder in the Vallée de Gaube. It made a cozy refuge for sheep that grazed nearby, together with pale fawn cows with floppy dewlaps.

Long before sunrise next morning we stumbled across a boulder moraine towards the foot of the Vignemale. Still half asleep, we roped up in silence; Bill Marks and me on one rope, Bill Turrall and Mark James on the other. By alternating leaders we quickly followed a long steep crack leftwards. After three hours climbing with space between our boots, the rock angle eased and we moved up the open face like flies on a wall.

The thrill of such climbing comes from confidence in dealing with danger; terror paralyses a climber, and a "head for heights" is a myth. Scaffolders and steeplejacks, before feeling comfortable on tall buildings, would do well to learn rock climbing skills on airy mountain faces. Climbers need constant practice, otherwise each venture onto rock is like starting over again. Some, like Bill Turrall, have innate skill; others, like me, get there by hard apprenticeship.

As we rose higher on the Vignemale we could scan the entire Central Pyrenees. On the summit we were satisfied, having overcome our fear of the formidable north face climb. We hurried down the glacier to our bivouac, packed up, and hiked back to the roadhead. Then we returned to Gavarnie and our farewell to the Vergez family, celebrated in his cellar with champagne.

\* \* \*

Mark James and I wanted to explore the canyons on the Spanish side of the range. Bill Turrall decided to stay in Gavarnie to climb with Bob Chambers, who had hitch-hiked over from the Alps.

Visas were mandatory for entrance to Spain. As Mark and I had none, and they could not be acquired locally, Pierre Vergez wrote a note to his frontier guard colleague, asking him to let us pass—a talisman in which we had total trust. From the wooded Gavarnie valley we followed a mule track through alpine meadows towards the Col de Boucharou. Beyond the Spanish frontier, rolling limestone canyons merged with the distant sun-scorched plains of Aragon. Soft green beech trees replaced dark pines in France to the north. Hillsides were yellow with gorse, once-red azalea blooms drooped a dreary brown, and wild blue irises grew in dense patches like mountain pools. As we ran down towards the village of Boucharou, edelweiss, gentians, and violets unavoidably fell under the tread of our boots.

Near the head of the valley, needle-shaped aiguilles formed the jagged horizon of Mont Taillon. We broke out of dense bush and gorse scrub near the river where a single-arched stone pack-bridge led to a dozen buildings clustered round a small church. From above, ochre-tiled roofs of the village looked higgledy-piggledy. The river clung to the left side of the valley and flowed towards a ravine leading to Torla. On farmhouse balconies, streamers of washing hung out to dry. A flat-roofed modern building, plastered outside, had two barred windows on either side of a wide central arch where a flag surmounted a crest inscribed *Guardia Civil*.

It was siesta time. Not a soul stirred; even the dogs were asleep. At the top of a flight of a dozen steps, a guard lounged in a shabby deck chair, apparently dozing. An Alsatian dog with a spiked collar lay at his feet. We crossed the bridge and walked brazenly past the guard post. I was wearing my grandfather's kilt as it was so pleasant to hike in.

"*¿Senors, a donde van Usted?*" (Where are you going?) he croaked from under a heavy black moustache that overhung his upper lip and curled round the corners of his mouth. He stretched out his hand and languidly waved us up the steps murmuring, "*Pasaportes.*"

We produced our documents. He thumbed through them and turned each over again before handing them back.

"*Visado. No se puede entrar sin visado,*" he said, shaking his head. (Visa. You can't enter without a visa.)

I handed him Pierre's note, which read: "*Au Chef de police à Torla—prière de laisser passer mes deux amis anglais qui veulent aller par Torla à la Vallée de Razas. P Vergez. Comptrolleur Frontière, Gavarnie.*" The guard shrugged his shoulders and pointed back towards the Col de Boucharou. The verdict was final.

Mark and I returned to the bridge and dangled our feet over the parapet; we kicked them aimlessly while contemplating our options. The only way to bypass Boucharou was across the river by a path that led along the foot of a steep hillside in full view of the police post. We set off hoping to appear as if we were returning to Gavarnie by way of Mont Taillon. Soon a piercing whistle announced the policeman running breathlessly after us in his carpet slippers. After remonstrating for a fruitless half hour, we turned back up the path we had descended from the Col de Boucharou.

Five hundred feet up we looked down on the village and realized that if we traversed under cover of some bushes we could drop down to join the Torla path at the mouth of the gorge. After half an hour picking our way carefully across the steep, overgrown hillside we reached a scree slope in full view of Boucharou. Two men were talking on the balcony of the inn.

We dashed across the scree and sheltered behind a small shrub in the middle of the chute. A dislodged stone clattered off downhill. Alerted by the noise, one policeman scanned our hillside with binoculars. The other went off to the guardhouse and returned with a rifle. A heavy shower of cherry-sized hailstones fell on the recently sun-bathed valley, and sent him scurrying for shelter. Mark and I raced down a gulley and through a coppice to the river. While boulder-hopping across in full view of Boucharou I missed my footing and fell into a deep pool, where my kilt splayed around me.

Mark and I wrung the water from our clothes and laughed hysterically. We knew that there was no going back. To avoid the Torla track, we climbed over fallen trees and crossed streams that dashed towards the ravine. While eating wild strawberries we heard pounding hoofs. We dived back into the bushes, and a moment later a horse and rider galloped past. We guessed they were going to report us to the police at Torla. As we hurried along the path in gathering darkness, moon shadows loomed ahead and stars flashed messages across an ebony sky.

We reached a hut in a clearing at the junction with the Torla-Razas road. We pushed open the door and stepped into inky blackness. Suddenly a flashlight shone in our faces and five soldiers surrounded us. By hand signals we asked for somewhere to sleep. They pointed beside their barrack room to a shed where we burrowed into some wood shavings. Soon a big dog joined us.

Next morning the soldiers gave us half a loaf of bread. We walked two miles to Torla, set among terraced vineyards. On the balconies of old houses round the central square, pots of geraniums stood out against whitewashed walls. Two uniformed men approached from a side street and beckoned us to follow them into a café.

"*¿Visados?¿Donde sus visados?*" they asked. (Visas? Where are your visas?)

A small crowd gathered and peered through the metal fly chains. The corporal left after muttering a few words to his colleague, who sat on the edge of a table swinging his leg and fingering his pistol. His cap badge depicted the fascist emblem. Twenty minutes later the Inspector of Police arrived. We handed him Pierre Vergez's note, which obviously did not impress him. He pointed towards France and clapped his wrists together, suggesting handcuffs. His message was clear.

We left Torla and walked towards Razas, a canyon about ten miles long and a mile wide. Limestone walls carved into tall, grotesque pinnacles rose from the thickly wooded valley floor. We intended to spend a peaceful night high on the mountain at the Réfuge de Gaulis, and to cross into France next day. On pushing open the door of the refuge we were confronted by the barrel of a rifle. Four green-uniformed frontier guards paraded us against the stone wall outside with our hands above our heads. Four years before, they had shot at a friend of mine who had trespassed in the same area, but in our youthful arrogance we did not consider this. We dreamed of holidays spent quietly, and wisely, by the seaside.

The sergeant clapped his wrists together—now a familiar gesture—and pointed to the frontier with his gun, muttering, "*No visados.*"

Back at the Hotel du Cirque, Pierre Vergez was annoyed that his note had been to no avail. We just presumed that the border guards were new and did not know about Pierre Vergez.

\* \* \*

Soon after we arrived at the hotel, Bill Turrall and Bob Chambers stumbled in looking gaunt and haggard. While we had been adventuring in Spain they were playing out their own drama on the walls of the

Cirque. It was a story that needed telling urgently, and so upstaged our own story.

They had set off to attempt the north face of the Tour du Marboré. The near-vertical first pitch took two hours to climb. Bob was leading over a holdless bulge when he fell, bounced past Bill, and ended up thirty feet below him, tight on the rope. Luckily Bill's leather gloves prevented friction burns of his hands, but his neck suffered a painful rope burn. Both of them were severely shaken and retreated to the terrace where they had bivouaced.

As they brewed tea and washed their abrasions, they heard a distant thunder clap followed by a prolonged roar. Looking up, a huge avalanche of rock and snow cascaded down the very corner they had just descended.

"*Si vous n'auriez pas tombé, vous seriez tous les deux morts?*" said Madame Vergez rhetorically. (If you hadn't fallen, you'd both have been killed?) "*C'est la destinée. Ça, certainement, c'est la destinée.*" (That is destiny. Yes, certainly, that is destiny.) Destiny it was.

We all bade a sad farewell to Pierre and Marguerite Vergez, our adopted mountain mentors, and headed north for home with a volume of new experiences and gratitude for our safe deliverance.

\* \* \*

On returning to Cambridge for my third and final year, life and work took on a more serious aspect as there were important exams to pass. In Clare Memorial Court I occupied my previous rooms on R staircase. Ted Maden and Bill Turrall shared rooms in Trinity Hall. Bill had transferred from classics to theology and bent himself without compromise to his new course, often staying up all night preparing a tutorial essay. We noticed a disturbing change from his previous light-heartedness, and he had little time for frivolities like climbing.

Bill was a driven man. Partly it was by religion, partly by the need to impress his father, Guy, who was working in Africa in yet another temporary contract job. Bill recounted to him his alpine adventures in long, strangely impersonal letters—"Dear Guy. . . I don't know that you're actually receiving my letters at all . . .Will you have time to write in the near future? . . .Yours ever, William." A note in his diary reads, ". . . had a couple of unusually friendly letters from my father recently." Bill bore the burden of his parents' separation and he felt responsible to try to get them back together so they could be a "normal" family again.

Bill introduced me to the poetry of Gerard Manley Hopkins, especially his favourite, "The Windhover." For my birthday he gave me General Wavell's book, *Other Men's Flowers*, which I subsequently carried on many climbing trips. The intensity of our friendship gradually moderated as he immersed himself more deeply in theology, while I was rejecting the Christian fundamentalism that had so stifled me. Also there was less time for climbing since both of us were making up in study for the time we had frittered in the mountains.

However, on a whim, we did one more stupid piece of night climbing, innocuous in itself, but still at risk from the proctor. St John's College has two courtyards, one on either side of the River Cam, which are joined by the Victorian neo-Gothic Bridge of Sighs. The hazard of its traverse was to fall into the river. Starting on the side of the New Court Wedding Cake, Bill traversed round a corner and, straddling the gap, pulled up on some metal bars from where he danced across to the other side. I followed him. Then we climbed up to a small window. We had asked the undergraduate occupant's permission beforehand to use this exit, and he agreed to leave the kitchen window unlocked. Once inside, Bill and I tiptoed across the kitchen when a blinding flash convinced us of our Armageddon. The owner of the room stood holding a flash camera—just one for the record.

One Sunday Dick Marsh and John Chater invited me for lunch to

Ridley Hall, where they were studying theology. I sat next to the vice principal, also the chief proctor of the university, whose "bulldogs" had booked us for rowdy behaviour outside The Mill pub the previous evening. He graciously pretended not to recognize me, although he could not have failed to know that we had met before.

Whenever Launcelot Fleming, then Bishop of Portsmouth, visited Cambridge we met to play squash. He tried tactfully to warn me about the inclinations of a fellow bishop whom I had got to know. I became alerted when that bishop, a college fellow of Trinity, invited me to lunch in his rooms and started delving into my boringly innocent intimacies with my girlfriends. He announced that I needed beating and ordered me to prepare for it. Launcelot's warning sprang to mind and I quit those rooms in a hurry and decided thenceforward to cool my friendship with the bishop. I later discovered it was this sadistic yen that caused him trouble in his diocese abroad, which he left under a cloud, thereby forfeiting the strong possibility of high office.

Peter Barbor and I still had no reason to exchange telegrams on the state of our non-existent love-lives. I listened avidly, but to no avail, for the ladylike crunch of feet on the gravel outside my window, and I would sometimes pedal two miles against the prevailing wind down the Huntingdon Road to Girton College, where once I found my adored entertaining a rival to tea. With the university's ratio of ten men to one woman, I realized then how low were my chances of being the lucky one.

Francis Walker, my neighbour, was then squiring the younger daughter of the professor of engineering, himself an avid rugger fan. I was also invited for tea to the home of the Bakers, 100 Long Road, where I met and fell for the prof's elder daughter, Joanna, a physiotherapist at St Bartholomew's Hospital in London. Our close, and chaste, friendship lasted with great happiness for four years.

By my third year I had become confident of my place in the university hierarchy, backed up by the kudos of being in the Hawks' Club. Edward Platts was a member of the nearby Pitt Club, a gathering place for social toffs, who even ran their own pack of beagles.

Because I had won the university rackets singles competition I was automatically in the first pair for the match against Oxford. At Queen's Club in London, my partner, Jeremy Hogben, and I beat the Oxford doubles pair of Roddy Bloomfield and Michael Scott by four games to two. Hogben, a natural stylist, beat Bloomfield in the singles in a fast, low-hitting match; I narrowly lost to Scott. But our combined scores gave us the overall match, the first time Cambridge had won in many years. We celebrated with dinner at a smart restaurant in Piccadilly— one of the greatest days of my three Cambridge years.

At Easter, with final exams looming, four of us, Simon Dean, Andrew Elkington, Bill Marks, and I went to the Lake District to the Wasdale Head Hotel to study. Wilson Pharoah, the owner, had become a good friend over the years since I was on my first Outward Bound course. As we were the only guests, it being the lull before the season opened, Wilson gave over the small lounge exclusively as our study. We were totally undisturbed and could leave our books and papers out on the tables.

For ten days we sat down at our books by 8:00 a.m. and worked through till 1:00 p.m. with only a break for coffee made by Frieda, the longtime chief housemaid of the hotel. In vacant moments I would stare at Green How, sweeping off the back of Scafell towards Hard Rigg and Burnmoor Tarn. We walked or climbed all afternoon and were back at our desks after tea for another couple of hours' study. In the bar after supper we listened to Wilson tell his characteristically larger-than-life stories.

With this routine we studied hard and enjoyed relaxed afternoon rambles over the Wasdale hills. At the end of the week, by way of reward for our single-mindedness, Bill Marks and I climbed Central Buttress on Scafell, a classic route graded Very Severe.

I returned to London urgently in order to seek a place in a teaching hospital. My rejection by Edinburgh had knocked me sideways, and meanwhile all my friends had found places in hospitals like Bart's, Thomas's, and Guy's. On emerging from the Underground at Hyde Park Corner, I looked up at St George's Hospital, writ large across the portico of the Wilkins' neoclassical building that stands on one of London's busiest roundabouts—at mile zero.

I asked the whereabouts of the medical school. A porter directed me round the corner to a tall Georgian building: Number 9, Knightsbridge. By chance the dean, Dr Alastair Hunter, had no particular engagements, so the secretary ushered me into his office for an interview. He was tall and athletic, with a boyish face and crinkled sandy hair grey-flecked at the temples. Shy for someone so powerful, he exuded a passionate love of St George's. He was a cardiologist and a keen cricketer and a musician. His medical partner was Aubrey Leatham, son of the school doctor at Charterhouse, H. W. Leatham, one time amateur rackets champion— a good start for me.

"Have you heard of Edward Wilson?" Dr Hunter asked.

"Yes," I replied. "He was doctor on Scott's last expedition. He's my hero."

"He was a student here," he said. "Come and I'll show you something interesting."

Downstairs in a study room hung several framed watercolours Wilson had made during that fateful expedition.

"That's the one I like best," said Dr Hunter, indicating a pencil sketch of five men man-hauling a sledge, bent over and bowing their heads against the howling wind. "That was the last drawing he ever did.

It was found on his body in the tent where they died. And to think he nearly left St George's because of bad health—tuberculosis, it was. The dean, Dr Rolleston, tried to persuade him to take up pathology drawing instead of medicine, because he was already quite famous as a bird artist."

"I once spent an afternoon in Cambridge looking through the Scott Polar Research Institute's collection of his paintings," I said. "That was before they were locked away."

Dr Hunter told me then and there that he would accept me to start at St George's in the autumn provided I passed my Cambridge exams.

Back at Cambridge, I had little time for climbing because of finals looming. Between lectures, my climbing friends and I dreamed up ambitious expeditions for the coming summer, and pored over maps in undergraduates' rooms and in coffee houses. John Longland and some friends planned to climb Pumasillo, an elegant pyramidal peak in the Cordillera Vilcabamba of Peru. Roger Akester, a lecturer in the university zoology department, invited me to form a team of three climbers to join an expedition he was organizing and leading to the Tibesti Mountains in the middle of the Sahara to study their geography, geology, and natural history. I was thrilled with the invitation and the chance to visit some very wild country and to climb some unexplored mountains. For our team I chose Bill Marks as a strong climber, and Rod Tuck because, although not an experienced climber, he was an Olympic pentathlete and one of my oldest friends.

In my final exams I gained a third-class pass, which was lower than I would have liked but probably what I deserved considering my many distractions.

The May Ball was Cambridge at its romantic best. I wore with pride my rackets blue blazer. Joanna and I danced in a marquee erected in Clare Old Court and punted to Grantchester for breakfast. Nostalgic tunes of *Salad Days* wafted from gramophones; *Beyond The Fringe* was launched in The Strand with Jonathan Miller playing alongside Peter Cook, Dudley Moore, and Alan Bennett. It was a heady ending to three unforgettable years.

# TWELVE

THE TIBESTI MOUNTAINS RISE UP to over 11,000 feet from dead centre of the Sahara Desert; in the southwest corner lies Chad, once French Equatorial Africa, with Libya to the north, Sudan to the east, and Niger to the west. The denizens are the Tebu, an Arabic people isolated from mainstream African culture.

In the course of researching our expedition in the library of the Royal Geographical Society, Wilfred Thesiger featured large. Few travellers had ever been to Tibesti before him, so I wrote to ask if we might meet to discuss our project. He invited me to his flat in Tite Street, Chelsea, for tea. A wrought iron lift took me sedately to the top floor of Shelley Court, a solid Victorian block of flats. At 4:00 p.m. exactly, as the invitation made clear, I knocked at the door of Number 15. I was slightly nervous about meeting the desert traveller famous for his journeys across the Empty Quarter of Arabia. A housekeeper showed me into the living room where a tiny, wizened old lady sat in an outsize armchair.

"I'm Wilfred's mother," she said. "Do come in. Wilfred will be here shortly. He had to go to the Travellers Club to collect his mail. Do you want tea?"

The room was lined with books and ivory knick-knacks, and a silver sword lay on an elegant sideboard. A wide window looked over the roofs of Swan Walk towards the River Thames, and with a glimpse of the Albert Bridge. Immediately below lay the high-walled botanical garden of the Chelsea Garden of Physic that belongs to the London Society of Apothecaries. Briefly I explained my business.

"Wilfred's been on camels all his life," said the little old lady. "His father was in Abyssinia as British Adviser to Emperor Haile Selassie. We used to ride camels from Djibouti to reach Addis Ababa. Before Wilfred could walk he'd sit on the saddle in front of me and shout 'Yallop, Mummy, Yallop.' When he went to school in England later on he had lots of tales to tell his friends about hunting lions and so on. But they all said he was a liar."

The door opened and a tall man dressed in a dark suit entered.

"Sorry, I'm late," he said. "Couldn't find a taxi at the Travellers. I'd prefer to go by camel any day. At least they don't break down. If a camel stops, you kick it; and if it doesn't move, you eat it."

He sipped tea from a china cup, a contrast, I imagined, to sitting cross-legged in a black Bedouin goat-hair tent drinking sweet mint tea. He lived chameleon-like between London and Arabia, but evidently his heart was in the desert where he felt most comfortable.

I studied his face as we—or rather he—talked. A large aquiline nose, bent by a fracture when boxing for Oxford, projected from his craggy face. Crows' feet radiated from his eyes, his brow was furrowed, and one deeply etched line ran from his right cheek to the angle of his jaw. A warty growth projected from the right side of his chin. Bushy eyebrows overhung deep-set blue eyes that stared right through me.

"I was in Tibesti in '38," he said. "I had to take three months' leave from my job in the Sudan. It wasn't much time to cover such a distance. But we did it by forced marches. Sometimes we spent eighteen hours a day in the saddle. Camels, of course."

Thesiger was then stationed at Kutum, Darfur Province, as Assistant District Commissioner in the Sudan Political Service, the élite of colonial administrations.

"Most people thought it was a rotten appointment to be posted to such an out-of-the-way spot. But I loved it. The desert was wild in the west of the country and I was used to similar people in Ethiopia."

He went to a bookcase and lifted down a photograph album.

"We took three months' supply of food to Tibesti," he said. "Just flour, dried meat, onions, tea, and sugar. I had my hunting rifle so I knew we wouldn't starve. Water was the real problem. To my surprise we found plenty of water holes on the way. Our caravan passed Fada in Ennedi, and then we crossed to Faya-Largeau. That's where the French colonists administered Tibesti."

He casually turned the pages of photos. All were taken with a Leica camera—his trademark and one of his few concessions to modern technology. The stark desert's contrasting shadows suited his black-and-white images, which have become classics of exploration photography.

"That's Tieroko," he said, pointing a gnarled finger at a jagged mountain massif. "I didn't manage to climb it myself, but we saw it from Modra. It's the finest peak in Tibesti. However, we slogged up Emi Koussi. Its huge volcanic crater is the highest point in the Sahara. Then we travelled up to Bardaï and Soberoum. If I were you, I'd aim for Tieroko. No one's been there."

After such advice I needed no more encouragement. Not wishing to outstay my welcome, I rose to leave.

"Come and visit any time," piped up his mother, hunched in the corner seat. "Even if Wilfred isn't here, I enjoy visitors. But phone first to make sure I'm home."

* * *

At the end of June 1957 our expedition of Cambridge men set out from Tripoli for the 1,500-mile journey across the desert to Tibesti. We comprised the leader, Roger Akester, anthropologists and geographers and ourselves. We were supported by a Royal Army Service Corps convoy of three trucks and two Land Rovers, along with their own driver-mechanics. The mountaineering team, comprising Bill Marks, Rod Tuck, and myself, travelled in a truck together. The canvas canopies were chequered white and black to show up clearly from the air in case of emergency, and we slept on them because it was cool and safe from scorpions and snakes.

Just before leaving London I realized that I had forgotten to pack a textbook that I needed for revision. I phoned the daughter of the dean of Charing Cross Hospital (sister of Guy Warner, my rackets partner) and asked her to rifle her father's bookshelves for a copy of Samson Wright's *Applied Physiology*. I told her I would pay for the taxi ride if she would bring it to me at Victoria station. My gratitude was unbounded when I received the book just before the train drew out of the station.

\* \* \*

The Mediterranean coast road turned due south towards Sebha, capital of the Fezzan, seven hundred miles distant. The Libyan desert, a kaleidoscope of ochre, dun, red, brown, and black, rolled gently past. Only an occasional rocky outcrop broke the horizon. The land appeared uninhabited but whenever we stopped for a break, after a few minutes, a shepherd boy would silently appear as if from nowhere.

The constructed road ended at an active French Foreign Legion fort that dominated Sebha oasis. Thereafter we followed the tracks of Tunis Automobile Transport Company trucks, which regularly ran south carrying supplies to desert communities and trading with the bigger centres. We navigated open sand from one stone cairn, or pile of old truck tires, to another. Along the way lay abandoned vehicles of General Leclerc's force, which, in 1943, reinforced Montgomery's Eighth Army advancing on the heels of Rommel.

We crossed the unstable sand sea of Murzuq in the bitter cold of early morning when the surface was relatively firm. If a vehicle bogged down axle-deep with tires spinning, we pushed perforated metal sandchannels under the wheels to give grip. The driver would accelerate onto the sand surface and roar off alone in order to keep up his momentum. We would then have to hitch a ride from a following vehicle.

On the other side of the sand sea lay Al Qatrun. This small battlemented fort had an ancient Italian howitzer positioned beneath each corner tower. A French Tricolor flag flew over the central, heavy wooden gate. White-turbaned Arabs in flowing white djellabahs squatted in the shade of palm trees. Barefoot boys climbed the knotted trunks to reach swags of dates ready to harvest. Flat-roofed, whitewashed houses, attached to each other at random, made a burrow of narrow streets. The local sheik, riding a caparisoned horse, pranced by holding open a black umbrella. One could easily imagine Beau Geste sallying out of the fort's gates.

Black-clad women balancing earthenware ewers on their heads walked gracefully towards the water hole, the social hub of village gossip. A pulley set in a rickety wooden frame held a braided rope connected at one end to a leather bucket, at the other to a donkey. An old man, with every muscle taut, drove the donkey up and down a ramp to lower and raise the bucket. By pulling on a string he could empty the water bucket into a wooden sluice, from where it flowed into a holding tank. There the women filled their pitchers with murky, greenish water covered with a thick scum. We filtered it through a shirt to remove most of the solid matter before boiling the water to drink.

Rod, Bill, and I each bought a goatskin water carrier. We gave them names—Charlie held seven gallons, Annie and Jezebel five each. After beheading, eviscerating, and curing, the legs had been tied off with rough cord. Water was then poured into the hole at the neck and tied securely. The water kept cool by constantly seeping through the skin and evaporating. However, the acrid flavour of goat remained—a fair return for cool water.

Beyond Al Qatrun, sand dunes gave way to a stony lunar landscape of rounded and conical hummocks. Mirages of distant sculpted sandstone towers rose from dried salt flats, and shimmered as if suspended over a boiling lake. We usually stopped for a couple of hours at midday and strung a tarpaulin from the side of the truck to offer shelter from the scorching sun. Deep glowing sunsets made exotic colours in the sand; then the temperature plummeted into gelid night.

On the neck of a gigantic soft sand dune, we crested the Korizo Pass. Undulating hills ahead rolled towards Zouar, an oasis on the western fringe of Tibesti. Not far distant lay Bardaï, the largest village of the region that would become the focal point of our travels. On the way between the two oases was the Trou au Natron, an extinct volcanic crater measuring five miles across with near-vertical, two-thousand-foot walls that offered no easy way down. Pic Toussidé towered over the Trou that looked as if some gigantic excavator had deposited the contents of the crater there. Three smaller, more recent, black volcanic cones rose one hundred feet from the crater floor.

Rod and I carefully descended the escarpment to the crater floor that was scattered with white crystalline salt deposit. Larval bubbles crunched under our feet. With darkness approaching, we climbed one of the small cones and built a fire of brush to let our party on the crater rim know we were safe. We hoped that the flames would keep away snakes, tarantulas, and scorpions, which the local Tebu had warned us often crept into shoes and sleeping bags at night. Dressed only in desert clothing, as we had originally planned to make it only a day outing, we passed a bitterly cold night. We were happy to be on our own, away from the main expedition. We looked forward to being, along with Bill, an isolated group of just three mountaineers when we set off into the mountains to climb and survey. A full moon cast eerie shadows across the white floor of the Trou au Natron. Only the buzzing of insects broke the silence.

* * *

We found the oasis of Bardaï nestled between the volcanic walls of a gorge. Prehistoric paintings on the walls showed men hunting with bows and arrows and throwing knives, along with many animals—elephant, giraffe, rhino, camel, gazelle, oryx, antelope, cheetah, and ostrich. Evidently this region had previously been more fertile.

Bastille Day fell on the day of our arrival in Bardaï. The resident French colonial troops were delighted with company from the world outside and invited us into the lime-washed fort to celebrate with them. A bugle call rallied from the gaol a parade of black colonial troops and prisoners who acted as the officers' slaves. A few ancient Tebu with badges from bygone campaigns, and some half-naked children gathered in order to hear the lieutenant-in-charge speak some stirring words about fraternité (liberté and égalité being notably absent).

Afterwards some colourfully dressed dancing girls from the local brothel, evidently the officers' Tebu mistresses, served us a feast in the mess. Cooled by whirring overhead fans, we hacked hunks of roasted meat off a barbecued goat carcass and dipped them in spicy sauce. The French troops challenged us to a soccer match, which created clouds of dust, much sweat, and camaraderie.

At sunset, flamboyant white-turbaned Méharistes, an élite roving native police camel corps, gathered for a race. They sat on bright saddle carpets with ancient Lee Enfield .303 rifles and leather bandoliers slung across their shoulders. They wore long, voluminous white djellabahs belted with a scarlet cummerbund over black baggy pants. Their sleek racing camels were quite unlike the tired old pack animals we had met so far.

Méharistes roamed throughout the mountains of Tibesti on camels, constantly on the move, sometimes alone, other times in patrols of two guides and ten riflemen. Being absent from their command posts for six-month tours, they lived a hardy, independent life. Recently a missing Méhariste patrol was reportedly found dead near a water hole, after a sandstorm had obliterated their tracks. The men had killed their camels, extracted a few pints of murky brackish stomach water, and crawled inside the carcasses for shelter from the scorching sun, awaiting death that eventually visited each of them in turn.

Tebu, the sole denizens of Tibesti, have blood groups racially different from other sub-Saharan Africans and northern Arabs, and their tongue has no affinity with any other Saharan language. They bore no allegiance outside their fiefdom, although they had been nominally under the control of the French colonists who had their Foreign Legion troops stationed in the area. So our presence among them was not totally strange.

For centuries, bands of Tebu have forayed from their secure mountain retreats in order to steal camels and capture slaves from passing caravans of Senussi from the north, blue-turbaned Touareg of the Hoggar to the west, oasis-dwellers of Kufra towards Egypt and Sudan, and black Africans from tribal lands to the south. After marauding, pillaging, and looting for several months they would return to the mountains. Some old slaves still hobbled about Bardaï, their Achilles tendons having been cut to prevent their escape. Herodotus recorded troops emerging heavily depleted after disappearing for several months, ". . . towards the land of Ethiopia"—the Fezzan Desert.

By day Tebu men lounged in the shade of date palms talking and gambling and being waited on by their women. The men wore a white cloth turban, one long end hanging loose over a shoulder to mask their lower face against blowing sand. Long, loose white shirts cover baggy trousers gathered at the ankle. A tapered dagger lay hidden under the shirtsleeve in a scabbard attached by a leather band just above the elbow. A long metal pin in the scabbard acted as a toothpick or as an implement to dig thorns from callused feet. These intermittently bellicose brigands never adapted to an agrarian lifestyle, and were lawless long before French colonial troops arrived.

Tebu women had delicate Arab features and glistening ebony skin. Finely braided hair, greased with fat and intertwined with goat hair, was parted in the middle and hung to their shoulders. Black workaday clothes were ornamented with bangles, and a bandanna encircled the forehead. When in their finery, they dressed in a single piece of bright-coloured material wound round their body with a sash at the waist. They wore large gold rings in their noses, bangles at their wrists, and necklaces of kauri shells and coral. Painted fingernails were a sign, originating in the harems, that they were menstruating. Girls tended to marry between the ages of nine and twelve years, but the husband would keep his wife for only a few years and, after she produced several children, divorce her for a younger woman. Single and divorced women lived communally in an *oggu*, a matriarchal powerhouse that ruled the life of the village.

\* \* \*

The expedition left Bardaï and travelled south towards the mountains. The track wound through volcanic canyons and traversed dry wadis towards Bini Erde, a village at the foot of Emi Koussi, the highest peak in Tibesti, which had been climbed by Wilfred Thesiger. Frequently the vehicles bogged down in sand to their axles and could be moved only by hard digging, pushing, and revving over-heated engines. A storm in the mountains caused a flash flood, which turned the usually arid wadi that some of us had just crossed into a raging brown torrent. This subsided as quickly as it arose and then allowed passage of vehicles.

In an area of open desert our guide Gunneyi (meaning "born on a camel") spotted two delicate fawn gazelles with white underbellies and graceful horns curved inwards at their tips. At midday gazelles usually lie up in wadis in the shade of camel thorn trees, and appear only in the cool of evening. Having eaten no fresh meat for nearly a month, we chased them. Even at forty miles per hour on the flat, they outran us. Gunneyi finally shot one animal, still running like the wind at two hundred yards distance. While uttering the appropriate prayers to Allah, he cut its throat just behind the jawbone and drained the blood into a bowl for eating later. That evening we feasted on tender gazelle steaks cooked on our campfire.

We broke the journey to Bini Erde at Yebbu Bou, a small oasis in view of Tieroko, the mountain massif we planned to explore later. Some thirty huts stood on a rocky spur surrounded by a circle of palm trees, while the rest of the village lay half a mile away in a gorge, approachable only on foot.

I wandered off alone and was soon joined by a young Tebu man, who led me down into the gorge. We entered a swampy bamboo jungle that opened into a palm grove, where fig trees and succulent plants grew beside irrigated fields prepared for planting corn. My guide parted some bulrushes and proudly showed me a crystal lake set in the mouth of a narrow defile on one side of which rose a cliff where doves nested in rocky crevices. Moorhens swam among watercress and nested in the reeds—a paradise the more exciting for its clandestine approach. I fetched Rod and Bill. We swam naked in a rock pool along with a host of village boys who were amused by our white buttocks in contrast to our sun-bronzed torsos.

On returning through the village, our Tebu guide invited us into his house, beside which stood a couple of black goat-hair tents. A roof of matted palm leaves was laid over a conical beehive framework and tied down to a circular low stone wall with palm fibre rope. A low doorway led into an antechamber off the main room. Our hostess, who had tightly plaited hair and a brightly coloured dress, motioned us to sit on a reed mat on the gravel floor. She then blew the fire embers into life so flames licked close to the tinder dry reed wall. When the kettle boiled she began the lengthy ritual of brewing tea from mint leaves. She served the tea sweetened with sugar chipped off a block. By tradition we had to drink three small cups before we could politely adjourn.

A leather camel bridle, harness, and trappings decorated with kauri shells hung from one wall. She kept in a padlocked metal chest standing in a corner her treasures, one of which was a broken mirror with a picture of Jane Russell on the back. Her dresses and headgear were strung from the roof. Two dozen garish enamel-stencilled tin washing bowls, with "Made in Czechoslovakia" stamped on the bottom, hung in rows on the wall. They displayed the householder's wealth and were, like kauri shells, tokens of currency.

* * *

In Yebbu Bou we met a Tebu man who always walked around under an open black umbrella. We learned how some years before, his skull had been trephined to let out evil spirits. This was probably because he suffered from epileptic fits. Wrapped in blue cloth in an old sardine tin he carried some charms and two circular pieces of bone, which bore skull suture lines and impressions of brain blood vessels on their under surface. On unwrapping his turban he revealed two healed depressions in his scalp where blood vessels of the underlying brain pulsated visibly. The two pieces of bone filled exactly these depressions.

The local medicine man, Adele, was an expert in trephining skulls.

We persuaded him to perform the operation on a goat so we might observe and film his technique. He negotiated a fee by hard bargaining, using camel droppings as counters and drawing figures in the sand. The agreed sum was only a fraction of his original demand. Meanwhile the village chief, wearing a faded scarlet fez, moved a few yards off with an enamel bowl and washed his feet, to no obvious purpose.

A goat was brought to a sandy patch outside the chief's hut. From an old carpetbag Adele produced his instruments, which he laid out on the sand; two metal gouges with wooden handles, an old French army jackknife, and a polished six-inch nail. He made a fire of camel dung and warmed a tin of oil on the smouldering embers.

Two Tebu, with turbans pulled over their mouths like surgical masks, held the nose of the goat firmly in the sand, almost asphyxiating it—a very primitive anaesthetic. With the jackknife, Adele swiftly incised a cross over the scalp and tied dried grass strings to the flaps, which his assistant held open. Despite a pool of blood, Adele swiftly gouged out a circle of skull, then carefully levered away a circular fragment of bone and separated it from the underlying brain covering.

At this point Rod became sallow and retched; Bill ogled intently, quite unfazed. For me, as a medical student, this was utterly fascinating raw surgery. I had been appointed expedition doctor, but I had so far done nothing more than paint wounds with gentian violet and wash ringwormy children's heads with potassium permanganate. So this activity was unusually exciting, especially for me.

Finally Adele scattered some camel-dung ash on the open wound and mixed it into a sticky consistency with butter. He then tied the four strings in a knot to bring the flaps together and sprinkled a little sand on the head of the goat, who staggered to its feet and tottered away to join the flock, its devils expunged.

* * *

At Bini Erde we hired, for the journey to Emi Koussi, some scrawny mountain camels that travel well over the rough volcanic terrain. They were quite unlike the sleek Méhariste racing camels, or the big-boned beasts used by baggage caravans. We acquired a riding camel each, and with practice I learned to hang on tight to the saddle pommel when it rose to its feet from lying down. First it would lurch forward raising its rump, then straighten its forefeet, and finally rise on its back legs. Like riding a bucking bronco or hanging onto a frisky sailing dinghy, it left one feeling as though tea, lunch, and breakfast might regurgitate successively. One steers with a single rein using pressure from feet crossed over the camel's neck, which I found difficult, not being an experienced horseman. The fluid walking rhythm of a camel comes from its leg-bone sinking into its ankle and rebounding like a shock absorber. "Ship of the desert" is apt. Camels drink every four or five days, filling their stomachs to capacity whenever they come across water. Between waterholes they browse on tough spines of camel-thorn trees and graze on succulent scrub found in wadi beds.

We started our routine of marching—I preferred to walk rather than ride—in the cool of early morning long before the sun's red orb rose above the horizon. When high enough to be unpleasantly hot, we stopped under a camel-thorn tree for a long siesta. By midday the fireball overhead cast no shadow and the ground was too hot to walk on. Rod usually wrote his journal, Bill slept, and I studied for a physiology tripos exam I had to take in September.

For two days our caravan, that consisted of the entire expedition, wandered through the wadis and canyons at the base of Emi Koussi. After a steady climb we reached the rim of the volcano at 11,204 feet (3415 m). The only other Westerner to have climbed Emi Koussi before us was Wilfred Thesiger. The shallow crater measured eight by five miles across and was 1,000 feet deep. From this highest point in the

Sahara we looked out across range on range of gunmetal-grey volcanic shapes drifting towards a bluish horizon as if the whole Sahara Desert flowed away from this focal point. As we were very short of food, we hunted small birds with Rod's .22 rifle, skinned and roasted them, and then ate them in a Ryvita sandwich.

After returning to Yebbu Bou, we three mountaineers set off to explore Tarso Tieroko, as Thesiger had advised. Our two local guides from Yebbu Bou, Angerké and Mohadé, brought six baggage camels to carry food and gear for two weeks. For the first time Rod, Bill, and I were truly apart from the body of the expedition and able to decide freely our own routine and speed of travel. With no named leader, and since we were good friends, we made decisions by consensus and settled quickly into an efficient unit.

We were now bronzed and fit. We wore shorts to the amazement of our guides, who always dressed in loose-fitting trousers and long off-white shirts. Floppy bush hats protected us from the sun. My head, shaved in Sebha for ease of managing hair, was now a brush-cut, easy to wash and to keep free of nits. Rod didn't have much hair anyway, like his father and his grandfather who were bald in their mid-twenties. Bill had a thick mat and a bushy beard. My beard was scrawny with bald patches so I shaved it off.

After three days marching across the desert north of Tarso Toon we reached the edge of the Tieroko massif and made our base camp in an empty wadi. About a mile away, a cirque of rock joined a large peak to the left with some tall pinnacles. During the next week we made daily excursions from our camp, climbing any peak that would help us understand the geography better in order to make a map of this contorted land, and to discover exactly which peak was Tieroko. The mountain shapes were quite different from any volcanic cones we had encountered so far. We had the rare privilege and thrill of charting country none of which had been mapped or climbed.

One evening at our base camp as we were brewing our staple supper of couscous maize on an open fire, an old man appeared from the distant village of Modra. He showed his battle scars, inflicted many years before in fights with rival bandits, accompanied by animated signs. His left forearm was useless from a deep gash in the muscle, a swollen knee had a loose-floating patella, his neck bore a knife wound, and a jagged scar extended down his back. He mimed a warlike scenario, which demonstrated the fate of intruders into his territory—the very history of Tibesti's indigenous tribes. He danced wildly round the fire, brandishing his spear and knife, making menacing gestures. Angerké and Mohadé replied with their own mime showing how to creep up on a camel thief, draw a long knife from its scabbard, and sever his Achilles tendons.

Then we sat round the fire and shared with our visitor a meal of couscous, along with chunks of fresh gazelle and sun-dried goat meat. The actors murmured their prayers facing the setting sun, tropic darkness fell quickly, and the fire burned to embers. Lying in our sleeping bags under an inky sky, we watched meteors streak overhead and uncharted galaxies reduce our busy lives to an infinitesimal scale.

Next day we climbed to the cirque behind our base camp, mapped all we could see, and named several geographic features. Tieroko, the highest peak in the massif, lay in an adjacent valley. We set out from our base camp with Angerké carrying a full goatskin of water, not knowing whether we would find any during our possible absence of several days.

We found a clear stream flowing into deep pools surrounded by greenery in the floor of a neighboring wadi, which we named Paradise Wadi. An hour spent splashing around in a pool of cold water was a benison after two months of arid desert where every drop of water was precious. We sent Angerké back to base camp to await our return. Then we climbed over some house-sized boulders and skirted rocky pools in the dark and chilly two-hundred-feet-high canyon of Paradise Wadi. Eventually a rocky headwall forced us to exit the gorge. Some delicate climbing on rotten rock brought us out into scorching sunshine at the base of Tieroko from where we scrambled up a ledge below the summit cone. Equatorial night fell suddenly as usual, so we bivouaced under an overhanging rock, ready to tackle the final pyramid of Tieroko next morning. Under stars in an indigo heaven, a fire of dry scrub warmed us against intense cold.

Tieroko, however, proved elusive. The steep, rotten wall above our bivouac offered only tiny holds of conglomerate knobs and no belays. We rounded a corner that hung over another valley system to the south of Tieroko, but the top was out of our reach. Chagrined, we gave up. Several years later, Doug Scott, then a member of a Nottingham University expedition, traversed round the same corner and found a ramp leading to the top. Our timidity thus denied us the first ascent of the most handsome peak in Tibesti.

We returned to our base camp from where a day's march led across the plain to the village of Modra set in a deep gorge. We looked back to Tieroko, as Thesiger had, satisfied at having explored and mapped its massif. Our only regret was not reaching the very summit.

On our return to Yebbu Bou we stopped a mile outside the village to wash and smarten up after our three-week adventure. Angerké and Mohadé produced from their saddlebags clean white turbans, long white shirts, and black baggy pants. Angerké slung a long hunting knife from his shoulder; to impress his friends, Mohadé held—upside down—an old copy of *Punch* magazine. Rod polished his sunburned pate, Bill combed his beard, and my hair was still a brush cut. We looked like tramps compared to our guides.

From Bardaï we drove north to Aozou in order to climb Pic de Wobou, a needle-shaped spire of sound rock we had seen frequently from afar in previous weeks. From the top we had a panoramic view of the ground we had covered in Tibesti. Thirty years later this strip of barren rock and desert would become a war zone between Libya and Chad for its uranium riches.

Finally we walked over the hills from Bardaï to Soberoum with five donkeys, because all local camels had been moved to the lowlands for better pasturage. Hot medicinal springs covered a dozen acres of rolling hillocks of coloured minerals—green, brown, and golden-orange. The ground was pockmarked with deep holes that steamed and boiled, fizzed and whistled, emitting pungent sulphurous fumes. In pits twenty feet across and ten feet deep, boiling grey mud bubbled and burst, then collapsed with a loud *plop*. The wadi bed was caked with green and yellow salt; underfoot, soft crystalline rock broke into acid powder.

Six white-clad Tebu clustered round a fire built in a small stone circle beside an active hole where people bathed in clouds of steam. The ground seethed, spat, and belched sulphur, and rumbled and erupted gently every few seconds. With closed eyes it sounded like Paddington Station; open, it looked like the gates of hell.

The expedition foregathered in Bardaï and set off driving north by the way we had come. We looked back at Tibesti from the top of the bump that is the Korizo Pass, a strange untravelled land that we had explored for two happy months. It was unlikely that we would ever have the chance of reaching the middle of the Sahara again.

# THIRTEEN

WHILE IN THE EMPYREAN OF Cambridge I could not imagine that I would ever become a doctor, and deal with live patients rather than just anatomy specimens. After moving to London I underwent a metamorphosis from callow, baggy-pullovered undergraduate to medical student in starched white collar and gold-plated shirt studs. Days of punting on the River Cam and wandering carefree and head-in-air along the Backs suddenly changed after my first contact with real people suffering from real illness and the horror of it.

Five Cambridge friends and I planned to share a flat. Scanning the advertisement pages of the *Evening Standard* led Andrew Elkington and me on a trail to Number 38, Cleveland Square. Once a genteel part of Bayswater, it was now a seedy, run-down haunt of tarts, who solicited around nearby Paddington Station. The owner of the flat was a retired Jewish businessman.

"You're all nice boys, I'm sure," he said. "But I didn't have in mind letting to students."

"Please may we just look round to see if it would suit us," said

Andrew, flashing his most melting smile. "Then you can decide whether we'd suit you."

"All right, come on in," said the owner reluctantly.

"We're not like the ones in *Doctor in the House*," said Andrew reassuringly. Richard Gordon's book by that name had just been published, portraying the high jinks of rowdy young doctors in training, so our prospective landlord's concern was understandable. Andrew's smooth manners befitted St Thomas's Hospital, by repute one of the classier medical schools. Fair, wavy hair and handsome looks led to his being adopted by several well-connected, elderly bachelors who spoiled him outrageously, much to the envy of his friends.

The flat was on the third floor of a large Victorian building that flanked the south side of Cleveland Square, the gardens of which were kept for the exclusive use of the tenants, mainly for walking their dogs. Built at the turn of the century for the middle class merchants of Paddington and neighbouring Bayswater, the flat was spacious beyond the aspirations, and the pockets, of most students. But shared between six, the rent didn't seem outrageous. There was a huge sitting room, a kitchen that reeked of kosher cooking, two double and two single bedrooms, and a bathroom with a deep tub. The furniture was of dark mahogany throughout, light fittings drooped like lianas in a tropical forest, and chairs all bore antimacassars. A large aspidistra grew in a brass pot standing in the hall beside a rack holding canes, umbrellas, and a shooting stick.

Over a weak cup of tea, without even cake or biscuits, Andrew exuded such charm that we became tenants of the flat for two years while Mr and Mrs Goldstein moved to their retirement bungalow at Frinton-on-Sea. Each of us put one pound a week into a cracked teapot on the kitchen mantelpiece. We withdrew money as needed for communal flat expenses, which were signed into a notebook.

All our flatmates were medical students except Bob Thomson, who worked for a Dickensian firm that made manhole covers in South London. When phoning Bob at work one had to wait for him to give his introductory blurb: "Elkington Gattick non-rockable watertight covers recessed for your concrete fillings." His termagant supervisor, Miss Gurney, kept him working at his high office desk where we imagined him writing in a ledger with a quill pen. A talented cellist and chorister, Bob joined a prestigious madrigal group, The Elizabethan Singers. When emotionally charged he would break into falsetto alto plainsong. He relished High Church ritual. "I'd really like to be the Archbishop of Canterbury," he once announced. "I think I'd look splendid in the cathedral, dressed up in all those gorgeous vestments and regalia." Little did we realize then that Bob would eventually become much better known in medical circles than any of us. After a thorough apprenticeship of twenty years in the lower clerical ranks, he became Secretary of the Royal Society of Medicine, where he was on first name, hobnobbing terms with many medical lords with whose nod we would have been thrilled.

A St Bartholemew's trio comprised Basil Middleton, David Gibson, and Simon Dean. They helped to moderate the food bills by buying scrag end of beef and lamb from a stall in Smithfield market, just round the corner from the hospital.

Simon was of Suffolk stock with the ruddy visage of a farmer. His large, silent, and genial father was a retired colonel in the county regiment. Motherly Mrs Dean, ever pragmatic, once announced in a loud voice, "After a weekend visit by Simon's friends, if there are no stains on the sheets, I worry that they haven't enjoyed themselves." Simon was destined for a career in rural general practice like his maternal grandfather, an old-fashioned country doctor who made home visit rounds in a pony and trap.

Simon was manager of the household and guardian of the cracked teapot. His laconic wit and waspish tongue kept us all in our places. He was also a talented watercolour painter. Shortly after moving into the flat he caught chicken pox, the worst case I have ever seen, with vesicles all over his body. As he was hairy as a gorilla, the scabs became entwined and matted with his hairs, and his convalescence was painful and unpleasant.

Basil was the eldest of us—all of twenty-five years. Urbane, attired in an immaculate three-piece suit, not a hair out of place, he never raised his voice. But his response to adversity could cut to the quick. On cloudy days he always carried an umbrella, just in case. He eventually became a fashionable general practitioner in Montpelier Square, convenient for the society folk who lived around Harrods. If one or other of us was in crisis, it was to Basil we turned because he was solid as a galleon riding a turbulent swell.

David just did not look old enough to be near becoming a doctor. He had dark hair, a peach-fuzz face, and a constantly startled look behind spectacles that he wriggled up to the bridge of his nose by wrinkling his brow or, if that did not work, with the stab of a finger. David was our Lothario, the only one of us to have made out with a girl, and thus an object of awe and esteem. A natural actor, he had trodden the boards with the Cambridge Footlights, and could imitate each of us unmercifully. One day Simon chided him for his forgetfulness. "That's nothing," David replied. "When I was four my mother drove into Banbury and left me in the car while she went shopping at Sainsbury's. When finished she took the bus home—alone."

The sixth member of the flat was Mike Snell, a St Mary's man, who came and went haphazardly. Brought up in Nyasaland in southern Africa where dress was usually shorts and sandals, Mike, out of habit, dressed from the feet up for fear of getting jiggers of bilharzia between his toes. Early one morning the front door bell rang so, clad only in his socks, he went to the door and opened it to his cousin's girlfriend, who was in floods of tears after a domestic tiff. This gained him the nickname Screwball, which stuck into later life even after he had become an eminent surgeon at his own teaching hospital. We never quite knew whether to expect to find Mike in the bed or his St Mary's compatriot, Luke Zander. Luke was one of a large and diversely talented Jewish family. His grandfather insisted that all his children take trade apprenticeships before they went to university as backup against tougher days where brawn would be more marketable than brain. Luke's siblings were of genius calibre whereas he was just an elegant cricketer and a normal extrovert who played the violin.

We quickly and happily settled into our new home, like an extension of Cambridge college life, which eased our transition to the vast, amorphous city. We gathered some of the more hideous house fittings and ornaments into a hall closet for safekeeping. While tidying a cupboard we found a notebook, evidently the diary of a previous tenant. The reminiscences of this unnamed, faceless girl, who had arrived in London from a sheltered home in the Midlands as an innocent seventeen-year-old, read like following a Hogarthian *Rake's Progress*. The pages were soon laced with cryptic entries and initials graded with stars and marginal comments. Her avalanche into seamy London life culminated in coded financial transactions written beside the names. Shortly thereafter the entries stopped and we were left wondering what became of her.

Our immediate neighbours on the floor below were Robert and Andrea Samson. Robert, a young Lincoln's Inn barrister, had risen meteorically under the scales of justice at the Old Bailey. The Botticelli face and sleek legs of Andrea, a fashion model, often graced the front pages of *Vogue* magazine. The overflow from our bathtub connected with theirs, and acted like an old-fashioned speaking tube, common in restaurants for the waiter to call orders down to the basement kitchens. As we lay in our bath we could hear Robert's booming expletives and Andrea's indignant ripostes as clear as if we were in the same room.

Simon allocated cooking duty to each flatmate in turn. Wednesday was my day and somehow I learned to make fish pie with white sauce, decorated with a sprig of parsley and a slice of lemon on top. (Once when courting my wife-to-be I boasted of my skill, but sadly I have never been able to replicate it, nor she to forget it.) Andrew directed washing the dishes without getting his hands wet. The problem of cleaning the flat was solved in a roundabout way by an attack of virus pneumonia that confined me to bed in my own hospital.

A minuscule, ancient cleaning lady with a moustachioed upper lip and tufts of hair growing from her ears, came into my room. She seemed to take a liking to me and spent unduly long polishing around my bed. Raising her head, she peered at me through pebble spectacles.

"Hello, Doctor. I'm Edie," she said in broad Cockney. "Just giving your floor a once over."

"Please don't call me doctor," I replied. "I'm just a student."

"Never mind, Doctor. You're all the same to me in them white coats."

She began polishing the floor with more energy than seemed possible with such spindly arms. When she stood up her tiny form barely topped the table over the end of the bed where I lay with the sheets pulled round my chin, gazing at the London fog through wilting daffodils.

"I wish I could get out of this bed," I said. "I'm bored stiff."

"You soon will if you're a good boy and do what staff nurse tells you," Edie said. "Bye for now."

She disappeared into the corridor, where she began swinging a heavy floor polisher and continued gossiping to herself. As soon as she had gone, the door was flung open by the bossy staff nurse at the sound of whose tread I cowered. She thrust a thermometer into my mouth without so much as a by-your-leave, and left it to cook. When she had gone, the elfin figure of Edie appeared again, clad in a green jumble sale coat, knitted woolen scarf, and a felt beret pulled down over her ears.

"I'm off now, Doctor," she said. She delved into a worn plastic bag, pulled out an orange, handed it to me and said, "Don't let 'er catch you." Her mischievous eyes glinted.

About a month later, when I was fully recovered, I met Edie in the hospital corridor, still swinging her floor polisher.

"Will you come and clean our flat once a week?" I asked. "We'll pay you."

"Love to, Doctor," she replied. "When can I start?"

This was the beginning of a love affair between Edie and the six of us at Number 38, Cleveland Square. Every Wednesday she took a bus from her basement single room in Chelsea to the Albert Hall. Then she walked through Hyde Park "for a little bit of fresh air." She cleaned the flat, and cherished us, for ten bob a week taken from the teapot kitty. The flat sparkled when she was done, and usually she stayed until after five o'clock in order to see us when we returned from our respective hospitals. If we were late back, we would find some prank to remind us of her visit—a hairbrush down a bed or pyjama legs knotted together.

However, she would have nothing to do with Bob Thomson because he was not a doctor. Soon she came a second day each week, at no extra pay, to do "light work" such as washing down the walls of the kitchen or scrubbing the bathroom ceiling, which eventually fell in. Simon, wearing rugger shorts, cleaned up the mess. Without Edie the flat would have been a shambles. Her love for us nevertheless filled a gap in her otherwise lonely life, and was utterly reciprocated by all of us.

* * *

With our move to London and the beginning of our clinical studies, life took on a more serious aspect. No longer did vacations last for months on end when I could climb wherever the whim took me. I had to abandon my grandiose expectations of a fortnight in Scotland, the Lakes, or Wales at Christmas and Easter, and a summer season in the Alps arranged at the drop of a hat. Suddenly we were limited to a meagre four weeks of holidays a year, closely monitored by the Dean's secretary, and to be taken only when the time fitted suitably between teaching assignments. Rocks to climb on, still the ruling and exclusive passion of my life, were even farther away from London than from Cambridge.

There were other compensations, however, and living in London was new and exciting. Each day I walked from our flat across Hyde Park to St George's Hospital. The hospital and the medical school stood at the very hub of London's metropolis—mile zero—on the west side of Hyde Park Corner roundabout, in the centre of which stood the Royal Artillery Memorial.

I would enter Kensington Gardens at Marlborough Gate, opposite Lancaster Gate underground station. I could then choose to follow one or the other path on either side of the Serpentine. On the south side of the lake, I soon entered a shrubbery where stands the lithe and graceful statue of Peter Pan. The "Boy Who Wouldn't Grow Up" wears an elfin costume and holds a curved pipe in his left hand to summon, from Neverland, Tinker Bell and other fairie maidens, rabbits, and other small animals festooned around the roots of the tree pedestal on which he stands. Ducks congregate at the nearby concrete slipway down which they launch themselves into the Long Water.

To the right, avenues of elms lead towards the Round Pond, haunt of model yachtsmen, migrating geese, and uniformed Norland nannies from posh Kensington homes, pushing their wards in soft-sprung prams as smart as Rolls Royces. The lakeshore path converges on Rotten Row where the Household Cavalry, whose barracks stand on nearby Carriage Drive, exercise their horses. One misty morning from the Serpentine path I heard the pounding of hooves coming from the direction of the bridge. Peering into the mist I saw a troop of Horse Guards trotting across the entire span of the bridge. The plumes of their helmets bobbed up and down, and their blue capes swished in rhythm with a rise and fall in the saddle. White-blancoed leather gauntlets held their drawn swords erect. Then the mirage disappeared into the London fog. Only the *clip-clop, clip-clop* lingered above the distant hum of motors.

My path dived into a narrow tunnel below the Serpentine Bridge and emerged beside the Lido, a public bathing area where health fanatics, some white-haired, swum year round as a sort of self-flagellation to cleanse body and mind—a very English form of masochistic puritanism peculiar to boarding schools. If I chose a route along the north side of the Serpentine, I kept more to the centre of the park. I passed a boathouse where one could rent skiffs by the hour, and a bandstand where military musicians performed in summer. The sky glowed orange from the streetlights of Marble Arch, Park Lane, and Knightsbridge. The muffled background hum of traffic stayed beyond the rim of night that encompassed my very silent, private world where, wrapped in inky blackness, I was temporarily king of my domain. Apsley House, former home of the Dukes of Wellington, stood opposite St George's Hospital. Suddenly the cacophony of traffic would rudely shatter an illusion of peace I had enjoyed in the middle of the park, when for a precious half hour I was transposed from the busy city to a world light years away. Especially was this so at night when I returned home to the flat.

To exit the park I needed to avoid the ladies who emerged at dusk to patrol the penumbra and to solicit passersby. I got to know them quite well—on nodding terms—because they kept to their regular beat, mostly centred on The Dell, a glade of trees and herbaceous flower beds at the end of the Serpentine, where they had every corner staked out. The shrubbery rustled as I passed. Gentlemen wearing raincoats occupied every bench, their bowler hats perched on briefcases on their laps into which the ladies appeared to delve. It was also a favourite spot to pick up young guardsmen, the downfall of many a public figure.

* * *

In order to avoid busy traffic in Knightsbridge I ducked into a subway and emerged beside St George's Hospital. Designed by Sir William Wilkins in 1827, the elegant neoclassical building had a central portico with a pediment supported by four square columns, above which the hospital name was inscribed in Roman letters. Wide steps led up to the main door that opened into a hallway. There hung leather fire buckets full of sand used in the previous century. Swing doors straight ahead led into the boardroom where lay the couch on which John Hunter, father of modern surgery, collapsed and died from a massive fatal haemorrhage. He had experimentally inoculated himself with syphilis, which caused an aneurysm of his aorta that ruptured.

The medical school was housed in a tall building—Number 9, Knightsbridge—adjacent to the main hospital. Behind its Georgian facade was a warren of temporary army huts and underground corridors that splayed out to occupy the entire well of the hospital. There could be found, by good navigation, various departments of the medical school, lecture theatres, and the library. St George's was small in numbers and its academic record inconspicuous, yet its atmosphere was intimate and friendly.

The consultant teaching staff, registrars, and students shared the clubroom on the first floor of Number 9. Tall, elegant windows looked out across busy Knightsbridge to Hyde Park, where banks of crocuses and daffodils grew in springtime, tramps and sun-worshipers lounged in summer, and golden leaves of plane trees lay in autumn. Comfortable chairs were scattered around the common room and newspapers lay on low tables. The walls were decorated with caricature portraits of senior staff painted by the plastic surgeon, George Elliot-Blake. In an alcove off the main room stood the bar where students and registrars would share a beer with their bosses after rounds. Such informality was practically unknown to my friends in other, more prestigious, London teaching hospital medical schools. It was a hallmark of St George's that bred respect rather than familiarity.

We were apprentices in a system that essentially left individuals to search out their own medical education. Lectures were of uneven standard and spottily attended. Teaching ward rounds were spasmodic because chiefs were often detained by private patients or because they were still down in their country residences. Many had been co-opted onto the hospital staff after the war when the government instituted the National Health Service. Thereby they held safe tenure until retirement. Some, however, were excellent teachers with small firms of half a dozen or so students.

Some of our best teaching came from the registrars, poor fellows bent on climbing the professional specialist ladder. While waiting to fill dead men's shoes they worked long hours for a pittance with burdensome responsibility. They were close enough in time to our own situation to empathize with our difficulties and frustrations. Though teaching sessions were obligatory, it was up to students themselves to glean what extra they might. The students in our year were particularly bright; several of my contemporaries went on to distinguished academic careers—Peter Richards in medicine as dean of St Mary's, Paul Millac in neurology, John Bancroft in psychiatry.

During a medical lifetime I have formed over-simplified and exaggerated prejudices about how doctors choose their specialties according to their own personality traits. Looking around a classroom of students you could almost pigeonhole them into the specialist slots where they would fit. Physicians tend to be gentle philosophers, who think long before acting. They don't seem to vary much whether their interest is in heart, chest, or the endocrine system. Neurologists are strictly academic, pinpointing the exact anatomical site of disease, but all too often neurosurgeons are unable to do anything about it because it is so close to the clockwork of the brain. Dermatologists don't like getting out of bed, but they have a yen for creepie-crawlies and often get saddled with running venereal disease clinics as penance for undisturbed nights. Psychiatrists tend to acquire some features of their patients, whether because they entered the field to solve their own problems, or through osmosis.

Extroverts veer towards surgery, where they perform at centre stage under spotlights, and with, in the penumbra, a galaxy of acolytes, young and beautiful nurses, or doltish students. Their histrionic behaviour is commensurate with the drama of their chosen type of surgery. General surgeons are cut-and-thrust, action first, thought later; cardiac and thoracic surgeons have life-and-death panache when dealing with an open pumping heart and bellowing lungs, and they tend to throw instruments; orthopaedic surgeons with big hands and bluff mien are carpenter-like, at home with hammer and chisel, brace and bit; the eye makes the surgeon as myopic as his view of life; plastic surgeons are gentle men who move skin with the delicate touch of an artist and approach problems in an aesthetic vein.

Gynaecologists fall into two distinct types: either they are ladies' men identifying too well with their patients, or ambivalent misogynists getting back at them. Radiologists are good with the patient on the end of a needle or of a lens, but generally they prefer the company of the X-ray viewing screen. Pathologists and bacteriologists are happiest closeted in laboratories well out of reach of patients, dealing with excretions and secretions rather than their personal problems. General practitioners, considered the lowest on the totem pole, have the hardest job of all. Patients come in off the street with a multitude of complaints, weighty to themselves, mostly mundane to us in the profession. Keeping alert for the serious among the plethora of dross demands constant attention. No patients of family doctors are filtered and already diagnosed, as they usually are for the referral specialist. The canvas on which the general practitioner paints is vast; that of the specialist, by definition, is quite narrow.

My comments above notably relate towards men, because female students used to be rare. Nowadays the balance is appropriately adjusted and they occupy about half of medical school places. Gentler by nature, their personality traits do not seem so extreme as those of their more aggressive counterparts.

At St George's we had a host of interesting and eccentric bosses whose foibles we could appreciate in the bar of Number 9, Knightsbridge. The doyens of the older general physicians were Doctors Robson, Dow, and Hunter, men of well-considered opinions and sound diagnostic skills. An immaculate Harley Street gentleman, Charles Robson, was one of the royal physicians; he seemed to breathe rarefied air. James Dow was more like a country farmer. The easiest of the three for me to relate to was Alastair Hunter, gentle and thorough but never so intimidating one dared not risk making a fool of oneself by asking ignorant questions. They taught us how to take histories and thereby establish rapport with patients, to examine them carefully and observantly, and to draw conclusions on which to base our diagnoses. It was heady stuff: listening with my own brand-new stethoscope for murmurs arising from abnormal blood flow in a heart; percussing a chest with the middle finger of one hand tapping that of the other in order to detect solid areas in the underlying lung; feeling an abdomen with the flat of a hand while keenly observing the patient's face for wincing. The signs we sought were legion; their interpretation, art versus science.

A group of younger physicians, dashing whiz kids who had only just risen from the ranks of senior registrars themselves, seemed positively human. John Batten—youthful, handsome, fun loving—was just starting a meteoric rise eventually to become Physician to the Queen. I later worked for him as his houseman.

Another younger physician was Aubrey Leatham, who made his name by recording heart sounds and murmurs on paper, and by designing an eponymous stethoscope. His father, the school doctor at Charterhouse, had been amateur rackets champion in the twenties. Aubrey inherited his father's enthusiasm for the game but less of his skill. We teamed up as a St George's Hospital rackets pair and played some pleasant matches against schools, notable more for camaraderie than success.

I was slow to appreciate physicianly wisdom. Since childhood I had been more interested in surgery. "Nic" Nicholls, the senior surgeon whose houseman I became later, was a member of the Magic Circle. Coasting towards retirement, he would come into town from his home in the Cotswolds on Tuesday, do a round of his patients and a short operating session. Nic's surgery consisted mostly of cystoscopies that entailed looking into the bladder with a telescope. It did not require too steady a hand; his had a marked tremor. Then on Thursday he would return to the country, leaving the firm in the capable hands of his senior registrar, Malcolm Robinson.

Another surgeon, Sir Ralph Marnham, for some minor sin of omission fired his house surgeon on the front steps of the hospital whither his house surgeon had escorted him as usual in order to hold open the door of his Rolls Royce. "Go away, boy, I never want to see you again," he said. "But remind me, what's on the operating list for tomorrow?"

Rodney Smith—co-author of a classic surgical textbook, king of the pancreas, county cricketer, and champion bridge player—was always in a hurry. He would dash into the hospital with athletic grace, do his ward round or operating session, and dash out again, not to be seen for another week. He later became President of the Royal College of Surgeons, thus fostering his wealthy Arab clientele, and he left his senior registrars on their own to gain much valuable experience in pancreaticoduodenojejunostomy. Victor Riddell and Hugh Anderson were two antipoles. Riddell was the thyroid and breast surgeon, always dressed in newly ironed greens, utterly punctilious in his mutilating radical mastectomy technique, demanding an audience of adulating students and nurses. Anderson was short, with crimped grey hair and a ruddy face, blustery, coarse but warm-hearted. He slammed doors like Troyte in Elgar's seventh Enigma Variation.

The St George's thoracic surgeons were also opposites. Negating my theory, Harold Siddons was quiet and self-effacing even when immersed in the chasm of a chest. He was a civilized man, fond of music, the outdoors, and his home in Church Street, Chelsea. Charles Drew was busy in those early days of deep-freeze cardiac surgery. The job of us students was to pack ice round pre-operative patients, who were then brought into the operating theatre in a bathtub on wheels. When their core temperature had fallen below 28° centigrade, Drew could stop the heart for forty-five minutes. So he had to do his work mighty swiftly. This caused a level of tension that led him to swear and throw instruments when the going got rough. He apparently had a gentler disposition when not in the theatre.

Larry Kirwan-Taylor, a debonair and foppish gynaecologist, would stroke the hands and soothe the brows of many a distressed pregnant society girl from Belgravia. His silver hair was feathered over his ears. He wore hand-tailored suits with a carnation in the buttonhole and carried a monocle on a black silk string. His lectures, the academic content of which was slim, were always packed with students hoping for some gratuitous pearls about sex. His advice was: "If you're taking a gal out to dinner, better to make love before rather than after." His examinations always ended with a discreet application of Johnson's Baby Powder and a pat on the patient's bottom as he pulled up the draw sheet. He once told us, "The only important quality for success in medicine is always to be available." Needless to say, his patients adored him.

George Gwillim, by contrast, was a rough, rude, tempestuous Welshman. He was a brilliant technician, especially at vaginal hysterectomy for which he was world-renowned; he was also a qualified barrister. He appeared to scorn women and treated them with contempt. He would tetchily wrinkle his stubby nose to raise his glasses up his face before unceremoniously up-ending his patient under the scrutiny of half a dozen peering students. One woman began breathing heavily when he was inserting the examining speculum; he casually observed to us, "She's just having an orgasm." I found to my cost that Gwillim was a bad enemy to harbour. One day his seminar room was occupied during a teaching round so he stormed into the nearby hospital chapel. I brazenly told him that his show of pique was in poor taste. Gynaecology was fortunately not my avocation, but strangely we became quite amicable thereafter.

The orthopaedic surgeons were a comic double act of Bobs. Bobby Burns, like an elegant British bulldog, would send people off to physiotherapy with instructions for "heat, light, electricity, and magnetism." Bob Young came from the South London brewing family that still delivered its beer using drays pulled by Suffolk Punches. He was popular with the students for arranging annual tours of the brewery.

\* \* \*

A pleasure of being a student at St George's, right in the heart of London, was the view, enhanced for me during rounds on Drummond (urological) ward situated on the top northerly corner of the hospital where the windows looked both over Hyde Park and down Picadilly. If you glanced to the right of Constitution Hill, the trees in Buckingham Palace garden came into view. At eleven o'clock each morning the gleaming silver-breasted Household Cavalry rode past on their way to change the guard at Horse Guards Parade in Whitehall. If this hour fell during rounds, I was drawn irresistibly and would edge myself towards the window in order to watch the spectacle.

There were many other visual pleasures, not least the student nurses. St George's had a reputation as one of the finest nursing schools in London, certainly on a par with the Nightingales of St Thomas's. Dame Muriel Powell, the matron, had her pick of the rosebuds of England. Her busy air and starchy look, when I saw her in the corridors, was one of unchallenged authority. Her nurses were subject to discipline as rigid as any National Servicemen in the armed forces. The student nurses all wore starched white aprons—each nurse had twelve aprons kept in a trunk—that were changed twice a day. Their blue-and-white striped uniforms were in keeping with their convict status. When their black lisle stockings holed or laddered they would paint their white skin showing through the hole with black ink rather than throw them away. Later when they went out in street clothes, their legs looked mottled. Another ruse was to draw a line with black eye shadow down the backs of their calves to imitate a stocking seam. One of Miss Powell's predecessors liked her nurses to have pink underwear because she thought it radiated happiness. She also believed that a green light she saw hovering over St George's kept everyone safe.

Staff nurses wore plain blue dresses, Sisters dark blue; both had antique Victorian silver buckles on their belts, some of them very ornate. Their caps were folded fan-wise and pulled together with a bow at the back. Sisters had starched white cuffs that, when they got down to heavy work, they changed for puffy cuffs round their rolled-up sleeves. So strict was the military hierarchy of the nurses that it made us medical students look quite casual. But an equalizer on St George's Day was a charming tradition whereby all members of the hospital wore a red rose in a buttonhole or pinned to their apron.

Sister sat at her throne-like desk in the middle of the thirty-bed ward from where she could see every patient at a glance. Each bed had a curtain that could be pulled round for a modicum of privacy, but they were usually left drawn back. A central grand fireplace, no longer functioning, acted as a counter on which urine specimens were boiled in test tubes. A hint of Scutari still hung over the wards.

Grosvenor Ward hosted the Grey Lady, a ghost who would appear in the stairwell when anyone was about to die. Nurses were not allowed to put red and white flowers in the same vase because that also presaged death.

At first I kept quite distant from the probationer nurses; then three years later I fell heavily for one, met independently at a friend's wedding, and have been happily married to her ever since. But that's another story, for later.

# FOURTEEN

IN THE MIDDLE OF MY TIME AT ST GEORGE'S I managed to squeeze a meagre couple of weeks' holiday between teaching firms. Rod Tuck and I laid plans, at barely twenty-four hours' notice, to visit the Atlas Mountains of Morocco in September. Rod was then a lieutenant in the Royal Marines, serving in the Special Boats Section on an aircraft carrier. Whenever he was on leave in London we would meet at the salad bar of the Lyons Corner House, Marble Arch. For half a crown we could feast on as much salad as we could pile onto a plate.

During idle moments on our camel journey in Tibesti, Rod and I had dreamed up several grandiose adventures.

"Let's ride camels from one side of the Sahara to the other," I had suggested. "I bet it's never been done before. We could start on the Atlantic coast, traverse the Atlas, and make for the Hoggar. Then we'd cross to Tibesti, and finally end up in the Sudan on the Red Sea." However, time and opportunity dictated that we attempt something more modest, and the Atlas it was to be.

We flew to Gibraltar. While climbing The Rock, apes bombarded us with a fusillade of stones, so we retreated for a meal at Smokey Joe's

Eating House. We slept under the stars on the ferry pier and had two disturbing visits during the night. One was from a dog that took a dislike to Rod, the other from the chief of police, who was investigating reports of vagrants.

Next morning we crossed to Tangier on the ferry and, while still offshore, an exciting waft of the orient reached our nostrils.

An express bus ran down the coast to Rabat and Casablanca; then it turned inland towards Marrakesh. A festival was under way in the Medina, the vast market square in the city centre where an almost exclusively male galaxy of Berbers and other Arabs had congregated. They came from all parts of Morocco to pray in the shadow of the high minaret of the Koutoubya mosque, to discuss world affairs, and to watch displays of acrobats and conjurors. The voice of a muezzin wailed over loudspeakers five times a day at the hours of prayer. Then everyone would face Mecca and touch their foreheads on the ground while murmuing prayers and clicking beads. Men wearing broad-brimmed, tasselled hats circulated the crowd, clanking bells to announce they were selling drinking water, which they poured from skin bags into brass cups.

From the Medina we could see the distant snow-capped Atlas Mountains—a view often painted by Winston Churchill from his hotel balcony. In the old part of the city we wandered round the souk, a narrow warren throbbing with life, where brightly dyed skeins of wool hung to dry. I bargained hard for a silver filigree bracelet, which I eventually bought for a fraction of the asking price.

After a couple of days in Marrakesh, Rod and I packed our rucksacks onto the roof of a decrepit, overloaded bus that headed south towards Asni, a village at the foot of the mountains. There we met the proprietor of the Grand Hotel du Toubkal, a charming Frenchman named André.

"We'd like to climb Toubkal," Rod said. "Then we will cross the range to the Sahara side. Can you please find a muleteer and a mule for us?"

"No problem," said André. He immediately set about issuing orders and making arrangements. That same evening he drove us to Imlil at the head of the valley, where we met Asine, a sturdy Berber tribesman who would be our guide.

Asine unrolled a rush mat and we lay under a vast heaven flashing with stars, awaiting the arrival of Muhamed, the muleteer. On the hillside opposite, lights shone from a fortified kasbah; the plangent sound of voices rising and falling in excited chatter was muffled against the rumble of a stream that flowed beside the village street. On all sides tall mountains rose, deceptively close in the crepuscular light.

An hour passed; we settled into a leisurely Arab timelessness, sipping sweet mint tea as the heat of Moroccan day gave way to freezing Saharan night. After two hours the mule arrived with Muhamed, who reshod it by the light of a carbide lamp. A white molten ball of moon rose from behind a peak above us, flooding the valley with silvery light. We were keen to get started so we persuaded the men to load our baggage into ample pannier baskets set astride the mule. Then we set off into the hills towards a refuge that lay under Toubkal.

The first mile above Imlil our path passed through woodland of twisted pine. As we ambled upwards behind our silent caravan the moon shone through chinks in the foliage, casting mottled patterns on the ground and lighting each figure for a moment before he passed into blackness. Soon the valley widened and we entered the Cirque d'Aronde below Sidi Charamouche. We climbed steadily and the mountains, instead of getting closer, became more distant and vast. At a shepherds' encampment the valley resounded with wild barking of guardian pye-dogs.

After midnight we arrived at the Refuge Likemt. It was locked so we bivouaced on the grass nearby wearing all our spare clothing against a cold wind that blew down the valley. Our teeth chattered. I woke during the night with the hoof of the mule that had loosed its shackle planted near my face. Before sunrise we ate breakfast of hard tack biscuits and sardines and set off for Toubkal with Asine. We instructed Muhamed to cross the pass of Tizi n'Ouanoums with the mule and to meet us later in the day beside the Lac d'Ifni on the far side of the mountain.

A long climb up steep scree and rock brought us to a col lying below the final ridge of Toubkal, whose summit stood above us flanked eastwards by cliffs. It was more a slog than a technical rock climb, but tough nevertheless because neither Rod nor I was as fit as Asine, who set a relentless marathon pace up the mountain. Soon we stood at 13,840 feet— the highest point in North Africa. Rod, despite being in training for the Olympic pentathlon team, became tinged a sallow shade of green; I was panting, headachy, and tired because my only recent exercise had been pounding the wards of St George's Hospital and the occasional game of squash. We were undoubtedly suffering from acute mountain sickness, an as yet undescribed malaise caused by our sudden rise from the plains into the oxygen-thin atmosphere on high. We had recently moved from sea level to 13,000 feet elevation and found that it takes much longer to acclimatize than this rapid ascent allowed. But with the spectacular view laid out before us, we soon forgot our malaise. Ridge after ridge, peak on peak of great mountains stretched north towards the pink plain of Marrakesh that lapped the foothills of the Atlas and tailed away southwards into the arid, rolling brown hills of the Sahara. Somewhere eastwards over that horizon lay Tibesti—Tieroko, and Paradise Wadi— special places that Rod and I had explored together a couple of years previously.

In three hours we descended 5,200 feet to the Lac d'Infni and suddenly felt much better – the specific treatment. There we met Muhamed with the mule waiting beside the deep blue lake, sparkling like a gemstone, nestled in a drab brown volcanic crater. We plunged into the ice-cold water and felt much revived. After a snack we ambled off along a rugged track behind the mule. In late afternoon we descended into a green cultivated valley but, in contrast to Tibesti, there were no palm trees. Man-made leats chanelled water along the hillside to irrigate terraces where grew fruitful crops of maize. A local waterman controlled the sluices that rationed the flow to each farmer.

All was verdant compared with the barren brown rock that rose above the leat-line. Women with children on their backs picked peaches; boys climbed walnut trees and beat the branches with long poles to dislodge the nuts; barefoot children fed the cattle with leaves from the beaten trees. Stronghold kasbahs, built on the hillsides down the length of the valley, housed up to twenty families living together along with their livestock.

Towards late afternoon we reached a kasbah where Muhamed, without explanation, disappeared inside leaving Asine, Rod, and me picking blackberries in a streambed. Muhamed returned and signalled us to follow him. The local Berber headman had been forewarned of our arrival and welcomed us into his kasbah. He was a kindly, jovial old man with a scraggy beard and a shaven head. We entered through the cattle stalls on the ground floor, climbed a dark winding staircase, and reached a roofed open gallery well above ground level. Off this led another room, the heavy walnut door of which bore a brass hand-knocker. The kasbah was built of several galleries, one above the other, the roof of one forming the floor of the one above. Stone walls were plastered with brown mud, and the only ornament was a white surround to the windows.

We took off our shoes and passed through a heavy walnut door studded with polished metal bolts and a brass knocker into a small room where a beam of light shone through one small ornate wrought iron window, grilled and half-shuttered.

"*Solo malekum*," he greeted.

"*Ali kumah solo*," we responded.

"*Labas, Labas, Labas*," he said shaking our hands. He touched his lips with his forefinger and conferred blessings all round. We sat down in a circle on a large purple-and-scarlet carpet, reclining against bolsters covered with light blue silk. I could just discern a bilious green-and-white picture of the Sultan of Morocco, one hand resting paternally on a beggar's head, the other raised heavenward receiving a gift from an angel pendant in midair. The sun set fast and darkness crept up the valley leaving only the tops of the high mountains tinged with its last glow. The light of flames flickered from open galleries of kasbahs across the valley.

The headman's brother, a Berber wearing a brown djellabah, brought in an ornate silver tea tray mounted on four legs and bearing three silver boxes—one for mint, one for tea, one for sugar. Another family member produced a pottery urn made of baked earth that held a charcoal fire over which he placed a copper kettle. When the water boiled our host poured it onto a ladleful of tea in a teapot; he added a handful of mint after smacking it against the back of his hand to bruise the leaves; next he added sugar scraped from a conical block. The teapot then replaced the kettle on the heater and brewed for some minutes.

He poured a glassful of tea, tasted it with loud sucking noises and, as the brew evidently did not meet his approval, returned it to the teapot with a deft flick of the wrist. He added more sugar and repeated the tasting. Finally, when satisfactory, he poured out a glass for each of the men present. They slurped, grunted approval, and belched. The whole tea party took more than an hour and was a prelude to the main meal of mutton, chicken, gravy, and potatoes. After an hour some women brought an enormous platter of couscous. They hovered and flitted around in the penumbra refilling cups of tea.

"*Bouffe, bouffe*," commanded the headman. (Eat, eat.)

The men tucked in, tearing a chicken limb from limb and making balls of couscous in the palms of their hands. Afterwards, they wiped their hands on their trousers. Finally we cracked walnuts and almonds between two stones, drank some more tea, and sank back replete against some cushions. Rod puffed contentedly at his pipe, a tiny red glow against the starlit heaven. I reflected how lucky I was to be in this place so far removed from Hyde Park Corner.

When the sun rose illuminating the other side of the valley, Asine was still asleep wrapped in a large army greatcoat, with Rod's balaclava pulled down over his face, only his nose and moustache showing. Cocks crowed, cattle lowed, and figures—mostly women—busied themselves with the new day.

After breakfast of milk, coffee, flat unleavened bread and butter, we took leave of our host. But first the mule had to be re-shod as it had lost a shoe on the rocky terrain of yesterday. We departed as sunlight flooded the valley floor and walked down to a watersmeet at Amsouzert. Then we struck up another valley. By contrast with our climb of Toubkal, it was a lazy, relaxing day sauntering behind the mule and admiring the verdant scenery. We ground our way up a mule track to Tizi n'Ourai at 9,000 feet, from where we had fine views of Toubkal. It seemed we were a lifetime away from civilization. On the far side we descended to a long valley where small brown trout were plentiful in the pools.

\* \* \*

For seven days we walked behind the mule, crossing rough stony passes that skirted the Oukaimeden mountain massif. Streambeds, ravines, pastures, and steep terraced slopes varied the barren scenery. In springtime when the mountains are snow-covered, the country must seem much less desolate. In each valley floor where water ran, a kasbah stood surrounded by a green oasis. Figs, walnuts, maize, and blackberries abounded. Farmers working in the fields invited us into their houses and entertained us with lavish hospitality.

On top of Tizi n' Likemt, we saw Toubkal covered in storm clouds of squally evil vapours that rolled up from the Sahara. We hurried down to the Ikiss valley where a cloudburst sent us scampering for shelter in a cattle barn. Rod and I had spent a week wandering through the heart of the Atlas, alone except for the company of Asine and Muhamed (and the mule) and our Berber hosts. It was as far removed from our normal lives as we could imagine. We had done it with simplicity—no fuss, little organization. We were exploring at a most fundamental and enjoyable level, and taking time to renew our friendship.

That same evening we returned to Asni. The clouds rolled away leaving a cotton-wool streamer sticking to the summit of Aksqual above us, like the snow plume that blows off Everest before the monsoon. Puffs of high cumulus scudded off in the high wind, making an ever-changing pattern across the sky. The sun cast its waning rays onto the clouds, which glowed and then grew pink as evening fell on the tranquil world of High Barbary.

# FIFTEEN

WITH THE MOVE TO LONDON, my climbing friends were scattered widely and the close camaraderie of the Cambridge University Mountaineering Club no longer held us together. When I did manage to snatch a free weekend, I would extract George Fraser from his engineering job and drive maniacally up the old A5 road to Derbyshire gritstone or to Wales. However, I found myself out of practice, unfit, and unable to do climbs I used to find easy in my Cambridge years when I spent so much leisure time on rock. Somehow the magic had gone, and with the lack of confidence, I lost the ecstatic pleasure of standing on small toeholds looking down between my feet at the valley far below.

Ted Maden migrated south of the River Thames to King's College Hospital in the backwoods of Camberwell. Along with him went Edward Platts, who regarded all climbers as social retards and never hesitated to let us know it. John Longland's heart had never been truly committed to medicine so, after his successful Pumasillo expedition, he remained for some time in South America. Eventually he joined the ranks of Lever Brothers selling soap, which seemed to us a retrograde step. Bill Norton entered the Foreign Service and was posted to Beirut to learn Arabic. Jo Scarr organized a successful all-women expedition to the Himalayas and wrote a book about it.

I gradually lost touch with Bill Turrall. At Cambridge he had switched from reading classics to theology, and became more and more caught up in evangelical religion. In order to give himself time to sort out his confusions—especially his own sexuality—and to plan his future, he went back to Eskdale to instruct at the Outward Bound Mountain School. At that time John Lagoe had taken over as warden from Eric Shipton, who left under the cloud of marital musical chairs that resulted in a broken marriage.

Bill then went to Bradford to work in industry. In his spare time he took apprentices climbing and hiking over the Yorkshire Moors. I spent one happy weekend with him in Wales when he came to help me lead an outing of an outdoors club, the Edward Wilson Group, that I had just started at St George's. It was named after the doctor on Scott's last expedition, an alumnus of the hospital. We took a dozen medical students to Ynws Etwys, the Climbers' Club hut in the Llanberis Valley. Teaching novices let me repay some of the benefits I had gleaned at university from so many excellent climbers. The weekend rekindled my dampened enthusiasm for climbing.

Harold Siddons, the senior chest surgeon at St George's, accompanied our group. Bill and I were leading parallel routes up Crib Goch, and through the mists I heard Bill's voice, "Put your foot on that knobule, Sid. Then step up." Sid was very relaxed with students, and Bill's naïve informality was a far cry from the hierarchy of London teaching hospitals.

Bill gained a place at Ridley Hall, a theological college in Cambridge, with the aim of becoming a priest. However, he was unable to accept some of the doctrines of the Church of England—for him the issues were too big for compromise. As Ted Maden said of him later ". . . some measure of compromise was necessary for survival in the real world." Bill just didn't have it.

Because Bill could not make concessions and steer a middle course, he left Ridley Hall without taking holy orders and returned to work in industry in the Midlands. I almost lost touch with him at that time. He became a recluse and no longer answered letters, and severed contact with his friends. I should have recognized that these were the signs of a deep depression into which he was slipping. Although I suspected he was very unhappy and lonely, I was too far away from him to be of much help.

Bill's favourite poem was Gerard Manley Hopkins's *The Windhover*. I learned it by heart, and grew to love its magical onomatopaeic sound of the words: "I caught this morning morning's minion, kingdom of daylight's dauphin, dapple-dawn-drawn Falcon in his riding . . ." I was studying calligraphy in an evening class taught by Ann Camp at the Holborn School of Art and wrote out *The Windhover*, illuminated the manuscript with gold leaf, and drew a falcon hovering at the top of the page. I sent it to Bill and received back a very grateful letter, which seemed to retie the bond of our friendship.

I was quite unaware of the internal struggle that he then fought, attempting to sublimate in religion the jarring social and sexual conflicts that were slowly tearing him apart. During all our friendship I had barely realized he was homosexual. He had no close girlfriends, but he always related comfortably with the women students in the Magogs climbing club. Our own friendship was always intense, founded on our common passion for climbing. I had no intimation in Bill of any homosexual attraction towards myself or any of his other friends, of which I would have been well aware after spending my adolescence at Charterhouse. His sexual ambivalence is nevertheless amply evident in hindsight.

In a cataclysmic gesture of despair, in July 1963 Bill threw himself in front of a train at a suburban railway station—a violent final solution for so gentle a man. One can only imagine the depths of despair to which he must have sunk to be so overwhelmed that he would carry through with such a tragic scream for help and understanding. At twenty-nine he had barely begun to realize his potential. Those of us who loved him, and there were many, were devastated by his death and wracked with remorse for not noticing his problem of sexual identity and his slide into melancholy from which we might, had we known, have tried to extricate him.

* * *

Back in London my colleague Peter Richards and I produced in the first year of the Edward Wilson Group a full slate of lecturers—Wilfred Thesiger on "Arabian Sands;" Wilfrid Noyce on "Climbing in the Karakoram Himalaya;" Dennis Kemp on "Caving in Somerset and South Wales;" and Kevin Walton, one of Sir Vivian Fuchs' team, on "The Crossing of Antarctica."

I was elected to the Alpine Club whereby I kept in touch with other climbers. Lecture meetings were held on Tuesday evenings in its hallowed premises at 74 South Audley Street behind the Grosvenor Hotel on Park Lane. The formal setting was antithetic to my customary casual attitude to climbers and climbing. Long leather-covered benches flanking the walls of the lecture hall were kept for the attending throng of ancient alpine greats. At the mention of Everest, George Finch would jump up and turn the discussion to oxygen, once his speciality, now fifty years out-of-date. Howard Somervell blinked modestly as he recounted doing a dozen major abdominal operations a day in South India: "Billroth (the pioneer of gastrectomy for cancer of the stomach) told me I was the only person he'd ever met who had done more gastric surgery than himself." Odell, erect as a guardsman, urbane as a diplomat, always had some tale to tell of pre-war Everest expeditions. Eric Shipton's blue eyes, shielded by bushy overhanging eyebrows, stared as though surveying some distant range. John Hunt, a soldier-mountaineer used to rubbing shoulders with royalty since the climbing of Everest, seemed quite a youngster by comparison with such doyens. These men were the stuff that history books are made of, and yet in the warm environs of The Alpine Club they seemed pleasant, normal people, driven by a shared love of mountains.

Women were not yet welcome except on certain assigned nights.

\* \* \*

As we delved more deeply into our clinical studies I spent more and more time at the country branch of St George's Hospital, formerly the Tooting Grove Fever Hospital. I had done only marginally well so far and was in danger of the boot from the dean of the medical school unless I abrogated my obsession for mountains and turned my attention fully to medicine. The final straw was when I produced an appalling mid-term bacteriology exam paper. I was summoned by Professor Elek, a Hungarian refugee, squat and Pickwickian, who spoke with a thick accent. I could not distinguish the specifics of his tirade, only the general tone, which was hostile towards my ignorance of Staphylococcus pyogenes, the microbe closest to his heart.

I admit to a lifelong aversion to microscopes. I never understood the fascination of the miniature world I could see only by thirty-fold magnification; even amoebae and protozoa had failed to enthrall me at school. Professor Elek also knew my uncle, Charles Lack, a fellow bacteriologist. "Your uncle would not be pleased with you," he said in his deep guttural voice.

Thereupon I decided to do something radical to correct my poor image. I chose to move to Tooting where I was due to spend the next six months of clinical apprenticeship at The Grove Hospital. I hoped thereby to impress the Dean that I really meant to turn a new leaf, and incidentally to avoid the lure, and attendant distractions, of a newly-met nurse.

All the Cleveland Square residents were getting more involved in clinical work and living in, or near, their respective hospitals. So we decided, with great sadness, to close down the harmonious partnership and hand over the lease to a group of Cambridge friends from the year below us. Bob Thomson stayed on as the landlord, and Edie kept coming to clean the flat.

Edie was thin, but she began to lose weight and the hollows became more prominent in her wrinkled, weather-beaten cheeks. Eventually she had an operation that showed an inoperable cancer of the bowel. Over the next weeks we took turns to visit her in her tiny basement flat in Chelsea. Then she entered St Joseph's Hospice, Bethnal Green, where she received the ultimate in dedicated care. She remained cheerful, poking fun at one or another of us who was absent, and always talked of returning when she was better, so that she could put us to bed "if anyone got drunk." Soon she died, leaving no relatives or friends, so we decided that as many of us as possible should attend her funeral.

Six of us arrived at the Hospice in our best suits and Mother Superior gave each of us a cup of tea.

"Don't be surprised, boys," she said. "It may not be quite the sort of funeral you expect; Edie was a pauper, d'you understand?"

While we were trying to figure out what she meant, a man wearing a huge black overcoat came in.

"You the mourners?" he grunted. We looked at each other for reassurance, and nodded. "Follow me then, gentlemen," he said, leading the way to an ancient Rolls Royce. We climbed in and drove behind the hearse that was a plain black delivery van with a gold cross painted on the side. Our cortege wound a timeless course through the suburbs of north London and eventually arrived at last at the gates of a cemetery set in flat open marshland, where gasometers and canals broke up the empty spaces.

The van stopped at a gatehouse lodge. A small, white-haired man bustled out pulling a creased and grubby surplice over a cassock, blue-green with age, below which showed mud-stained trouser turn-ups. The undertaker passed him a slip of paper.

"One-three-seven. Yes. Follow me." He set off at speed towards a chapel surrounded by conifers as dark as the glass in its narrow pointed windows. We all got out of our car and walked up an avenue of leafless trees under a grey sky. We kicked the dead leaves to allay our disquiet. A chill wind blew across empty marshes that stretched away beyond iron railings.

The chapel doors were loose on their hinges and patched with corrugated iron; as they creaked open, a waft of stale air met us. The tiled walls inside were a dirty cream colour, and the only light a single bulb. The undertakers placed Edie's plain wooden coffin on a pair of trestles in front of some chairs. The parson hurried up the pulpit steps and peered at us over his spectacles. He opened a prayer book, the pages of which were loose from frequent thumbing, and began to read in a monotone that sounded like a worn-down gramophone record. Simultaneously we were struck with hysteria at this ridiculous charade; tears flooded our eyes and we bit our tongues to stop us laughing out loud. The parson, thinking we were racked with grief, doubled his oratory, exhorting us to courage and faith in the Hereafter.

His platitudes over, the coffin was wheeled on a trolley down a path between graves decorated with plastic flowers in marble jars on green granite chippings. A small graveyard was set apart behind a privet hedge that separated the main cemetery from a gardener's tool store and a compost heap. We gathered round a long trench and the sexton lowered the coffin into it. After a mumbled blessing the parson sprinkled a thin layer of soil into the grave that was now ready for another pauper.

"Thank you for coming," said the parson, shaking his head. He gave us a pamphlet advertising a local monumental mason and extended a hand. We shook it in turn; three fingers were missing. He pulled a cloak round his shoulders and hurried off down the path.

As we reached the gate lodge, two more large black cars drew up. In the lodge a newspaper fell; the surplice was lifted off its hook. We drove off into thickening fog believing that Edie would have laughed, too.

*  *  *

To reach The Grove Hospital one crossed the River Thames by Battersea Bridge, skirted Clapham Common, followed Balham High Road which led into Tooting Broadway, the very heartland of that jungle of South London that some denizens never leave in a lifetime. It has a cockney flavour all its own, despite being well beyond earshot of Bow bells, and a social structure poles apart from my own privileged upbringing.

I went down to Tooting on a reconnaissance for somewhere to live. On the corner of Garratt Lane and Fountain Road, which led to The Grove, stood The Fountain, a tall, red brick, Victorian pub. Just at opening time I pushed open the engraved glass swing doors of the public bar.

"Do you know anywhere I can find lodging around here?" I asked the publican, who was drying beer glasses with a damp dishcloth. "I need a place to stay for a few months."

"Hey, Molly," he called to a buxom woman who was on her knees scrubbing the floor, piano-shaped legs projecting from under her skirt. "This gent wants a place to stay. Would yer mum 'elp 'im out?"

"Try Number 39," said Molly, scrubbing circles of bubbly soap with her bristle brush so the tiles gleamed. "Out the door; turn left. 'Er name's Mrs Lucas. Everybody calls 'er Gran."

I thanked them and walked down Fountain Road, flanked by identical, two-up-two-down, slate-roofed terrace houses. Such as these were home to millions of working class families in Britain before bland, featureless estates of council houses usurped the low-cost housing market. In front of each house was a pocket-handkerchief-sized patch of grass just big enough for the neighbourhood dogs to foul.

Sitting on the low wall of Number 39 was a man with a bald pate, rimmed with a silvery tonsure that shone like the dome of St Paul's Cathedral. One of his legs was stretched out and a pair of crutches leaned against the wall of the house. His other trouser leg was folded back just below the thigh and held in place with three safety pins because the lower leg was missing.

"You must 'ave come from The Fountain," he said.

Having taken less than four minutes to walk from the pub, I realized that Tooting had a fast bush telegraph. Pop, as he was known, stuck his thumbs under his braces that overlay a rough and prickly undershirt with buttons at the neck. He hitched up his leg and rearranged it on the wall for comfort.

"Lorst it at the Somme," he said. "But I got medals from the king to show for it. They're in a glass case in the parlour. Go inside an' 'ave a look. Gran's expectin' yer."

Gran Lucas looked me up and down, wiping her soapsud-wrinkled hands on her floral pinafore. Her stockings hung crinkled round her ankles, she was hunched over with age, and her grey hair was tied in a bun.

"Come on in," she said. "I'll show yer the room upstairs. It'll cost yer three quid a week with breakfast and dinner. And I'll do yer laundry."

The room was tiny. Against the wall stood a single bed, so narrow it put to rest any lustful ideas of entertaining in it. A thin, guillotine window looked out over a small park and playground where some kids on swings were howling abuse at each other in Tooting dialect, as strange as any foreign language. In front of the window stood a card-table desk under which I could just fit my knees when sitting on the rickety wicker-seated chair. This hermit's cell was ideal for a period of retreat from worldly diversions and for meditation on the texts of clinical medicine *Gray' Anatomy* and the "pale, bulky and offensive" tome of Bailey & Love's *A Short Practice of Surgery* could stand on the mantelpiece over an empty fireplace that was stuffed with newspaper to keep out the draught.

I intended to seclude myself here for the months before my rapidly approaching Finals, the thought of which caused my knees to wobble and a damp patch to appear in my crotch. Besides, it was a deal at three pounds a week all found, so I accepted it without hesitation.

From that moment I became the adopted son of the household and, moreover, of the entire street. For the first few days the kitchen was never empty of visitors who came to inspect this toff, wondering what he was doing settling into their community.

"You gonna be a doctor?" asked Tommy, a scrawny teenage nephew who came to inspect me. "Gawd, yer must be brainy."

I hated to disabuse him of this idea, and to tell him that I was in this suburban wilderness for voluntary monasticism. Indeed, this Tooting enclave was to prove as tight-knit, parochial, yet fiercely loyal a community as I have ever lived in.

Pop was the sage and guardian of the street. Passers-by would call out, "Mornin', Pop." Some would stop to exchange news. Each morning he would see me off with a cheery, "Take care, lad," as though I might be waylaid on route to The Grove Hospital.

The Grove was down the street and turn left past the high blue iron gates of the Fountain Hospital that was the regional centre for mentally defective children, a veritable zoo of human misery that we visited during our paediatric course. Children drooled in corners of the barrack wards, rocked to and fro, smeared faeces on the walls, and grunted unintelligibly at the battalion of dedicated nurses who strove to nurture any glimmer of humanity in their imbecile charges. This visit left me haunted with nightmares.

Across the road stood The Grove, an old fever hospital that had almost become redundant since the advent of antibiotics. Block upon block of prison-like buildings were set widely apart and spread across expansive grounds, unlike the crowded precincts of Hyde Park Corner. The wards were linked by long corridors and built on brick footings three or four feet off the ground on the premise that bugs could not jump that high. Across the road, in view of and a constant reminder to patients, was a vast acreage of the Lambeth Cemetery, a marble jungle of headstones, vaults surmounted by winged angels, and graves splashed with year-round colour from plastic flowers.

I set myself a program of diligent study to make up for time frittered away so pleasantly in Glencoe, on Mont Blanc, or in the Pyrenees. Since Tooting offered a wide range of physical signs, I tried to examine as many patients as I could in order to become familiar with a wide spectrum of clinical conditions.

Each evening when I returned to 39 Fountain Road, barring a downpour, Pop would be sitting on the wall to greet me.

"Ow's them bodies, lad?" he would ask, expecting some ghoulish tale. However, at peril of failing morbid anatomy and pathology, I avoided the mortuary because the stench was appalling and the sights grizzly. "When I were in t' Somme there were bodies and mud and blood everywhere. Stank, it did."

Pop hitched up his amputation stump and adjusted his trouser leg. His accounts of the trenches became lavish with an audience, so I hurried indoors because the boiled vegetables Gran had ready for my dinner needed a settled stomach. She was always "busy as a hedgehog," just like Mrs Tiggy-Winkle, and she looked after me like a mother.

"Evening, Gran, what's for supper?" I would ask rhetorically. I usually ate by myself since she and Pop had already partaken of high tea by the time I returned from the hospital. The plastic tablecloth was decorated with garish printed flowers. I sat down to an unchanging menu of roast beef, boiled potatoes, boiled cabbage alternating with boiled peas—boiled everything. The kitchen always had a musty, boarding school smell of dirty socks. Gran hovered over me wearing her pinafore like a second dress that she never removed except when eating. As part of our deal, she also laundered my clothes in a little lean-to shed attached to the porch, which occupied half of the back garden that was not much bigger than the front.

* * *

On some weekends I was able to escape from London to my brother's farm in Sussex. After he finished an apprenticeship with some successful local farmers, the Renwicks, my brother bought a small farm at Codmore Hill just north of Pulborough. The three-hundred-year-old farmhouse was built of mellow grey sandstone encrusted with lichen and moss. Barns and outbuildings were surrounded by fields, copses, and the River Arun. Across the horizon stretched the South Downs where I sometimes walked along undulating cart tracks. The stone for the house was quarried from the farm grounds leaving a hollow with steep walls where I explored several short climbs, a pale imitation of real rock climbing. Wilfrid Noyce came over from Charterhouse to try them out for his regional climbing guidebook.

I wandered in a prolific bluebell wood, a most romantic place in which to gather armfuls of bluebells while doing some mild courting. I was still impressed with the virtues of virginity acquired through my flirtation with evangelical Christianity and reinforced by my promise of a telegram to Peter Barbor, so I passed up many a chance of rapture in those bluebell woods. The birth control pill had only just become available, and many women could not tolerate it because of side effects, so fear of pregnancy was still the driving force in keeping girls virtuous. French Letters we considered were unpleasant things designed to stop the fun and for sailors to wear as prophylactics, not as a sensible form of birth control.

My brother got married to Jane, who became a lynchpin in our ever-shaky relationship and thereafter he tolerated me more agreeably than before. He was always jealous of me—on what account I know not—perhaps because I was younger and more carefree. He took our parents' deaths even more harshly that I did; in fact, it remained throughout his adult life a millstone that he never came to terms with. However, he was extremely popular, jovial and funny with his farming and cricketing friends, a side of him I never saw as he was always the bossy older brother when we were together alone.

\* \* \*

As part of our clinical course we had to do a one-month firm in psychiatry, neurology, and neurosurgery at the Atkinson Morley Hospital in Wimbledon, the regional head injury centre for South England. For a month Joe Boerema, Robin Sellwood, and I moved into student quarters located in a wing of the nurses' residence. Joe's father was an eminent surgeon in Holland and I never quite understood why he chose small St George's for his medical school. But, like the rest of us, once there he was so happy he wouldn't have changed.

Robin I knew by sight at Cambridge as a small, fair-haired dreamer. He bought shares in a barge moored on a muddy eddy of the Thames at Chelsea Wharf just opposite some posh houses on Cheyne Walk. To reach his barge you picked a course through geranium pots and bicycles across several neighbouring decks. The belly of the barge was spacious but so low I had to remain stooped. Musty damp air caused fine mould to grow on anything that stood too long in one place. Robin shared this dwelling with a variable number of art students; it befitted their bohemian lifestyle.

Daily we went up to the hospital for teaching rounds. A corridor ran the length of the building; right for the neurosurgical wards where Wylie McKissock was king; left for the rest. It was a place of high drama, with patients arriving by helicopter from all over the south of England suffering from subarachnoid haemorrhage or other intracranial trauma. They were rushed into surgery where McKissock clipped the offending blood vessels and, as soon as they could open their eyes, discharged them back to their referring hospital in order to make room for the next serious head injury. Some never did open them and remained in a coma for weeks. While there we admitted Kwaku Hudson, a Nigerian house surgeon at St George's, who was in a car accident. He spent six weeks in a coma from which he suddenly emerged, happily with no residual effects.

Between our quarters and the hospital was a riding school compound run by "The Major." Joe, Robin, and I signed up for lessons, none of us having ridden a horse before. We made such progress that we became the pride of The Major. However, we were the despair of Mr McKissock, who looked out of the window from his wards and saw his students cantering round the jumps instead of studying.

The psychiatry wards were on the upper floor of the hospital. Aversion therapy was then being used to treat alcoholics. The patient was left in a dimly lit room surrounded by his own cigarette butts in overflowing ashtrays, and empty bottles of unlimited booze he had drunk. The theory was that at some time the patient would become so disgusted that he would want to give up drink, and the memory of his experience would avert him from ever wanting to return to it. The acrid smell of stale beer and stale cigarette smoke was unforgettable. A pallid creature lay on a mattress on the floor surrounded by pails of vomit. The success of treatment in that Hogarthian hell-hole was dubious, and aversion therapy is no longer used.

Another spooky new experience for me was seeing hypnosis used clinically. One psychiatrist was skilled at putting suggestible people into a trance. He hypnotized one patient and made her revert to earlier stages in her life. For instance, when told she was a three-year-old, she talked and acted like a child of three. The psychiatrist then took her up through various ages and repeated commands, so the patient behaved and talked appropriate to that age.

The psychiatrist used post-hypnotic suggestion with a different patient. When under hypnosis he was told that five minutes after being awakened he would climb on the table and sing "I'm the King of the Castle." Exactly five minutes after awakening, he started fidgeting and became embarrassed. Then he said "Excuse me," climbed on the table, and sung the song. We were reassured that it was not possible to suggest a criminal action uncharacteristic of the person.

While we were at the Atkinson Morley Hospital we visited some of the vast and gloomy mental hospitals that lie in a ring around Epsom, several communities of a thousand or more shut-aways with bizarre mental conditions who were never likely to return to normal society.

* * *

After my sojourn at Wimbledon I returned to Tooting and continued my studies with diligence. Then one day Pop took a stroke and died. He was laid out in a shiny oak coffin in the front parlour. An undertaker did an artistic make-up job to give Pop's cheeks a ruddy glow, and his silvery hair a fresh sheen. Beside him stood the glass case that held his medals, and some empty .303-cartridge shells from a Lee Enfield he used at the Front before his leg was shot off. Nearby were some porcelain mugs inscribed "Torquay" where he and Gran had spent their only far-away holiday.

"'E looks so peaceful," said Gran in the parlour where she led me in order to admire Pop. "I so likes 'im in 'is suit. 'E never would wear it for me, not even on a Sunday. Dearie me, I'll miss 'im so." She lifted up her pinny, which she still wore over her black widow's dress, and wiped tears from her eyes.

Even more than before, the house became the focus for the Lucas clan as they joined the ongoing wake. The ladies lamented over tea; their menfolk and assorted hangers-on consoled themselves with ale brought by Molly in crates from The Fountain. Meanwhile children made merry playing tag around the coffin, knocking over wreaths and flowers in their chase. The coffin lid was slid towards Pop's foot, and empty teacups and beer bottles lay on it once there was no more space on the mantelpiece and sideboards. As I passed the parlour door and headed for my room, I glimpsed the halo of Pop's tonsure and thought how piratical he had looked in life, now so seraphic in death.

Gran assuaged her grief by cooking endless meals for seemingly half of Tooting who gathered for one of the best free parties of the year. Daytime activity made the house convivial, but this gave way to night-time quiet and the gloom of Gran nursing her sorrow and the happiness of a half-century of togetherness.

I found the propinquity of Pop downstairs in his coffin too spooky so I moved back to Cleveland Square, as a guest, until the funeral was over. However, my time at Tooting was drawing in and I had to return to St George's, Hyde Park Corner, for the run-up to finals. The clock was ticking and all of us were working hard towards the climax of our past six years of study.

* * *

The relentless grind of book study in the medical school library was

interrupted by a two-week clerkship in forensic medicine, an obligatory ingredient of our clinical course. Nevertheless it was an unlikely
source of one of its most entertaining chapters. Dr Donald Teare, the
senior morbid anatomist and pathologist at St George's, was also one of
three forensic pathologists for the inner London metropolitan area. His
job entailed visiting certain mortuaries in the southeast part of the city
to perform autopsies in suspected criminal deaths. He would then give
evidence at the Old Bailey, London's Central Criminal Court. He shared
this beat with Dr Keith Simpson of Guy's, and Dr Francis Camps, whose
morbid lecture at Cambridge three years previously had left such a mark
on me. Now Keith Simpson came to lecture at St George's with a similar warped sense of humour and morbid amusement in his job.

So when the two-week forensic medicine firm rolled around I was
not enthusiastic. One Friday afternoon Peter Richards, Paul Millac, and
I went down to the hospital morgue to get our instructions for meeting the boss the following week. Donald Teare was mellower than his
two braggadocio colleagues. Short and stocky, he had tightly crimped
grey hair and a plethoric face. Over the top of horn-rimmed half-glasses
he fixed us with eyes that squinted in different directions—one at the
corpse, the other at the clock.

"Meet on the front steps of the hospital at eight on Monday," he
said. "John will be there to pick you up."

At the appointed time we stood surveying rush-hour traffic as it
wove a wiggly course round the Artillery Monument. It was an autumnal morning with tree leaves changing to gold in Hyde Park across from
the Duke of Wellington's Gate. A shiny black Bentley drew up and a
uniformed chauffeur rolled down the window.

"'Op in," he called. "The boss is down at 'ammersmith. 'E goes
there straight from 'is 'ome in Wimbledon. We'd better get a move on
or 'e'll be finished before we get there. The doctor don't waste no time."

John whisked us through the traffic as we sat back in unaccustomed lordly state. Peter and Paul had both been up at Cambridge with me, but each was at a different college. They were comforting companions with whom to be embarking on this new adventure. We had become firm friends since starting at St George's, where Peter's father had been a student before him. Paul and I had ended up in this easy-going, somewhat chaotic, little-league medical school by chance. Our common adversity of trying to glean an education bound us closely.

Hammersmith Mortuary is tucked behind the Broadway. A police constable opened big wooden gates that led into a narrow yard where John parked the Bentley between a police car and a hearse. In the morgue Donald Teare was already up to his elbows in work under floodlights suspended from the ceiling. Usually he dressed in a dark pinstriped morning suit, but at work he shed his jacket and shiny black leather shoes and donned a rubber apron that reached to the floor. He wore elbow-length rubber gloves below rolled-up sleeves, and a pair of knee-high Wellington boots.

The morgue had an odour of disinfectant, quite different from the formalin smell of the dissecting room in Cambridge. To save his boss's skilled time, Donald Teare's attendant was preparing another body on an adjacent porcelain slab, below which a channel led blood and the washings of a garden hose towards a central runaway drain.

"Come in, boys," Donald Teare said. "I had to get stated. We've to be at the Old Bailey at noon."

I tried to absorb our bizarre surroundings. "This one was murdered over the weekend," He continued, delving into the entrails. "Officer, please tell the boys the details."

A plain-clothes policeman whispered from the corner of his mouth, either out of sleuthly habit or because of a palsy. He recounted the tale of the lady on the slab, who had been found in the early hours of Sunday

morning half-dressed in an alley behind the Palais de Danse. This macabre tale set the tone for the next fortnight.

Donald Teare's skill was as impressive as any surgeon we had spent
so many weeks watching sycophantically in the St George's operating
theatres—not for nothing are they so called. After making a long inci-
sion to expose the vault of the skull, he pulled the scalp hair down over
the eyes like a mask. Then he sawed open the skull to display intact
brain. Finally he opened the body from neck to pubis so that all the contents were accessible. He could disembowel a belly with a few slices of
his long, razor-sharp pathologist's knife. He flopped liver and kidneys,
heart and lungs, onto a weigh scale that stood on a table over the body.
Then he cut them into sandwich-thin slices in order to inspect the tissue
minutely for tell-tale pathological changes. Every skin bruise had to be
accounted for. Entry and exit sites of knife and bullet wounds told him a
story that would appeal to the logical mind of Sherlock Holmes.

While he dissected, Donald Teare dictated a report of his findings
into a microphone hanging from the ceiling. The on/off switch cord was
greasy from his gloves. A police officer assigned to the case was present to supply details for compiling evidence; a photographer clicked
away in the background, seemingly quite unmoved by the drama. Even
though we had attended many post-mortems in the hospital as part of
our pathology course, the atmosphere here was quite different.

"So, boys," he said at his last deft slice. "Off to court."

We hustled out of the morgue and into the Bentley. The real world of
living people thronged the pavements as we sped past. On arrival at the
Old Bailey, police with great deference ushered Donald Teare straight
into court in order not to waste a minute of his time. We were shown
to seats beside the assembled lawyers. In the witness box Donald Teare
was brief, to the point, and expressionless. He read his report, occasionally glancing over the top of his glasses at bewigged barristers and at the

judge, but because of his squint it was impossible to tell who was getting his signals. He crisply answered the cross-examinations of counsel, gathered up his untidy bundle of papers and, after a deferential bow to the dais, swept out of the court with a flurry of policemen and janitors opening doors for him. As part of his entourage we hurried along close in his wake. The elaborate protocol suited him and he appeared quietly to enjoy the theatre of it all.

We spent our two-week apprenticeship to Donald Teare going from one lavatory-tiled, privet-hedged morgue to another, skimming round back streets of London in his black Bentley, and having beer and sandwiches with our boss at dockland pubs overlooking the River Thames. Drama was ever round the corner. The infamous Podola murder of two police officers happened during our firm and we knew all the details long before they appeared in the headlines of the *Evening Standard* that we bought on the steps of St George's on our way home. We declined Donald Teare's offer to accompany him to Wormwood Scrubs to witness the mandatory post-mortem on a hanged murderer.

Donald Teare was a gentle man, an artist with a long-bladed carving knife, and one of our best teachers; his wife, a gracious, motherly lady, was a children's magistrate in South London. "If you think some of my work is bizarre," he said on the last day of the firm, "you should hear some of my wife's stories. They're far worse."

Life was mundane on returning to hospital life after our fortnight in the clouds and among the morgues of South London.

# SIXTEEN

S INCE MY MEDICAL STUDIES HAD taken on a more clinical and practical aspect, I read several biographies of medical men who inspired me. Albert Schweitzer's *On the Edge of the Primaeval Forest* delighted me when I was very young. Now, rereading it, I imagined myself single-handedly dealing with leprosy and the sleeping sickness tsetse fly at Lambarene on the banks of the Ogowe River in the Congo. While at Cambridge, visits to the Scott Polar Research Institute stimulated my interest in Edward Wilson of the Antarctic. I dreamed that I could become an expedition doctor on some far-off adventure.

Wilfred Grenfell's autobiography *A Labrador Doctor* led me to the International Grenfell Association in Great Peter Street, Westminster where Betty Seabrook, a vivacious middle-aged lady, ran the office. She exuded an infectious enthusiasm that enhanced the magic associated with the names of far-off Newfoundland and Labrador. In the '50s, and still for some time thereafter, staff for the former Grenfell Mission were mostly recruited from Britain. This was partly because, at an outport nursing station, a nurse also needed to be a midwife, a training not then common in Canada. Few Canadian doctors wanted to work in such a remote "hardship" post when big centres down south offered better-paid positions.

The old Grenfell Mission became the International Grenfell Association that was run by a board of governors and financed mainly by the Newfoundland government. The main hospital and centre of operations was at St Anthony, a small fishing town on the northern tip of the finger of Newfoundland that points towards Greenland. Because no road extended far south, patients came by small bush plane, on floats in summer and skis in winter, or by hospital boat, from the fishing outports of northern Newfoundland and the southern coast of Labrador. A smaller hospital at North West River on Hamilton Inlet—which on a map looks like the mouth of the dog that is Labrador—cared for fisher folk and trappers in isolated coastal communities as far north as Nain.

Besides medical work, the Grenfell Association carried over from the old Mission days running handicraft shops, a farm, and dormitories for children from the outlying villages who were attending senior school.

Betty Seabrook casually dropped into her conversation words that were evocative of The Coast (as it was known) like dog team, float plane, Eskimo, Indian, ice-floe, and so on. She sparked my enthusiasm, and I laid plans to work in Newfoundland for a spell soon after I qualified.

At that time overseas job listings occupied a full page towards the back of the British Medical Journal. I always turned there before attempting to read its indigestible academic papers. Those were days when the colonies thrived, albeit breathing their last. Nevertheless, medical officers were still wanted for two-year postings to places such as St Kitts and Nevis islands, the slopes of Mount Kenya, Tristan da Cunha, and the Falkland Islands Dependencies Survey working in Antarctica—all fodder for any adventurous young doctor. It seemed that a short spell in Newfoundland would give me experience of working abroad that would qualify me to apply for one of these exotic destinations.

So I would make occasional visits to Great Peter Street in order to keep in touch with Betty Seabrook. Each time, I came away more determined to go to that wild corner of Canada of which she spoke with such glowing zeal. Meanwhile my dreams of far away places were not getting me any nearer passing my final Cambridge tripos exams, which I needed to qualify as a doctor. Although I was doing my clinical training in London, I still had to take a Cambridge degree. This was a much more serious enterprise than my first degree, when after waiting for three years and paying five pounds I would upgrade my BA to an MA—which could all be done by mail.

\* \* \*

Following the success of our study holidays in the Lake District three years before, I suggested to Andrew Elkington and David Gibson that we do something similar in Ireland. I had learned of a remote Youth Hostel in the hills of Killarney, euphoniously named Macgillycuddy's Reeks, which sounded far enough removed from distraction to allow concentrated study. On arriving in Cork by ferry from Swansea, we went to the bus station.

Eventually the bus rolled out of Cork and wound through verdant country, well watered by constant Irish rain and mist. At Killarney we hired a boatman to row us across Lough Leane. When negotiating the price based on the distance across the lake, the boatman assured Andrew that " . . . an Irish mile is a mile and a bit, and the bit may be as lang again as the mile."

On the far side of the lake we took a pony trap over the Gap (pronounced Yap) of Dunloe, a pass that led across the mountains to the Youth Hostel. It being April, and the place so remote, no one else was staying there so we could spread our books out. We adopted our previous schedule of studying hard all morning and then, after lunch, hiking in the surrounding hills. Both David and Andrew were keen on hiking, so we climbed Carrauntoohill and several smaller neighbouring mountains.

After dinner at the hostel we went down to the local pub that was the parlour of a small stone family home. Dark brown draught Guinness, with an inch head of froth, slipped down easily. David, a natural actor and comic, became adored by the locals whose broad accent he imitated exactly.

During our ten days in Killarney we each achieved a solid core of study so on our return to London we felt refreshed for an ultimate push towards finals.

* * *

In June we had to return to Cambridge for the tripos exams. Shortly before finals I attended the wedding of the sister of a friend who lived in Cambridge. It was one of those posh garden party affairs with a marquee on the lawn, tailcoats, and champagne. I spent much of the afternoon wooing one of the bridesmaids in the rose garden. Finally the guests gathered outside the house to see off the happy couple on their honeymoon.

Beside me, standing on a concrete bicycle pad for a better view, was a girl in a blue polka-dot dress, hazel hair flowing to her shoulders, a startlingly pretty dimpled, smiling face. I introduced myself and asked her name.

"Sarah, with an *h*," she replied. "Sarah Fleming."

"Where do you live?"

"London."

"What work do you do?" Slotting people into their appointed places was typically British.

"I'm a nurse," she replied.

"At which hospital?"

"St. George's."

"You must be a staff nurse?"

"No. I'm first year," she said. "I chose St George's because I thought three years in central London would be fun. I've spent most of my training in the country at Tooting and Wimbledon."

I knew some of the nurses who roamed the hospital, but never before had I met one so pretty.

"I'm driving back to London this evening," I said. "Do you want a ride?"

"Yes, please," she said without hesitating.

Later that afternoon we drove off from Cambridge on an adventure that was, little did we know it then, to last our lifetime. At the Blue Boar transport café I learned about Sarah Fleming. She was born in Cyprus where her father was in the Colonial Service as an education administrator. Her life on the island was always sunny, with picnics at St Hilarion Castle, swimming on the beaches of Kyrenia, bicycling near their home in Nicosia, hiking in the Troodos Mountains, and sporting in the governor's swimming pool. It was wartime and people in Cyprus expected a German invasion, similar to Crete. As a result, many women and children were evacuated from the island leaving their husbands to man the Home Guard. Sarah's mother, Irene Fleming, took her two daughters to South Africa by boat. After two years as evacuees at Mossel Bay on the southern coast, they returned to Cyprus, and enosis—the post-war political division of the island between Greeks and Turks.

Max Fleming was shortly afterwards transferred to Nigeria, where he and Irene reluctantly exchanged the sun, sea, and snow of Cyprus for a humid equatorial climate of Lagos. Sarah returned to bourgeois England. At a very unconventional boarding school in Buckinghamshire, Sarah and her sister, Jean, drove tractors instead of playing hockey, watched the man from the Ministry of Agriculture inseminate the cows, and chased each other with billhooks through fields of rape seed, shouting that name at the tops of their voices. Sarah and Jean went out to Nigeria for one school holiday a year; for another Irene returned to their cottage in Suffolk; and the third, at Christmas, they spent skiing in Switzerland in company with several other families. Sarah became a fearless down-hill racer and gained a place on the British junior girls' team.

After leaving the Farmhouse School—undistinguished academically but strong on friendships—Sarah enrolled in a secretarial course at the Cambridge technical college. With the firm idea that marriage would solve her problem of having to work for a living, she boarded in the house of Dr Bevan, a local physician, whose wife ran a finishing school for rich foreign girls, leavened with a handful of ordinary English girls. Most of the girls attended language courses in between entertaining hulking oarsmen of the university Blue Boat that was coached by Dr Bevan.

Mrs Bevan ran a tight ship. Two rules were strictly enforced: no ladders in stockings, and no kissing boyfriends on the front doorstep. A Spanish princess was asked to leave after the doctor, on returning home with a senior member of the university, was forced to enter by the kitchen door because the girl was entwined with a rowing blue beside the front door.

The secretarial course was less successful than Sarah's social life. Her wise and tolerant mother eventually persuaded her to move to London to follow a nursing training at St George's Hospital, one of the finest nursing schools in the country.

\* \* \*

After a supper of greasy fried eggs and baked beans we drove on to London. In my arrogance I presumed that any girl who could put up with a transport café rather than a posh restaurant was bound to suit me and likely to enjoy rough climbing. In London we parted, Sarah to the nurses' residence in Montpelier Square, and Tooting Grove where she was working; me to my lodgings in Ebury Street. I had just moved into a flat recently vacated by Paul Millac. It was a pleasant room at the top of a slim, south-facing Georgian terrace house into which the sun streamed on clear days. The quiet street lay between Belgravia and Pimlico, a strange social sandwich. The landlady, Miss Garner, a bird-like, genteel lady, adored Paul; I was a pale comparison.

Despite the urgency of my studies, I just couldn't get Sarah Fleming out of my mind. While I was in Tooting for a teaching round I bumped into her under one of the covered arches that protected patients who were being wheeled on trolleys between wards. She was dressed in uniform with starched white apron and cap. She blushed to the roots of her hair, and I dithered, shifting from foot to foot.

Rod Tuck had invited me to a Royal Marine ball at the commando training depot in Deal, but originally I was not particularly keen, having no special partner.

"Would you come to a Royal Marine ball with me next weekend?" I asked Sarah. "It's in Deal on the south coast."

"I'd love to if I can get time off," Sarah said. "I'll find out today. How can I let you know?"

I gave her my telephone number. She got leave, and we drove down to Deal the next Friday afternoon. The ball was a colourful affair, with Royal Marine officers in scarlet monkey jackets, Royal Navy officers in white, and a few civilians in black dinner jackets. Sarah was radiant in a new dress. The big question was where to stay, since I had an aversion to hotels of any sort because of my addiction to climbing huts. I had brought my Meade mountain tent in the trunk of my car. Sarah seemed quite unabashed when I suggested we might camp on the beach.

In the early hours of the morning after the ball, Rod had us follow his low-slung, Morgan coupe sports car to the nearby White Cliffs of Dover as a moonlight experience. It was obvious that he hoped to impress and seduce his partner, a well-bred, double-barrel-named girl from London. On the cliff top a gusty wind blew her underpants away into the English Channel. Sarah and I camped chastely on the beach. Next morning Rod collected us to go to church, presumably to atone for his recent sins. A cloudburst caught us on the way and we had to sit through the sermon in a pool of water on the wooden pew.

I was gauche in those days and recall them with embarrassment and regret at opportunities lost. I quickly let Sarah Fleming know of my "five-year plan," which intimated that I had no intention of settling down for five years because I had so many mountains to climb and expeditions planned to far off places. I naively thought I was being honest and doing the gentlemanly thing by not letting her hopes rise. But events overtook me and we fell in love, which shattered my pompous plans.

I was studying hard for my approaching finals and Sarah was still working at the suburban hospitals in Tooting and Wimbledon, so our courting was limited to country weekends at her parents' home in Suffolk or on my brother's farm in Sussex. When work kept us in London for the weekend, we explored the City that was always deserted, having been a beehive of activity on weekdays. The criers of Billingsgate fish market were still, bowler-hatted stockbrokers no longer thronged the narrow pavements, and only the occasional chimes from the Wren church towers broke the silence. With Nicholaus Pevsner's architectural guide on hand, we tracked down most of the fifty-one Wren churches within the confines of the City of London, each different, each exquisite. We lunched at pubs on the Isle of Dogs, sitting on balconies that overhung the River Thames. We admired myriad cranes that pointed skyward, and watched big boats from exotic foreign destinations passing upstream towards East India Docks. We walked in Greenwich Park, explored Inigo Jones's Queen's House, and imagined ourselves dining in the banqueting hall of the Royal Naval College.

Sarah's parents had retired to Stansfield, a small village in the rolling pastoral farmland of West Suffolk between Bury St Edmunds and Clare. They lived at Bridgemans, an old farmhouse perched on a hilltop from where fields fell away to a small valley and a mediaeval church on the hillside opposite. A quiet retreat from the rush of London life, we went "hedging and ditching" in the lanes and fields, explored old churches, and visited country mansions and gardens that were open to the public.

* * *

Max and Irene Fleming had spent most of their married life on the move, so they could understand my restless whims that might eventually lead to their daughter roaming the globe, too. Max was a keen mountaineer when at the University of Grenoble, where he climbed with some of the best continental alpinists of the day. He started his working career in the Sudan Political Service, before going on to Cyprus and Nigeria. Max was a Mr Fix-it, a turnupstuffer, always tinkering at repairs necessary to maintain an old country house with a garden, herbaceous flower beds, large vegetable patch, an orchard, duck pond, and several outhouses. I was always a welcome audience in his workshop, but rarely as an active participant, similar to assisting my surgical chiefs at St George's.

On my visits, Irene would always put out pyjamas, thinking I had forgotten to bring them; but they remained folded owing to my habit of sleeping naked. They were passionate gardeners and widely read since both had studied classics at Oxford University.

The house was old and comfortable, but it was never warm because of large gaps under the doorsills and round windows through which cold

East Anglian winds blew. Most of the floorboards creaked with age. The only toilet was downstairs in the bathroom beyond the kitchen. During the night, in order to avoid using the china chamber pot in the bedside cupboard, I had to creep along the passage past Sarah's bedroom. Since every floorboard groaned and every stair cried out, I feared her parents might think I was up to no good. I eventually learned to walk silently on the firm outside edge of the stair.

On one of my first visits, keen to impress, I accepted an invitation to go riding with the Master of the local foxhounds whom Sarah and I had met at a party. He arrived next morning with a couple of restless hacks as sleek as racehorses. Still fresh from The Major's riding lessons at the Atkinson Morley Hospital, I confidently mounted the quieter beast, all of seventeen hands. Sarah, a competent horsewoman, took the other, a gelding hunter. For two hours we pranced around the lanes. My horse reared at every passing car and trotted uncontrollably whenever I relaxed my tug on the reins. On our return I had on each buttock an enormous blister that prevented me sitting in comfort. I spent much of the rest of the weekend lying prone and submitting to alcohol rubs by Irene and being powdered by Sarah.

I still harboured a sneaking suspicion—now unbelievable—that arriving virginal at the nuptials was important to future happiness. Sarah was less hung up on the idea. Back in London we eventually decided that abstinence was putting too much strain on us both. One weekend when my puritanical landlady was away in the country, we impulsively decided to spend the night together at my Ebury Street flat. We arranged that Sarah would meet me there when she came off duty at 9.30 p.m. I waited nervously in my small room, unable to concentrate on anything. Then from below I heard the door slam. She bounded upstairs and fell into my arms. No sooner was our first union furtively but happily consummated than we heard a slow, regular pounding of feet on the stairs. I knew that we were the only occupants of the house because all the offices on the floors below were vacant for the weekend. The steps came relentlessly nearer, and then a flash of light appeared under the door. Expecting the apocalypse, Sarah hid under the bedclothes while I grabbed a towel to my naked self and opened the door a chink. In the doorway two uniformed, helmeted London policemen confronted me.

"Excuse me disturbing you, sir," said the sergeant, "but we're doing a routine check. The front door was open so we thought we'd better investigate."

"I can't have closed it properly when I came in," I said. "Sorry for the trouble, officer."

The policemen turned back down the stairs, and the clumping noise of their boots echoed through the empty house. Sarah lay with the sheet pulled up to her chin and laughed hysterically at her carelessness in not closing the front door firmly, so eager was she for her tryst.

In a burst of guilt and paranoia, I imagined that the police would report the incident to my landlady, who might evict me. So at five o'clock on a drizzly London morning I turned Sarah out, a moment of selfishness I have never been allowed to forget. Because the nursing school doors were not opened until eight o'clock, she had to bide her time in the waiting room of Victoria Station.

As if this was not bad enough, soon after, we arrived at my brother's farm for the weekend to find a note saying the family had gone to a cricket match in a nearby village. Two hours alone in an empty house was too good to be true, so we hurried up to the spare bedroom. After an hour of passion I tried to flush away the condom that I had bought slyly from an all-night chemist in Picadilly. Being half full of air, it kept bouncing back. So I put it into the Aga coal stove and an acrid smell of burning rubber filled the kitchen and percolated through the house. Sarah and I rushed round opening windows and doors, frantically trying to fan a draught to clear the air before the family returned.

\* \* \*

Finals brought together all of us who were previously from the Cleveland Square flat but were scattered throughout the London teaching hospitals. We foregathered with nervous jocularity in those woeful days of reckoning, united against a common enemy—the examiners. Conscientious students faced them with confident equanimity; those less single-minded of us dreaded our comeuppance. We went up to Cambridge for the written papers and returned for viva-voce examinations two weeks later. Many of the examiners were from Addenbroke's Hospital, my former anatomy tutor, John Withycombe, among them. Soon after the last exam I heard that the results had been posted in the cloisters of the Senate House. I hurried over there, with a rapid heartbeat and a sick feeling in my stomach. It was a waste of time to look under the First Class Honours; unreasonable to scour the Two-ones; just a chance I might have scraped a Two-two; a Third class was most likely. There was my name in company with many of my friends. Some had edged into the Two-twos. One Clare man of our year actually got a First, but he was a swot who eventually became a distinguished professor in London.

My elation was a mix of unbelief, dismay, joy, and pride. I could now call myself Doctor, and write MB (Bachelor of Medicine) B Chir (Bachelor of Surgery—*chirugiensis*) after my name.

# SEVENTEEN

AFTER THE CAMBRIDGE FINAL exams I went to the south of France with two friends, Bill Skelton, chaplain of Clare College, and John Sheldon, a fellow medical student. I was alone because Sarah could not get off work. As I was doubtful of how I would adapt to a sedentary week of sand and sea, I packed my climbing boots—just in case. St Tropez, our destination, was full of expensive yachts. Brigitte Bardot lived adjacent to the harbour in a castle built on a rocky point inaccessible to peepers. Local beaches boasted the only nude bathing on the Riviera—avant-garde for the late fifties, the swinging sixties not having yet arrived. Near the town, nymphets lay clad in skimpy bikinis that gradually were shed the farther along the beach one went until clothing looked quite out of place. Police swooped regularly but failed to rid the miles of sandy beaches of naked bodies that quickly covered themselves, and then returned to worshipping the sun as soon as the law moved on.

For three days I lay on the hot sand trying to read, but was distracted by the gorgeous bodies that paraded past me. Being unaccustomed to so much sun, I burned my bum to the colour of a ripe peach and was continually uncomfortable because sand got everywhere.

Soon I became bored, so I donned my boots and took a bus along the Corniche, leaving my companions lazing, eating, and drinking wine. I bought a *quatrième classe* ticket to Corsica on a ferry where I shared deck space with cars, animals, and other young travellers.

At dawn next day we entered the Gulf of Ajaccio, heralded by the boom of a foghorn. Rain fell as the coast bus clattered out of Ajaccio town. Subtle smells of the maquis and eucalyptus trees permeated through an open window. Damp rose from rain-spattered pavements where dust congealed in small circles. Passing through Porto, we rolled north along the cliff-hung coast road and wound in and out of many small bays. Eventually we reached Calvi on the northwest corner of Corsica.

I climbed to the fortress citadel, a former bishop's palace, which I understood was a youth hostel. It stood high on an escarpment and commanded a view far out to sea beyond a crescentic sandy beach. In response to the sonorous thud of the brass knocker, a servant girl opened the iron-studded doors that were twice as high as her.

"Do you have a room?" I asked.

She nodded and silently beckoned me in and led me down a circular stone stair to a dungeon-like hall that was once the cellars, now a restaurant and bar. The owner, an affable man with a bibulous glow to his cheeks, welcomed me, unsteadily holding a wine glass.

"As you can see, business is slack," he said, looking askance at my scruffy dress. "But come in and we'll see what we can find for you to eat." The waitress brought me a lavish supper, which I ate at a table by the window looking out over the bay of Calvi. The patron joined me, bringing a bottle of wine.

"I fled Russia in 1917 after the revolution," he said. "After several false starts, I finished up in this place."

He tossed off this fact quite casually, so I was agog for more fascinating gossip. He recounted how Rasputin, a peasant debauchee who became the wizardly courtier of Czar Nicholas II and Empress Alexandra, was summoned to staunch the bleeding of hemophiliac Crown Prince Alexis. "Prince Yusupov, who poisoned Rasputin, was my cousin," he added casually. "Calvi became the hangout for White Russian aristocrats fleeing the revolution. They held wild parties here in the castle. They would ride their horses through the doors where you've just come in, then descend the stairs into these dungeons. They would get wild drunk, make the horses lie down on their sides lined up in rows, and dance Cossack dances on the flanks of the lying horses."

After midnight I reluctantly dragged myself away from his tales of the Russian steppes, of the Ural Mountains beyond Moscow, and of old St Petersburg. I pitched my little tent on the beach and slept with waves lapping near my ear.

I planned to walk across the highest mountains of Corsica to Corte, in the centre of the island. The bus creaked and huffed up a winding road of the Figarella Valley. Steam rose from under the bonnet so we stopped frequently for the engine to cool. Raindrops of a sudden downpour smote the windscreen. The flowers and leaves of the maquis shrubs gave off a strong, musty fragrance that can be smelt far out to sea, earning Corsica its name, "The Scented Isle."

I left the bus at Bonifacio and struck off the road on a path that dived immediately into the maquis. This dense undergrowth of bushes covers much of the island and is so thick and high that a fugitive is safe from discovery there. Hence the interior of the island has long provided refuge for brigands and bandits. I bivouaced beside a stream in resinous pinewoods. I lit a fire and lay on a mattress of pine needles under the star-bright vault. The peace of the mountains was a delight after the bustling, commercialized beaches of the Riviera. On waking I could see Corsica's highest peak, Monte Cinto, several ridges distant. Upland rugged rock held patches of snow in shaded gulleys, while forested valleys appeared carpeted with ubiquitous maquis. I climbed to the Col de Petrella, followed the ridge south to the Col d'Avartoli, then dropped into the Stranciacone Valley that drains the jagged cirque of peaks of which Monte Cinto is the crown.

At sundown next day, after twelve hours of scrambling over steep rock—but nothing that needed a rope—I surveyed the whole island of Corsica from the top of Monte Cinto (8,891 ft; 2,710 m). For protection from the cold night I dug myself into a dense bush of maquis just below the summit. I felt quite content at being on my own. Usually I like to have a companion with whom to share the highs and lows of an adventure, to exclaim over a sunset, or to discuss a problem. However, now I was alone and content withal. I was off on my own adventure in this rugged country. Any happening, any situation can be an adventure; they are always there, we just have to look for them. It is just the personal interpretation of it that matters and dictates the excitement we derive from it. For some it is Mount Everest or the South Pole, for others somewhere much less exotic but none the less of an adventure.

The following morning I descended into a valley where lay the village of Albertace. I stocked up with bread, cheese, and fruit, and set off to climb over the mountains again to reach the old city of Corte. At dusk I halted at a shepherds' encampment in an open alp below the top of the pass. The shepherds spoke a peasant patois akin to Italian. They invited me to share their meal and to spend the night in their rude shelter, a stone sheep pen roofed and thatched with maquis laid roughly on wooden slats. The entire space was filled with ruffianly men squatting round an open grate in the middle of the floor. They crouched under woolen, felted capes pulled round their shoulders. Acrid smoke hovered under the roof vault before escaping through cracks at the eaves. When seen from outside, the shelter appeared to be on fire because a wispy line of smoke rose along with steam made by the evaporating evening dew.

The shepherds evoked images of Prosper Mérimée's story "Mateo Falcone," which had first stimulated my interest in Corsica. Mateo, a child of seven, was in the yard of the family farm when a wounded bandit on the run emerged from the maquis and asked to be hidden from the police. Mateo hid the bandit under a pile of straw. The pursuing sergeant dangled a gold watch on a chain in front of Mateo, tempting him to tell where the bandit was hidden. The child eventually reached out for the watch, at the same time pointing to the straw pile. Mateo's father returned as the police were leading away the bandit, who cursed Mateo out loud for his treachery. The father, condemned by the bandit, marched Mateo off into a clearing apart from the house and made the boy kneel to say his prayers. The mother ran after him but before she arrived a shot rang out.

The shepherds' hospitality defied their roguish appearance. We ate mutton barbecued over open embers of a fire around which we all settled to sleep—they, wrapped in their capes, me cosy in my down sleeping bag. Lupine howls of fierce guard dogs interrupted the peace of night. Next morning I descended through a pine-forested valley that debouched on the ancient city of Corte.

Time was rolling on and I had to be back in England to catch the boat leaving for Newfoundland. I was also keen to spend time with Sarah before I went. So I took the fast train across France to the Channel ferry, and so to London.

\* \* \*

My dream of following the steps of Sir Wilfred Grenfell became real when I stepped on board a Norwegian iron-ore freighter, *M/S Evita*, bound for Bell Island, Newfoundland. Glasgow docks, where I embarked, were gloomy with mist that rolled down from the Highlands;

the only sparkle came from the city's wet cobblestones. In similar wet cloud and Highland mist, I had spent the previous night bivouacing in the lee of a rock on the top of Cir Mhòr, the highest point on the Isle of Arran. Then I narrowly avoided being trampled by a flock of sheep in whose path I slept.

Several Norwegian sailors were leaning against the dockyard railings entwined with Gorbals lassies and sucking a last farewell.

"Them Norskies is used to t' cold," observed the cabbie who took me to the ship. "T' climate dunna make moch difference to 'em."

The huge iron-ore carrier, tinged red with dust, was moored against the dock. I met Captain Egeborg, the skipper and a phlegmatic sea dog, who had his wife and two small boys aboard for the passage. The purser allocated me a berth in the owner's cabin next to the bridge. I ate endless meals of smorgasbord in the officer's mess, and had free run of the ship for the eight-day Atlantic crossing.

As we approached Newfoundland we encountered icebergs that floated south in the Labrador Current. They were destined to melt in the warmer waters of the Gulf Stream that sweeps up the eastern coast of North America from the Caribbean. The two currents converge just off the Grand Banks and create dense fog and dangerous waters redolent of *Captains Courageous*.

"What do people do for a living around here?" I asked the bosun as we approached the cliffs of the sparsely populated Avalon Peninsula.

"Fish in sommer, fock in winter, and there's not much fishing," he replied.

A stocky, bristly-chinned pilot came on board to guide *Evita* through the harbour narrows. After thanking Captain Egeborg and his crew for their hospitality, I climbed aboard the pilot cutter. The pilot's accent lay between Irish brogue and broad Devon, spoken out of opposite corners of his mouth, from which protruded a brier pipe stoked with pungent shag. At the age of twenty-one he had been master of a schooner with a teenage crew that sailed a triangle route from Newfoundland carrying salted cod to Spain, then sherry and port to the West Indies, and finally a rum run home.

"Give me sail any day, 'stead of those damned enjuns," he said. "Saint Jaans be full of 'em, and oi hates 'em. Oi loikes to loie in a 'ammock on the deck of a four-master running wi' t' southern Trades."

We passed a large schooner with her mast trimmed short and no longer used for sail. "In her praasperity she garn up to warmer waters," said the pilot, (convention being that on the Labrador one travels down north, and up south). "Oi used to cut spars for schooners long ago; now all I cut would make a picket fence."

The Grenfell hospital plane happened to be in St John's carrying Dr Gordon Thomas, the superintendent, on business. So I flew north on its return to St Anthony. The interior was a wild, rugged, and deserted forest of pine and spruce trees with few signs of habitation. We passed over myriad lakes that cover a third of the surface of Newfoundland. Along the coast, small fishing settlements nestled in every bay and sheltered cove of the inclement rocky shore.

St Anthony, a town of two thousand people, is built on the shore of the bight, a narrow-necked harbour protected to seaward by the cliffs of a high headland. This was then the headquarters of the International Grenfell Association that provided medical care for the northern finger of Newfoundland and the entire coast of Labrador. Wilfred Grenfell, a young doctor and evangelical missionary with the Royal National Mission to Deep Sea Fishermen, first arrived on that inhospitable coast in 1892 bent on serving the migrant fishermen and their families. He was so moved by the poverty and ill health that he devoted the rest of his life to improving their living conditions and medical care.

In the outport communities, fish was the mainstay of a depressed seasonal economy. Those tough seafaring folk still jigged for cod, using a long line and hooks baited with capelin. In winter some men trapped for fur in the interior, others stayed home to repair their nets and boats for the next year's fishing season.

Men and women from Scotland, Ireland, and the west coast ports of England have landed and settled for five centuries on this coast of Newfoundland. Each community faces the ocean and has retained its original local accent. Quaint names abound—Heart's Delight, Come By Chance, Joe Batt's Arm, Twillingate, Dildo Run, Bristol's Hope, Goobies, Harry's Harbour, Black Duck Cove.

Mail boats plied the coast delivering supplies and mail, a lifeline of each settlement. From St Anthony a single dirt road led south beside the Strait of Belle Isle that separates Newfoundland from Labrador. It only reached as far as Flower's Cove, where there was a nursing station, but it was later extended south to join the Trans-Canada Highway at Cornerbrook.

The hospital stood a quarter of a mile above the dry dock and the wharf where supply boats landed stores and equipment to maintain the Grenfell Mission complex of a dormitory for children attending school, a handicrafts store, and a farm. They came from "the coast"—that refers to any part of northern Newfoundland and all of Labrador.

Dr Thomas, the youthful, versatile superintendent of the hospital, trained in Montreal in general surgery, thoracic, and neurosurgery and so he was able to deal with a great variety of medical and surgical problems. Each morning I assisted at surgery and gained wide experience in doing procedures that would never have been possible at my teaching hospital. Mayo Johnson, the surgical resident, allowed me to do several operations under his tutelage. Having qualified only three months before, I was thrilled by the challenge of actually treating patients myself. My diary reads: "I cannot get used to being called 'doctor'. It still sends a shiver through me, half of pride, half of embarrassment, both fill me with wonder."

During afternoons we made rounds of hospital patients and then did the outpatient clinic. Tuberculosis was still a scourge on the coast, but less so than in the days of Grenfell. As drug treatment using streptomycin, isoniazid, and para-amino salicylic acid became more effective, surgery for TB had steadily decreased. Indian and Eskimo patients from the coast were treated and schooled in a sanatorium attached to the hospital.

Since I was the most dispensable member of the medical team, I often went by plane to escort patients back to St Anthony Hospital from villages on the coast. The red de Havilland Otter took off from a pond outside town. When we reached the outport, the pilot would fly over the nursing station to announce our arrival and to scout the best wind direction for a landing approach. Then bang-bang-bang as our floats crested the wave tops before settling into quieter water. While taxiing to a buoy, fishermen would come out to escort us to the wharf where villagers congregated. The plane was their communication with the world outside, and each flight was a magical event shared by everyone.

At the nursing station I met the nurse, and we would examine the patient together. Then we called the radio operator at St Anthony to report the patient's medical condition and our expected time of return.

Newfoundland women were accustomed to huge families and often preferred to have their babies at home or in the nursing station. Most nurses were British-trained midwives because at that time there was no special outport midwifery training in Canada. Complicated antenatal cases went to St Anthony for delivery, reducing the chances of obstetric emergencies. One day I delivered a woman of her twentieth child. During her long labour she kept up a steady, repetitive, mantra-like moan, "Oh moi, Oh moi, oi'm goin' to doie"—not an encouraging chorus for a fledgling obstetrician. After one heavy grunt in the third stage of labour, the baby suddenly appeared in the bed. Soon after, when it was swaddled in her arms she said, proudly smiling, "Oi loves 'em when oi gits 'em; but, oh moi, oi hates the havin' of 'em."

\* \* \*

On my afternoons off I would explore the town. Painted weatherboard wood-frame houses hugged the edge of St Anthony harbour. Wooden fishing stages, built on stilts, projected from the rocky shore so that fishermen in the long motorboats or flat-bottomed dories could land there directly onto the dock beside the filleting shed. They pitched codfish into boxes beside a bench on the landing stage, where several other men and women worked each at a specific job. The cutter would take a fish from the box, slit the throat and belly along its length with a sharp knife. Then the gutter decapitated the fish with a swift knock against the sharpened edge of the bench, disembowelled it with one deft stroke, and pushed the roes towards a hole in the bench where they slid into a barrel. Then he kicked the guts into the sea and tossed the heads to small boys, who cut out the tongues and cheeks—great delicacies. The splitter removed the backbone and threw the filleted fish into a barrow. Someone else wheeled the barrow to a dark shed on the shore edge and piled the fish with a heavy sprinkling of salt between each layer. In the fall of the year, a schooner from St John's came to collect the catch for market.

Later I would climb to Fishing Head at the entrance to St Anthony Bight. I looked out over the hostile ocean, and watched wild seas roll in from the Atlantic and crash on the rocks below in clouds of fine spume, just as I remembered the cliffs of north Cornwall when I was a boy. Several times I went by the hospital boat—the *M.V.Gould* under the command of Captain Small, an old-timer seaman—to do clinics at outport nursing stations of Conche, Roddickton and Englee. On the sea I became keenly aware of the hazards of navigating this savage, rocky coast, which the fishermen did so nonchalantly in the course of their daily work.

* * *

One weekend I went hiking with an American boy, newly arrived from Boston as a summer "Worker without Pay," known as WOPs, who were part of a long Grenfell tradition. We climbed to some ponds above the hospital where open ground led towards the White Hills. On the far side, the Parker River flowed down to Westerbrook on the road south from St Anthony, which seemed a feasible outing.

From the map it looked an easy day, but I had underestimated the Newfoundland bush, as thick as the Corsican maquis. In places it was so impenetrable that it was easier to wade along the edges of ponds and creeks than to fight through bush. My athletic companion made heavy going of walking along the water's edge, where willow and ground alder grew from the banks so there was no shore to follow. Our feet slithered on rocks as we clung to overhanging branches. By dusk we were still a long way from our exit to the road so we had to bivouac. I built a shelter of boughs, started a fire to dry our sodden clothing, and settled down to a long and uncomfortable night. I knew there would be much concern in the hospital because we were expected back that evening.

The next morning was clear so we set off past a couple of small lakes and started wading down the Parker River. We heard an aircraft drone overhead, and soon the hospital plane made a pass over us, returned for another look, and dipped its wings in recognition. My heart sank at the thought of explaining this foray to my boss. At the road we hitched a ride into St Anthony, where the staff were agog to hear of our adventures. Understandably, Dr Thomas was cool.

Not long after my escapade on the White Hills, I went sailing in St Anthony Bight in a gaff-rigged boat recently built by a local carpenter. Julie Johnson, wife of the surgical resident, asked to accompany me.

As we were leaving the dock, Mayo, her husband, told me to take care because Julie could not swim. After a few elegant tacks in the middle of the harbour, without warning a severe squall hit us. I let out the main sheet to spill the wind, but the boom hung up on one of the stays that was set too far aft to allow the boom full play. Consequently the boat headed up to wind, and heeled viciously so the sail dipped into the water, dragging the mast down after it. In a moment we were in the icy water. I had difficulty clinging to Julie with one hand, and the keel of the boat with the other. Captain Small, who was watching us from the *Gould* and had kept his engine running just in case we got into difficulty, promptly came out to rescue us. On the wharf, an anxious Mayo had watched the whole foolish epic.

Shortly after this incident, just as I had finished delivering a young woman of a baby boy, she said, "Was you the one in the sail boat?"

"Yes," I replied.

"Was you the one in the woods?"

"Yes, I was," I said. "How did you know that?"

"Oi s'pose everyone in St Anthony knows," she replied nonchalantly. I was suitably humbled.

Thereafter I restricted my adventures to walking over the headland on the cliff path to Goose Cove. It was "berry-pickin' toime," so we gathered pails full of berries that cover the ground in fall and add variety to the fishy diet of Newfoundlanders.

The three months I spent at St Anthony soon came to an end. I had made many friends and had a medical experience beyond any expectation. During my evenings while there, I laid plans to travel south through the United States to Mexico in order to climb Popocatépetl. The volcano's name had intrigued me since reading

Prescott's account of Cortez's Conquest of Mexico.

I left Newfoundland in late November and vowed I would return to the coast some day.

\* \* \*

I caught a Greyhound bus from New York to New Orleans following the western edge of the Appalachians. Then I flew to Mexico City, lying at over 7,000 feet, from where you can look through a jungle of church spires east over red-tiled rooftops towards two snow-capped volcanoes that lie on the horizon. To the right stands Popocatépetl—the Smoking Mountain—where steam rises out of its crater like a boiling kettle. To the left of Popo lies Ixtaccíhuatl—the Sleeping Woman—whose snowy cover appears as the profile of a woman's head, chest, body, and feet.

I was bound for Amecameca, a small village near the base of the volcanoes. I carried only the clothes and boots I stood up in, a sleeping bag, and a packsack with a climbing rope strapped on top. The bus rattled, and steam hissed from under the hood that was held in place by a piece of bent wire. I was wedged between hot sweaty men who laughed loudly and spat out of the window. In the luggage rack, chickens, tied by their feet, clucked disapproval. A farmer held a little pig, secured by a string round its neck. The driver pressed his hand on the horn and his foot on the accelerator so that the bus swayed and creaked round the bendy road.

A notice above the driver read "No pise los asientos" (Do not step on the seats)—which sounded like a strange thing to do. In the aisle beside my seat stood Miguel, with whom I conversed in fractured sentences of phrasebook Spanish. He grasped a plastic bag in the same hand with which he steadied himself against the baggage rack. At the corners of his mouth, a Zapata-style, bushy-black, droopy moustache grew out of an olive, stubble-bearded face. His pupils glinted through a dark forest of eyebrows. Platform-heeled, embossed-leather cowboy boots made him look taller than he really was. The black ribbon hatband of his high-crowned, curly-brimmed straw sombrero was greasy from the oil of his hair. Being short for his torso, and because his trousers hung loose from his hips, a hairy roll of fat overtopped Manuel's brass-buckled leather belt, showing a volcano-crater belly button.

We saw a crowd had gathered at the roadside round a demolished car lying in the ditch, the result of a recent head-on collision. All the bus passengers leaned towards the side of the wreck, groaned in unison, and murmured prayers while crossing their breasts. On the summit of a particularly steep and dangerous descent, the bus driver passed a hat round for a collection of coins to leave at the shrine to the Virgin that was embellished with sun-bleached plastic flowers.

We took the bend at the bottom of the hill at speed so all the standing passengers swayed outwards by force of gravity. Manuel leaned on his thin plastic bag, which ruptured, releasing a cascade of limes. At first they rolled along the rack's parallel metal bars, arranged like riffles in a placer miner's sluice box. Manuel lunged to catch the fruit, but another sideways lurch of the bus caused the limes to drop through a wider space in the bars like the balls of a pin machine. An avalanche of limes descended on two men in the seats below, who looked up in surprise. Again Manuel lunged. But the torrent had started and the whole bag of limes emptied into the rack. With each lurch of the bus, more limes fell through the gaps in the baggage rack. The two men below sat on the edge of their seats, ducking and weaving, laughing amicably. Other passengers cheered whenever Manuel caught a lime but, being large and not very adroit, he caught few. Loud encouragement came from the seat in front where the grey-haired senora in a flower-printed dress wore two watches on her gnarled and wrinkled wrist. A lime rolled under her seat. She leaned forward, deftly scooped it up, and started biting on it, meanwhile calling encouragement to Manuel, who was gathering most of his spilled produce that he transferred to a more substantial bag provided by the senora.

*  *  *

In Amecameca's main square, country peasants had congregated for market. Women wearing red pleated skirts and black knitted shawls squatted on their haunches beside fruit and vegetables laid out on reed mats. Men in straw hats turned up like cowboys, carried over their shoulders colourful wool-woven serapes. Chatter rose like the evening chorus of cicadas, whose shrill chirping is made by vibrating membranes on their thorax. At the prison in a corner of the square, a crowd of relatives passed food between tall iron bars to convicts herded into one large courtyard.

I asked a hotelier if he knew a guide to lead me up Popocatépetl. After long discussion he called a small boy from a back room and ordered him to take me to the house of Lucio Sedano who, I was assured, had climbed the mountain at least a hundred times. I followed the barefoot urchin down a narrow alley and through a maze of streets between high stone walls where lazy, mangy dogs snapped at us. Eventually the boy pushed open a door, beckoned me inside, and then disappeared. An old man with a drooping moustache sat mending a worn-out pair of boots with leather as gnarled as his fingers.

"I want to climb Popocatépetl," I said. "Can you show me the way?"

We bargained over his fee, and agreed to meet at 8:00 p.m. at Tlamacas, a hut built on a pass between the two volcanoes that Cortez crossed with his army. Five Spanish conquistadors "out of their wild love of adventure," climbed Popo, something the natives said no man could do and still live. It was reputed to be the prison of the departed spirits of wicked rulers, whose fiery agonies caused the billowing sulphurous steam and eruptions of lava that frequently spurted from its summit cone.

Alone, I began climbing up the road from Amecameca and started to feel sick as I neared Tlamacas. I had risen from sea level to 12,000 feet in less than twenty-four hours, which is very foolish in light of present knowledge of the physiology of high altitude and acute mountain sickness. At the cabin I cooked some maize I had bought in the market. Lucio arrived just before sunset and, as we sat looking out over the mountains, he told me the legend of the two volcanoes, Popocatépetl and Ixtaccíhuatl.

\* \* \*

Popo and Ixta were lovers. Ixta was a princess, the only and adored daughter and heiress to the throne of a powerful Aztec king. Neighboring tribes rose up to depose her father and to plunder his treasure. From his sickbed, the old king summoned his strongest young warriors and promised that whoever conquered his enemies should both inherit his kingdom and marry his daughter Ixtaccíhuatl.

Popocatépetl had been distantly in love with Ixta since, as a boy, he had seen her standing on the balcony of her father's palace during a festival. Popo never had the courage to tell her of his love because she had so many swains. However, he was determined to conquer the enemy to show he was the bravest man in Mexico and thus deserve the hand of Ixta.

After many bloody battles he won the war and set off home in triumph to claim his reward. But one of his rivals sent a messenger ahead of the victorious army to report that Popo had been killed in battle. Ixta was heartbroken. She could neither eat nor sleep and, despite all the witchdoctors' potions and sacrifices by the priests, she languished and died.

In ignorance, Popocatépetl and his army marched proudly up to the palace at Tenochtitlan and were greeted with the news of Ixta's death. Popo built a great pyramid on which he laid Ixta; inconsolable, he built another altar beside her and lay down to die, holding a lighted torch to illuminate his beloved forever. Snow fell and covered the bodies of the two lovers. Year-round they remain thus, standing out white above the surrounding green altiplano. People say the smoke of the volcano is the torch of Popocatépetl that continues to burn in memory of his love for his beautiful princess, Ixtaccíhuatl.

* * *

Before dawn next morning, Lucio and I set out towards the volcano. Ash covered the lower slopes, making them slippery—like climbing a sand dune. At the snowline Lucio pulled from his sack a pair of rusty old crampons that he bound to tattered sacking gaiters wrapped over his boots. He wore a tasseled serape and a felt hat pulled down over his ears. In the freezing morning air his nose dribbled, forming icicles on his moustache.

We climbed steadily. Lucio grunted in my footsteps and I realized that he, like his crampons, had not trodden a mountain for many years. I tied the climbing rope round his waist and, ignoring his protests, hauled him upward. I was breathless myself and could sympathize with Cortez's men who found "respiration in these aerial regions so difficult that every effort was attended with sharp pains in the head and limbs."

After four hours climbing, we gained the crest of the volcano rim just as the rising sun cast a pearly light on the snowy top of Ixtaccíhuatl, five kilometers away. Steam rose from pools of boiling mud in a crater a thousand feet deep, and acrid, sulphurous fumes made our eyes water. The sheer, grey-brown walls were broken by snow-covered ledges tinted yellow with crystals of sulphur. Here Cortez' men had cast lots to choose who should descend into the crater to collect sulphur to make gunpowder for their muskets. The lot fell to Montano, who was lowered in a basket at the end of a rope.

I climbed to the highest point of the crater rim at 17,800 feet and felt

abysmally mountain sick, with a pulsating headache and overwhelm-
ing nausea. I lingered only long enough to look out over all of Mexico.
Forest and rolling hills surrounded the great plateau, on which stand
the two most beautifully named mountains I know: Popocatépetl and
Ixtaccíhuatl. I then spent a couple of weeks wandering by bus round
Central Mexico, from Cuernavaca to Taxco, to Lake Pátzcuaro.

On my return to Mexico City, a telegram from Sarah told me that I
had got the St George's Surgical Unit house job, due to start in a week's
time.

I had promised a friend to collect his Alfa Romeo from a garage in
Hattiesburg, Mississippi, where it was being repaired, and drive it to
New York. I was stopped for speeding by a sheriff in Tennessee, and
was hauled in front of a judge and fined on the spot. Despite this delay,
I made New York in less than twenty-four hours, just in time for my
plane to London.

Sarah played truant from her nursing classes to come and meet me
at Heathrow Airport. Her sin was found out, reported to Dame Muriel
Powell, the matron, who sent her down to St George's neurosurgical
unit in Wimbledon as punishment. Meanwhile I reported for duty to my
boss, Nic Nicholls, in starched white collar and tie, about to start a new
and more responsible era in my life.

# EIGHTEEN

I RETURNED FROM MEXICO TO TAKE up the post of house surgeon to the Surgical Unit of St George's under Nic Nicholls. Any job at one's own hospital was prestigious, but this was one of its most prized. It boded well for the relentless surgical training ladder to which I then, in all my keenness, aspired.

When I was a student, Nic had showed uncommon kindness to me, and his interest in my career had virtually earmarked me for his job. He was coasting towards retirement and so he went down to his cottage in the Cotswolds on Thursday evenings and returned for his teaching round on Tuesday mornings. His only operating session was on Wednesday. His active surgical days were virtually past, partly owing to age, which dulls dexterity, partly to a tremor generally thought to be due to the large quantities of alcohol he drank while serving in the North African desert campaign as a colonel in the Royal Army Medical Corps. As an urologist, he was a renowned authority of gazing into the bladder through a cystoscope. To his assistants, a waving telescope caused much less anxiety than a shaking scalpel. Sensibly he left any cutting surgery to his capable and experienced senior registrar, Malcolm Robinson. But

Nic was still considered to offer a uniquely wise surgical opinion for sheer common sense and intuitive diagnosis.

Nic stood tall, his military moustache bristling under a hooked nose that sniffed the air like a periscope scanning the horizon. When in deep thought he would rub the side of his nose with a bent, nicotine-stained forefinger and then nibble the cuticle of its deformed nail. He smoked heavily, so business rounds were punctuated by rests outside each ward while he lit a cigarette, discussed any interesting cases we had just seen, and then tossed the half-smoked butt into a sand-filled ash bin beside the ward door.

Nic had a thriving private practice, mainly dealing with prostate glands. He would safely operate on them through a cystoscope by pulling back on a looped wire cutter that burned a swathe through the gland in order to relieve urinary obstruction or halt dribbling incontinence. While gazing into the bladder of a lord of the realm impaled on his cystoscope, he once said casually, "This'll make him a better peer."

For rectal examinations of the prostate, he kept in the waistcoat pocket of his dark three-piece suit some rolled latex fingerstalls, the stock-in-trade of urologists in the days before disposable plastic gloves made the examination more aesthetic and hygienic. Once during a cocktail party, Nic withdrew a lighter from his waistcoat pocket to light a lady friend's cigarette. A fingerstall, which he kept in the same pocket, fell at her feet.

"Oh! Dear, Nic," she said, "I can see you're not the man you used to be."

He was urbane, unpompous, and considerate towards his junior staff, and we responded with loyalty and hard work. I abandoned my sloppy student clothes for a dark suit and white shirts with detachable collars that needed starching, and collar studs and cufflinks. I wore over all a long white coat into the pockets of which I stuffed my stethoscope (a badge of office) and my essential notebook in which I scrawled long "to do" lists.

I would meet Malcolm Robinson, the senior registrar, in the front hall of the hospital at 1:30 p.m. before the business ward round on Tuesday and the teaching round on Thursday. We knew that Nic would not arrive for another half hour, so we had time to discuss each of the patients on our firm, and to have at our fingertips the results of all their tests and investigations. We sat on long benches on either side of the boardroom doors under the chapel balcony. Leather fire buckets, the date 1832 gilded onto them, hung from hooks above our heads. In the hall was a painting of John Hunter, St George's most distinguished forefather and founder of modern surgery. Inside the boardroom was the couch on which he lay bleeding and dying from a ruptured, syphilitic aortic aneurysm, acquired after experimentally inoculating himself with the disease. On pegs in the hall, his predecessors would have hung their top hats with urinary catheters conveniently curled into the brim.

Malcolm was a very gentle man and an excellent teacher, and we became close friends despite being widely separated by rank. Academically brilliant and a sage diagnostician, he was however only an average technical surgeon. I was lucky to have so wise and experienced a mentor, rather than a young registrar with blood lust and surgical bravado. Malcolm was caught in the post-war bottleneck of too many trainee surgeons for too few places available at the top of the pyramid. As a result, competition for consultant posts at teaching hospitals, particularly in surgery, was fierce for the many registrars and senior registrars who, after years of training, working, and waiting in the wings, were often redundant. They either left surgery to enter general practice, for which they were overtrained, or they went abroad to the dominions or colonies where surgeons were still in short supply.

At times the rivalry got nasty as trainees clawed their way to the top, and Malcolm just did not have the necessary aggressiveness. Being earmarked to fill Nic's shoes caused much resentment among his contemporaries. His wife, Liz, was also training to be a surgeon at a time when there were few women in the profession. This added a strain to their marriage that was hard enough to handle with both of them spending long hours by day and night at the hospital.

Ward rounds in the teaching hospitals were like funeral corteges led by the chief and the ward sister. Each had a train of a dozen acolytes, smartly dressed in their various uniforms, following in order of seniority. A rabble of students in grubby, short white coats brought up the rear. The procession moved from bed to bed, heads wagged sagely, and jargon befuddled the patient, who was rarely invited in on the discussion. One day Michael DeBakey, an eminent American vascular surgeon, accompanied us on rounds. My newly acquired beeper, the latest in high technology, sounded unexpectedly. Nic turned calmly to the astonished visitor and said, "Don't worry, Steele's just gone into orbit."

St. George's, like many London teaching hospitals, was a hothouse of Freemasonry. Several friends told me that joining the Lodge was virtually a prerequisite for getting a house job. However, Nic was one of the few staff members who abjured the Masons. I had therefore good grounds for rejecting the soliciting of those colleagues who spelled doom for my surgical career if I desisted. As it was, Freemasonry nearly caused my downfall. The hospital telephone exchange occupied one corner of the front hall, and in the evenings, housemen would drop in on the switchboard ladies for a chat. One night when the hospital was quiet as a mausoleum, two other exhausted housemen and I called by the telephone switchboard to catch up on hospital gossip. On the desk lay a thin, shiny black leather briefcase left behind by one of the consultants after a Freemasons' meeting in the Board Room. Unable to contain our curiosity, we opened it and found a piece of regalia embroidered with gold filigree; small silver balls hung on fine chains from the ruffed edge. I donned the apron—for that is what it was—and danced around the front halls as if wearing a jock strap, laughing hysterically. During these undignified hijinks, the owner, a very senior anaesthetist, returned to recover his mislaid case. He was not amused.

The resident junior doctors lived in a nine-storeys-high, red brick, Victorian building, wedged between the main hospital and the medical school. My room was on the fifth floor facing Knightsbridge and there was no lift. Buses drawing away from the bus stop outside my window would grind through their gears to gather speed. Light from the yellow street lamps brightened my room. So in order to exclude noise and light, I developed the habit, which persists to this day, of sleeping with a snuggly pillow drawn tight over my eyes and ears—not a romantic sight.

Because there was no lift, when the telephone beside my bed rang in the middle of the night I had two choices in order to reach the main hospital: descend five floors to the basement or climb four floors to the roof. I would jump out of bed, pull on my trousers, slip sockless into unlaced shoes, and wrap a white coat tight round myself. I then stumbled out onto the pitch-dark landing and felt for the self-timing switch to the stair lights. The mechanism was often faulty, so I would take the stairs two at a time to reach the floor below before the lights went out.

Once down in the hallway of the residence, I was among tomorrow's breakfast trolleys, standing beside a kitchen pantry dumb-waiter raised on a hawser—the only elevator in the building. I reached the bowels of the hospital beyond the swing doors of the basement outpatient department. A long corridor had pipes in the ceiling painted bright colours that gave the illusion of being in a submarine. I passed the window of the Special Clinic (for Venereal Diseases) where every evening gentlemen from Belgravia and tarts from Victoria would collect their anonymous waiting numbers. The Latvian émigré venereologist greeted each male

patient, whether in pinstripes or jeans, with the command, "Dvap ya
tvarsars. Now milk it." A huge hole in the pharmacy wall, a result of
recent construction work, connected the hospital to the Hyde Park underground station, and the sound of pneumatic drilling interfered with
listening for many a second heart sound. A stone stairway led to the
main hospital corridor. There the main lift, manned by a hunchbacked
Irishman, took me up to the surgical floor at the same altitude as my
bedroom but separated from it by yards of bricks and mortar.

Before long, an old-hand houseman introduced me to the roof route
to the hospital. Female doctors and students were cloistered on the top
floor of the residence, where a bathroom had a large sign—"Ladies
Only." Makeup bottles cluttered the mirror shelf and underwear hung
over the bathtub. A frosted sash window gave access to the roof. Once
out in the fresh air, I could see the canopy of Hyde Park tree tops and the
lights of Buckingham Palace reflected in the Queen's own private lake.
And there below me lay ". . . all of London littered with remembered
kisses."

On the road side, the gentle pitch of the roof sloped to a parapet
about two feet high that looked onto the tops of red, double-decker
buses swinging down Knightsbridge towards Harrods. On the opposite
side of the roof, an iron railing guarded a duckboard walkway that overlooked a deep courtyard two hundred feet below. The hospital was built
round this well where I could see the asbestos roofs of prefabricated
huts that housed the biochemistry laboratory, the typists' offices, and
the medical school library. After rain, the beechwood duckboards were
slippery from being weathered and covered with a fine layer of moss.
Six paces on, the walkway led to a brick wall on which perched a water tank. I looked down fifteen feet into a smaller well where a vertical
ladder was welded to the wall. I remembered how old Cecil Donne had
bawled me out at Cowes for going down a ship's ladder facing outwards

so I reversed and grasped the cold, wet iron handrail and started down feeling for every rung with my feet. One of the obstetric registrars, a good athlete, a month before had done a fireman's slide down the ladder and fractured his forearm. A plaster cast up to his fingertips made his job difficult.

The next few steps were crucial. A drainpipe led from the foot of the ladder towards the labour room, set at an angle on the wall opposite. By using a brick wall on the right for support and balancing carefully, like walking across a log bridge, I could reach the narrow, upright window in ten paces. A sloping glass skylight of the hospital kitchen filled the abyss to my left. A friend, new to the obstetric run, slipped off the pipe, crashed through the glass, and landed on the table where a chef was kneading bread. Shards of glass extruded from his abrasions for months afterwards. Having negotiated the pipe, one had to insert a knife blade into the window frame to flip the catch; then step over the sill directly into the labour room, hoping it was not in use. From there, a few steps led into the upper corridor to a flight of stairs down which lay the surgical wards. On returning to my room in the residence, all was well so long as the ladies' bathroom was unoccupied. I once was caught out and discerned through the frosted glass someone splashing in the bath and had to take the long way round through the basement corridors.

* * *

During my time as Nic's house surgeon, I became deeply aware of the responsibilities of being a doctor. This first came to me when I was looking after a young man, newly married, who had an aggressive, spreading, malignant melanoma from which he was slowly dying. His beautiful wife leaned heavily on me for support, which made me realize that often it is unspoken words that are most powerful. I had to learn how to give support with feeling, yet avoid getting myself caught up in the tragedy of it all, and also to stop getting emotionally involved with patient or relatives that might influence my medical judgment.

I was aware of this forcefully when I was on duty in the Accident department one night when a woman came in having had her face smashed into her car's windscreen. I got to work repairing the many cuts on her beautiful face, a task that I enjoyed as I was good at suturing, and I especially enjoyed plastic surgery procedures. Only after two hours meticulous work did I learn that the patient was one of *Vogue*'s top models, so probably I should have called in the plastic surgeon instead of tackling the job alone. However, the result of my labours was very satisfactory. Over the next few weeks I watched her face heal with huge relief, and with the approbation of Elliot Blake, the plastic surgeon, who I consulted after the fact.

One patient with whom I became friendly was the costume designer for the Sadler's Wells opera. After her discharge she invited me to her flat in Chelsea to choose one of her working sketches. "Help yourself," she said. I thumbed through folders full of sketches of costumes with samples of material attached. Finally I chose six drawings and she appeared quite disappointed at my modest selection and urged me to take more. I declined as I felt that I had already overreached her kindness.

* * *

Towards the end of Nic's house job, I proposed to Sarah in a fleapit cinema in Bermondsey. She accepted so we went off to a jeweller's in Knightsbridge, bought a diamond and sapphire engagement ring, and celebrated over a cup of coffee. A beaver skin hat in a nearby shop window caught my eye. I thought I would look rather dashing wearing it in my emerald green Austin Healey 3000 sports car that I had just bought from a former rackets player friend who was in the business of high quality, second-hand cars. The next weekend we drove down to Sarah's family home in Suffolk. Sarah and I suggested to her mother, Irene, that we should get married in six weeks time in their local church of Denston. We were quite oblivious to the amount of work involved, especially since we were both still busy working in London and had little time to help.

On 20 May 1961 Sarah and I were married in the fifteenth century church of St Nicholas, Denston, three miles away from the Fleming home. Sarah wore a long-sleeved white satin gown with a long veil, and she had gardenias in her hair. My black morning suit with tails and grey top hat came from the rental department of Moss Bros. Canon Charlie Moule and Bill Skelton, both clerics of Clare College, Cambridge, conducted the marriage service. Edward Platts, my best man, drove me to the church in his Rolls Royce; John Hamilton, a South African doctor, took the bridesmaids in his tiny two-seater Austin Seven coupé.

It was a cold, blustery East Anglian day. We were never warm, even in the marquee pitched on the lawn, but the chill did not lessen our joy. Sarah's Uncle Douglas, a Royal Navy captain, gave the reception speech while nervously grinding his fist into his opposite palm. I responded, and we cut a cake decorated with ice axes and coils of climbing rope.

After the reception, we and most of our friends from London congregated at the Bell Hotel in the nearby village of Clare, where we danced until the small hours of the morning. Sarah and I spent the night in the hotel and left the next morning for our honeymoon in Norway. I had kept the destination secret, but one of my friends, hearing she was packing her bikini swimwear, dropped the hint that it might not be a warm holiday. Sarah fondly imagined herself lounging on a beach in Corsica, but I had Norway firmly fixed in my mind as one of the mountain ranges of Europe I had not yet visited. Instead of a honeymoon in the sun she got a late Norwegian spring with snow still on the high ground. Even marriage barely assuaged my mountaineering machismo, to my eternal shame.

We drove in the Austin Healey to Newcastle to catch the ferry to Oslo, on which I had booked a first class cabin. The very rough North Sea crossing did not bother Sarah, who happily tucked into a smorgasbord cornucopia of seafood; I lay on our very expensive bunk with the world going round and felt nauseated by the thought of lobster, prawns, and shrimp.

On dry land we made a dashing couple in our sleek, emerald-green sports car. We each wore a traditional Norwegian *lusekofte* sweater, bought with wedding present money given us by my boss, Nic Nichols. Sarah's new sheepskin coat was handy against the chill that still hung in the late-May air. We drove south from Oslo to Arendal, where we visited the home of Captain Egeborg on whose ship I had sailed to Newfoundland the previous year. Then we headed north to fjord country and the Jotunheim Mountains.

Usually we stayed in bed & breakfast lodgings; occasionally we camped in my old Meade mountain tent. Sarah and I appeared so alike we were mistaken several times for brother and sister, which as honeymooners caused some confusion. At one hotel in remote rural Norway we fell just short of being accused of incest. We climbed on the glaciers of the Jostedalsbreen and hiked in the Jotunheim. Sarah never said she would have preferred to be lounging on some Mediterranean beach.

\* \* \*

On our return to London I took up the post of house physician to Dr John Batten at St George's Hospital, Tooting; Sarah stayed in Knightsbridge to finish her teaching block at Hyde Park Corner. We rented a flat at the top of a Georgian terrace house in Thurloe Square, opposite the Victoria and Albert Museum, a central location in South Kensington, very convenient for both our hospitals.

Our landlady, Lady Campbell-Anstey, once lived with her husband in a castle in Scotland. One day she invited Sarah into her private chambers; Sarah noticed a print of the same castle and remembered seeing a picture of it hidden in a thistle brooch belonging to her grandmother. Lady Campbell-Anstey was nosey about our comings and goings, which she liked us to restrict to mornings and evenings only. We once found cotton tied across the stairs, presumably to see whether we had crept in during the middle of the day. But at £9 a week, it was a small price to pay for being only a step and a jump down the road from Harrods.

Our little flat looked onto the treetops of Thurloe Square. The bedroom backed onto the Earls Court underground railway line as it surfaced from the bowels of London for a breather, and the rattle of trains in the night made sleep fitful. As I was a resident house physician at Tooting for those six months, I only spent half a dozen nights in the flat. What with the noise of the trains and my uneasy conscience at being absent from the hospital, nights at the flat were not restful. It was a strange way to start married life.

The atmosphere of St George's, in suburban Tooting, was much more relaxed than Hyde Park Corner. The hospital buildings, spread over a huge acreage, were widely spaced with grass and trees in between, giving the place a country air. A long, covered corridor joined each of the red brick ward blocks that were built four feet above ground level. So great was the distance between wards that I used to do my night rounds on roller skates.

The doctors' mess stood just inside the hospital gates in a low, temporary army hut with walls so thin you could hear the person breathing in the next-door bedroom. This was not ideal for newlyweds, especially as the single bed was so narrow Sarah and I each had to place our pillows on separate bedside tables. Nurses were strictly forbidden to cohabit with doctors, regardless of their married state, so our nights together, like secret assignations, added a piquancy to the romance.

The doctors' dining room served quality Savoy-style meals on tablecloths along with uniformed waiters and waitresses. This touch of civilization softened the rigours of resident life that for newly qualified doctors was tough going, with long hours and heavy responsibility. Eating separately from the rest of the hospital staff gave doctors the chance over lunch or dinner to discuss patients' problems informally, yet in confidence.

My chief, John Batten, a general physician, was one of a breed of bright young consultants. He also worked at the Brompton Chest Hospital, his particular interest being in lung disease associated with cystic fibrosis. Our rounds were done at a trot, as he darted through the wards with athletic grace, and a charm and courtesy that left nurses swooning in his wake. He was a handsome, youthful figure with black hair smoothed back from shiny temples, a deep voice that easily broke into a cackle of laughter, and staccato movements of his hands when he was not jangling the coins in his trouser pockets. Like Nic, J.B. treated me with the utmost kindness, and I count myself fortunate to have worked for two such thoughtful and considerate bosses—far from a common experience at London teaching hospitals. In return I was loyal and hard working.

Once during a ward round, after I had been up for several preceding nights, J.B. told me we should start injections of gold for a patient suffering from severe rheumatoid arthritis. I wrote down the order on the treatment sheet but, in my exhaustion, I put the decimal point in the wrong place so the patient ended up getting ten times the required dose. If I had had my wits about me, I would have been alert to the mistake, and certainly the hospital pharmacist should have questioned it. But the dose was given and I only noticed a week later when the patient's white blood cell count started to fall because the gold was depressing her white cell production—a potentially lethal situation. I immediately told J.B. what had happened. He never chastised me, but was supportive throughout the worrying period of watching the patient's white cell count slowly rise again to normal levels once the drug was stopped.

The Battens invited Sarah and me to dinner at their house opposite the Lion Gate of Kew Gardens. During an unforgettable evening we listened to J.B.'s brother-in-law through his wife's sister, David Attenborough, recounting the week he had just spent in St George's, Tooting, having his hernia repaired. 'Dave' was evidently adopted by the local Tooting patients, who, finding it strange to have such a toff in their midst, treated him like some sort of mascot.

Although destined to become a surgeon at that stage in my career, I was grateful for the sound foundation of basic internal medicine I acquired from J.B. He subsequently became a friend and has remained so, a transition in relationship between acolyte and master that is not easy to accomplish.

Another senior physician at Tooting who left a deep impression on Sarah and me was Charles McIntee, an Irishman, and expert in infectious diseases, especially poliomyelitis. He lived above the doctors' mess in an apartment where he would occasionally invite young doctors for a glass of sherry. He was a civilized man, well read, fond of classical music, and wide-ranging in conversation. Sarah said he was the only consultant who always opened the doors for nurses, however humble their rank, to pass through first.

Dr MacIntee's registrar at the time was Bill Shakespeare, who I met first at Clare College. Bill was a "small person" owing to achondroplasia, a condition where the limbs are underdeveloped, but the head and trunk are of normal size. He coxed the Clare rowing eight and was a close friend of David Jennings, captain of the university Blue Boat and an Olympian. Bill, when pulled up to his full height, reached only to his friend's waist. He owned a Sunbeam-Talbot sports car with extended pedals, and sat on a box placed on the car seat.

Bill's buddy at Tooting was a large-girthed Australian surgical registrar, Bill Macbeth; the pair was known collectively as Shakespeare & Macbeth. When wanting to talk to another adult, Bill would draw over a chair and climb up on it to be on eye level. He was much loved by the children patients, and at Christmas he dressed up as Santa Claus and drove a child's pedal car round the wards distributing presents. He married one of Sarah's nursing contemporaries.

Our weekends were precious since Sarah and I saw so little of each other while we were both working, especially with me being resident in Tooting. Her Uncle Douglas was then Commodore of Portsmouth Barracks, whither we were invited to spend a weekend. Arriving in our Austin Healey at the gates of one of Britain's largest Royal Navy establishments, we showed our invitation and were waved through, sailors standing to attention and saluting. Douglas and Doreen Bromley lived in Anchor Gate Lodge, a Queen Anne house surrounded by gracious lawns and trees. A sailor whisked our meagre luggage from the boot of the car. Sarah's uncle and aunt showed us upstairs to our bedroom, where Sarah found a naval rating tenderly laying out her nightdress on the bed. Such luxury was heady after the austerity of our daily lives in London.

We appeared before dinner for cocktails in the drawing room where, at the push of a button, a sailor appeared with a tray full of drinks. Since I was, as my uncharitable but truthful friends always said, "liable to get drunk on the sniff of a wine gum," I was cautious with the drinks, wanting to be on my best behaviour. Sarah nonchalantly knocked back several gin and tonics, a drink I had prissily associated with "loose women."

When the party of a dozen persons moved in to dine, being the newest married couple, by tradition Sarah sat on the right of the host, her uncle, while I was on the right of her aunt, the hostess. Soup came and went with one white-uniformed waiter starting to serve Sarah, another waiter came to me, and they each worked round their own half of the table. When the main course arrived, a waiter duly appeared at my elbow with the roast beef, pink and juicy in the middle, a little bronzed around the edges. Meat was a luxury we rarely had so I was salivating at the sight of this delicious pile. Without checking to see if Sarah was also being served, I tucked liberally into the meat, then tried to hide the mound under vegetables. Alas, there was no waiter on Sarah's side, and I, as first in line, had demolished a good portion of the platter. My hostess fumbled for a bell button under the table, a waiter appeared from behind the pantry swing doors, and a hurried conversation ensued. Meanwhile I sweated in embarrassment that my greed had been disclosed. In due course another waiter appeared with more meat and served the guests on the other side of the table.

Next day Douglas Bromley took us to visit Admiral Nelson's flagship, *Victory,* that was laid up in dry dock near his house. A smart Women's Royal Naval Service rating on duty at the gangplank jumped to attention and saluted. "Fine bunch, my Wrens," said Douglas.

Soon we had to return to the real world.

* * *

While at Tooting I became friends with Tony Warner, a medical registrar with whom I used to play squash. Shortly after marrying a nurse, he started having nosebleeds, which came from cancer at the base of his brain. It spread quickly, causing him to go blind. I used to read the British Medical Journal to him in his anticipation of the time when he would be better and could return to work. Sadly it was not to be and I watched him fade away, and beheld the living grief of his wife, who nursed him devotedly. Within a few months Tony died.

Not long after, Malcolm Robinson was appointed as a surgical consultant at St George's, Hyde Park Corner, in place of Nic Nichols, my former boss. Nic had groomed Malcolm to succeed him, much to the envy of the other senior registrars, waiting in the wings for their bosses to retire or die.

Doctors returning from the armed services all got jobs and hung on to them until the last moment, hoping for a fat National Health Service pension. No one moved from the top of the pyramid and meanwhile young surgeons were continually being trained and fed into the system with nowhere to go. This led to jealous competition for jobs. Within a few months of being appointed to St George's, Malcolm killed himself with an overdose of drugs. The anticlimax of at last achieving his goal, together with the open antagonism of his fellow senior registrars, drove him into deep depression. I had grown very close to Malcolm when we worked for Nic, and his death upset me deeply.

* * *

Around this time, several of my friends died climbing. Bob Downes, former president of the Cambridge University Mountaineering Club, became sick and died on an expedition to Masherbrum, a high peak beside the Baltoro Glacier in the Karakoram Himalaya. I was in the neighbouring room to Bob when I moved into Clare Memorial Court at the end of my first year at Cambridge. He was short, stocky, powerful, with curly hair, a quizzical grin, and a beaked nose like Mr Punch. Shy and reserved, I never got to know him well as he was two years my senior, but he was always friendly when we met on the staircase. Bob had done many difficult climbs in Wales, Scotland, and the Alps along with Eric Langmuir, Mike O'Hara, and Geoff Sutton, establishing a reputation as one of the strongest climbers in Britain. Normally fit and tough, he was at high altitude for the first time on Masherbrum, and suffered a pneumonia-like illness at about 23,000 feet. He descended to a lower camp and then to the valley, where he felt much better. So, unstoppable as ever, he returned to the mountain. At the same height as originally he fell sick, the same illness returned, and he died, overcome by fluid accumulating in his lungs. The sadness of this tale is that now, with hindsight (the condition was first fully described in 1960), Bob's illness was a classic case of acute mountain sickness complicated by high altitude pulmonary oedema. Descent was the correct treatment, but Bob should have stayed down in the valley and been forbidden to return to the mountain. Had he lived, he would probably have become a mountaineer of the same world class as Joe Brown and Don Whillans; his writing talent was only just emerging and had far to go.

\* \* \*

George Fraser and I became close friends after our magnificent Easter climbing holiday in the highlands of Carnmore and saw each other frequently in London. I always think of him forging ahead of Bill Turrall and me on our speedy ascent of the Brenva face of Mont Blanc, a climb we could not have done on our own without George's drive and experience. George was excited to be invited on an expedition to Ama Dablam, a spire-shaped peak that looks down on Thyangboche in the heartland of Sherpa country. He and his companion, Mike Harris, were leading the climb, far ahead and approaching the final steep summit cone of the mountain, when they disappeared in cloud. They were never seen again, nor were their bodies ever recovered. No one knows if they reached the summit and fell on the descent, or what was their sad fate.

\* \* \*

Wilfrid Noyce, on an expedition in the Pamirs, was descending from Peak Garmo with Robin Smith when they slipped on a patch of ice, not wearing crampons, and slid to their deaths. Wilf had sparked my interest in climbing when I was at school at Charterhouse, and I owe to his encouragement that I signed up for the Outward Bound School. He left a widow and young children. Although famous for his part in the ascent of Everest, Wilfrid was just becoming recognized as a serious poet and writer, a career that held much in store for him. Literature would have let him get out of teaching, for which he was never truly bent, being much too softhearted to deal with philistine adolescent schoolboys who never recognized nor respected his intellect.

\* \* \*

Around this time I became friends with John Emery, one of Oxford University's most aggressive young climbers, and a fellow medical student at St Mary's Hospital. We met when he was incarcerated there as a patient, recovering from a series of operations to reconstruct his hands and feet after being frostbitten on an expedition to Haramosh in the Karakoram—a unique survival epic.

While descending, two of John's companions, Bernard Jillot and Rae Culbert, fell through a cornice and plunged two thousand feet into a bowl. John and the expedition leader, Tony Streather, climbed down to help them, John falling and dislocating his hip, which he reposited with the utmost pain and difficulty. John and Tony had lost their ice axes during the fall, and had a terrible climb back up to the ridge from which they had fallen. Jillot and Culbert were ahead, approaching their camp. John and Streather were following their footsteps, which suddenly disappeared into space where a cornice had broken off. Streather and John, who was severely frostbitten, reached their tent and then had to climb down to the base of the mountain. Their companions must have died in their long fall.

John's subtle sense of humour helped to keep him sane during months of surgery and rehabilitation. He was determined both to return to climbing and to medicine. With skilful plastic surgery on both hands, he finally had a short thumb made by grafting a piece of bone from his forearm, a stubby index finger fashioned by cutting down between the metacarpal bones of the palm of the hand, and a pad of fat in place of his three smaller fingers. He could just wield a specially designed pair of scissors to dissect rats that he was using in his research into multiple sclerosis. During his final clinical viva he took delight in telling the examiner, "I'm afraid, sir, I'll have to do the rectal exam with my thumb." He was excused the procedure. He had also lost all his toes, which gave him an awkward gait, because without toes there was no spring in his step and he had to roll forward on the stumps of his feet.

John married Sara soon after he left hospital. He wanted to climb again, and I spent a weekend in the Lake District leading him up many of the easy climbs he would have waltzed over a year before. Now he had to muscle his way with willpower, trying to keep his balance in boots that had no toes inside them.

Returning to the Wasdale Head hotel one evening, he was in the hall struggling out of wet boots with his weird, clumsy hands. An old lady, removing sensible walking shoes, had also returned after a day on the hills. Looking aghast at John's stubby hands and bare, toeless feet that looked like two clenched fists, she said, "Poor boy, whatever happened to you?"

"I bite my fingernails, madam," he replied without hesitation.

John was so determined to climb well again, he had forged a special ice axe that he could hold in his stunted fist. On his second visit to the Alps, having completed the difficult traverse of the Weisshorn, he and his American companion were descending in a hurry to get out of a storm. They slipped to their deaths. John was buried in the churchyard at Zermatt alongside many other climbers, most notably those who perished in early attempts on the Matterhorn.

* * *

The sadness of my friends' deaths altered my view of climbing from then on. I was a reasonably good rock climber and a capable mountaineer—not brilliant, but steady and reliable. It was unlikely I was going to graduate to the ranks of the maestros, but now I lost all desire to climb dangerously. Sarah was relieved at my change of heart. I put to the back of my mind all those magnificent classic routes I had planned in the Alps. But my dreams of exploring the Himalayas and other far-flung ranges remained.

* * *

At this time Sarah and I made two chance encounters that radically changed our future. At a meeting at The Alpine Club we met Jim and Betty Milledge, both doctors, who had recently returned from working at a mission hospital in Nepal. They in turn introduced us to Barry and Lila Bishop; Barry was on the staff of the *National Geographic* magazine. He was one of America's foremost climbers and had just been in Nepal. We all had supper together and got to discussing the opportunities of working in Nepal. Both couples were unreservedly enthusiastic, and Sarah and I needed little goading to make a decision. On Jim's recommendation I wrote to the United Mission Hospital in Kathmandu asking if they had any jobs for a young doctor and a nurse. A reply came back: Yes, so long as we could find our own way to Nepal. We decided to drive overland in a Land Rover, a useful and popular vehicle for doing adventurous travel. But I would have to sell my Austin Healey to pay for it.

I was nearing the end of my house job at Tooting and in the course of telling our plans to my boss, John Batten, I mentioned that I wanted to sell my sports car. He offered to buy it from me, a decision he was to regret—fortunately for me, after I had left the country. First the gear box fell through the floor; then the car was stolen, the number plates changed, and the body repainted. It was found by the police abandonned with a load of gelignite in the boot, having been used on a "job." But J.B. never let this tarnish our friendship.

Sarah and I went up to the Rover Company's factory in Birmingham to collect a long-wheel-base, hard canopy Land Rover. We parked it outside the doctors' mess at Tooting, and in the evenings we drove it across the rough ground at the back of the hospital, practicing manoeuvres we had learned during an off-road driving course we took at the factory.

At this time our most momentous acquisition was a home. During weekend visits to Sarah's parents we scoured the lanes of West Suffolk, and the local newspapers, for a small house that we could have as a base once we left London. We focused on the rolling uplands between the mediaeval market town of Bury St Edmunds and the wool-rich village of Clare. One day we found ourselves standing in a stubble field of rich, heavy clay looking down into a shallow valley where stood a low, thatched farm cottage set in the middle of a long meadow—The Bakery, Shoemeadow Bottom. For £2,500 it was ours.

# NINETEEN

S UFFOLK SKIES STRETCH FAR TO THE HORIZON. They
seem higher, more open for lack of high hills, than elsewhere.
Cumuli that have fled the Siberian steppes and raced across
the wild Baltic find haven over this rural corner of England where
we chose to live. Our house in Shoemeadow Bottom lay where West
Suffolk rolls down to a hollow. A small stream starts its meandering
course through the oak and elm forest of adjacent Ickworth Park
to become the River Lark that works its way northwards to join
the Ouse and empty into the North Sea at the Wash. We were surrounded by fields of heavy clay that produce rich harvests of grain
and grass such as gave the wool merchants of the Middle Ages the
wealth to build the finest parish churches in England.

The Bakery, for that is what it had been before the cut-loaf gi-
ants flooded the bread trade, was approached by a lane full of pot-
holes and exposed flints that are knappped thereabouts for the polished walls of the church towers, many of which in this country are
round, as stone for corner quoins is scarce. A thick may hedge stood
on the left obscuring the house, and a ditch with abundant cow pars-

ley lay on the right. The house nestled into the bank standing quite on its own with its only neighbour a small white farm on a hill a half mile away.

The roof was in good order, having been relaid a year or two back by a master thatcher, who had set bundles of straw deeply, and put the sign of his hand to this modest work of art with decorated chevrons on the roof ridge. The wattle and daub walls had been lime-washed but it was flaking, so the timber frame stood out like gaunt ribs, and in places where the plaster had peeled, the sticks showed through.

George Jolly was our outdoor adviser. He lived beyond the village with his brother and sister-in-law in a solitary cottage that people rarely visited. He could remember the time before the bus service when a cart drawn by a Suffolk Punch left the village weekly to take villagers into the nearby market for a penny a head, and tuppence if one sat beside the carter.

George came over once a week in the evening after work to help hedge and ditch our seven-acre meadow, to advise on planting trees round the pond and along the brook, and to mow the grass. He looked like a gnome as he wheeled his bicycle, the handlebars of which stood level with his shoulders. His scythe was tied to the crossbar with bailer twine. His balding head was weathered by long hours in the sun and wind, and his hands were rough and horny from working pitchforks and muck shovels. When he smiled, his face screwed up at his own wit, crowsfeet spread out from the corners of his eyes like the rays of the rising sun, and he looked to heaven for another quip of wisdom.

"Can't have 'e whitewashed, sir. Stuff from them big cans ain't no good. 'E'll drip and run in no time."

"What should I do then, George?" I asked.

"Do you 'ave 'im washed with lime, I say," he replied. "pink's the colour for these parts."

So we settled on pink and drove to Lavenham to find George's friend, who was a single-handed builder with a small yard in the lee of the most magnificent of all Suffolk parish churches. In the yard stood two large drums into which the men heaped reddish clay, then a measure of lime, and finally a shovelful of cow dung, fresh and sloppy.

"That'll make 'e stick," said Billy. "Without it, lime'll flake away and you'll be painting 'im over again next spring."

The lime in the cauldron bubbled and the dung fermented as George and I mixed it ready for washing onto the walls with a long-handled scrubbing brush. George was still in his waistcoat, the sleeves of his cream flannel shirt were rolled up, and he wore no collar. We spread the wash on thickly with a delicious sloshing noise, and lime splashed on the grass round my feet. It went on an earthy brown, but in the sun it dried to a warm salmon pink that blended with the fresh green of the oak trees in the hedge beside our field.

George's sister-in-law came to clean our house once a week. Violet (Violent, we called her because of her appearance, in lie to her nature) walked a mile and a half across the fields from the village because that was the path she used to follow on her way to school fifty years before—across a farmer's field where now a large notice said "Private—no thoroughfare."

"Buggar thaat," said Violet, looking hostile. "That field's where my father died. Killed dead he was under that big elm there when the lightning struck."

She had caught George's habit of glancing upwards and away with a quizzical look, as though she had a cast in her eye, whenever she had made a profound remark.

"Never bin a storm like it since, and we children had to go an' fetch him in when the rain stopped. I never waits under that tree no more when there's storms about."

She wore a knitted woollen cap pulled down over her ears, winter or summer, a scarf covered the hairs on her chin, and her stockings hung loosely bellow her skirt, rose-patterned like wallpaper. Come rain or snow (but never thunder), Violet would cross the field in defiance of the farmer who lived in the large hall beside the church.

Then one morning she arrived in a state of excitement. "Oh, doctor, come quick, me bruvver-'n-law's 'ad a accident. We lives way yonder by the windmill past the village but there bain't no road to the house. We'll 'ave to go over by the fields."

So I set off walking behind her carrying my medical bag, not knowing what to expect. She strode ahead in her clumping brown leather shoes, mud splattering the backs of her baggy stockings and her flowered skirt swishing behind her in the breeze. The grass was wet with dew and deep wheel ruts cut into the track. Across another field stood a cottage, like our own but shabbier. The thatch was overgrown with moss, bald in places where sparrows had pilfered the straw for nesting, and patched with ugly corrugated iron.

We entered the kitchen where George's brother sat beside a cast-iron chimney grate watching for the kettle to boil. The tabletop was bleached with the scrubbing of many years, and a loaf of bread stood partly cut in heavy slices.

"'E's up yonder," he said, indicating the stair with a nod of his head. "Stupid clumsy idiot 'e is."

I climbed the narrow stair using a rope handrail and found a small bedroom at the top with bare floorboards and newspaper stuck to the walls to patch up draughty gaps. The only pieces of furniture in the room were a brass bedstead resplendent with large knobs on the posts and a curly pattern on the headpiece, a washstand with a large china jug and bowl, and a chair.

Lying in the middle of the bed, sunk deep into the feathery mattress, lay George with two huge black eyes peering over the sheets pulled up to his nose.

"What on earth have you been up to, George?" I asked, for I thought this to be a house of uncommon amity.

"Well, sir, it was like this. By the way, 'tis awful good of you to come," he added apologetically. "I was taken short in the night you see, and so I gets out of bed to get my little ole potty and I hangs onto the back of that there chair to steady myself and 'e slips and then I goes head first into 'er."

An ornate china jerry lay on the floor, the bowl rim intact but the bottom knocked clear out of it.

"You'll never believe me, doctor, but I was stuck fast there with my head in and not able to see out and so I calls me brother and me sis'r-'n-law and they tugs and heaves and then one of 'em knocks a 'ole in the bottom for they thought I was suffocating, and they pushes me head down through."

I looked at the bruised eyes and the grazes around his face, still with the crowsfeet spreading as he grinned.

"Awfully lucky it was empty, doctor," he said.

* * *

I was working in Bury St Edmunds doing an obstetric job so I still had lots of nights when I had to be resident in the hospital. But during time-off, Sarah and I planned our overland journey to Nepal and we spent many happy hours with the help of her father, fixing up the interior of the Land Rover so we could sleep in it.

Finally, one cold February morning we set off from The Bakery and drove across a frosty Newmarket Downs on the first leg of our three-month-long journey to Kathmandu, and the beginning of a new adventure.

THE END

# ABOUT THE AUTHOR

Retired doctor and mountaineer Peter Steele was born in England and lived in far-flung places such as Bhutan, the Sahara and Kathmandu before settling in Whitehorse, Yukon with his family in 1975.

Steele once ran the Grenfell flying doctor service in Labrador, travelling the coast by plane, dog team and boat. His first book, *Two and Two Halves to Bhutan*, tells the story of his young family's adventures in the Himalayas. He was Medical Officer to the ill-fated 1971 International Everest Expedition, an experience recorded in *Doctor on Everest*. He followed this with two books on medical care in the wilderness, and *Atlin's Gold*.

*Eric Shipton: Everest and Beyond*, a biography of the great British climber, won the Boardman Tasker prize for mountain literature. His latest book is *The Man Who Mapped the Arctic: The Intrepid life of George Back, Franklin's Lieutenant*.

peter.steele@northwestel.net

CPSIA information can be obtained
at www.ICGtesting.com
Printed in the USA
FFOW04n1307060116
20184FF